W9-BME-333

# ISO 9000

## An Implementation Guide for Small to Mid-Sized Businesses

Frank Voehl • Peter Jackson • David Ashton

Printed and bound in the U.S.A. Printed on acid-free paper.

**Library of Congress Cataloging-in-Publication Data**

Voehl, Frank, 1946–
ISO 9000: an implementation guide for small to mid-sized businesses / Frank Voehl, Peter Jackson, David Ashton.
p. cm.
Includes bibliographical references and index.
ISBN 1-884015-10-7
1. Quality control--Standards. I. Jackson, Peter. II. Ashton, David. III. Title. IV. Title: ISO nine thousand
TS156.V63 1994
658.5′62′0218--dc20 93-46440
CIP



A version of this book entitled *Implementing Quality Through BS 5750* was first published in 1993 by Kogan Page Limited, 120 Pentonville Road, London N1 9JN.

Direct all inquiries to St. Lucie Press, Inc., 100 E. Linton Blvd., Suite 403B, Delray Beach, Florida 33483.

Phone: (407) 274-9906
Fax: (407) 274-9927

StL

Published by
St. Lucie Press
100 E. Linton Blvd., Suite 403B
Delray Beach, FL 33483

# PREFACE

With all of the books and materials published on ISO 9000 over the past two years, why is this book needed and what makes it different and unique? Basically, there are two reasons for its being. First, it is specifically written for the manager and/or owner of a small business who is looking for a do-it-yourself guide to ISO 9000 certification, to the degree that this is possible and practical. Some things by their nature must be done by independent, objective external parties. In order for ISO 9000 to be effective, economical, and long-lasting, however, most of the activities relating to it can and should be performed by the people at work within the organization rather than by an external assessor who does not live or die by the results.

Second, this book represents a collection of both American and British thinking and experience. Accordingly, it represents the best of both worlds on either side of the Atlantic. We can all learn from one another, as well as build on each other's ideas, expertise, quality business models, and dreams for a better tomorrow.

It is in the spirit of building for a better tomorrow that this book is offered. If in some way it makes a contribution, then we can say, as Dr. Edwards Deming often did at the end of his seminars and lectures, "I have done my best."

**Frank Voehl**

# DEDICATION

***To Micki, my wife and friend***

Who never fails to lift my spirits
and keep me focused on the road ahead.

***And to the memory of Dr. Edwards Deming***

Who always taught me to do my best.

# CONTENTS

1

# WHAT IS QUALITY?

## INTRODUCTION

This book is written specifically for the small to mid-size business organization that wants to implement ISO 9000 as one of the building blocks of its quality system. It is also written for the organization that prefers the do-it-yourself approach. However, because ISO 9000 is also an accepted standard for quality, it is necessary to understand what quality means in a business environment and how it can be achieved.

During the past three years, there has been an explosion in the number of books in the field of total quality and ISO 9000. Yet in all the hundreds of books and millions of words written on the subject, there are few good working models and comprehensive yet concise overviews. This book offers a clear and simple systems model of ISO 9000 that can be used for certification (registration). The book takes a how-to approach and includes sample procedures and forms, where appropriate. Its intent is to demystify the ISO 9000 standards and to demonstrate their use in improving day-to-day operations of the small business.

## THE NOTION OF A QUALITY SYSTEM

Quality is defined as "the totality of features and characteristics of a product or service that bears on its ability to satisfy given needs." This implies that we must be able to identify the features and characteristics of products and services that relate to quality and form the basis of measurement and control.

Total quality consists of a set of philosophies and management systems aimed at the efficient achievement of the organization's objectives to ensure customer satisfaction and maximize stakeholder value. Total quality is accomplished through the continuous improvement of the quality system, which consists of the social system, the technical system, and the management system. Thus, it becomes a way of life for doing business for the entire organization.

It is a concept that says a company should design quality into its products, not inspect for it afterward. Only by having a devotion to quality throughout the company will the best possible products be made. As stated by Japanese quality control scholar and counselor for the Union of Japanese Scientists and Engineers Dr. Noriaki Kano, "Quality is too important to be left to inspectors."

Quality is also too important to take second place to anything else in the company's goals. Most importantly, it should not be subsidiary to profit or productivity. Concentrating on quality will ultimately build and improve both profitability and productivity. Failure to concentrate on it will quickly erode profits, because customers resent having to pay for products deemed to be of low quality.

The main focus of the quality system is on *why*. It goes beyond the *how to* to include the *why to*. It attempts to both identify the causes of defects and remove them. It is a continuous cycle of finding defects, identifying their causes, and improving the process to eliminate these causes.

Accepting the idea that "the next process is our customer" is essential to the real practice of quality. This means that each process should not only develop its own control charts but should also disclose its own errors to the next process in order to improve quality. However, it has been said that it seems contrary to human nature to recognize one's own mistakes. One tends to find the errors caused by others and to neglect one's own. Unfortunately, that self-disclosure is what is really needed.[1]

Too often, management tends to blame and then take punitive action. This attitude prevails from first-line supervisors all the way up to top management. In effect, workers are encouraged to hide the real problems; instead of looking for the real causes of problems, as required by the quality system, they look the other way.

## THE NOTION OF CONTROL

The Japanese notion of *control* differs greatly from the American notion; that difference of meaning does much to explain U.S. management's failure to adopt total quality management systems. For many American workers, control carries the meaning of someone or something limiting an operation, process, or person.

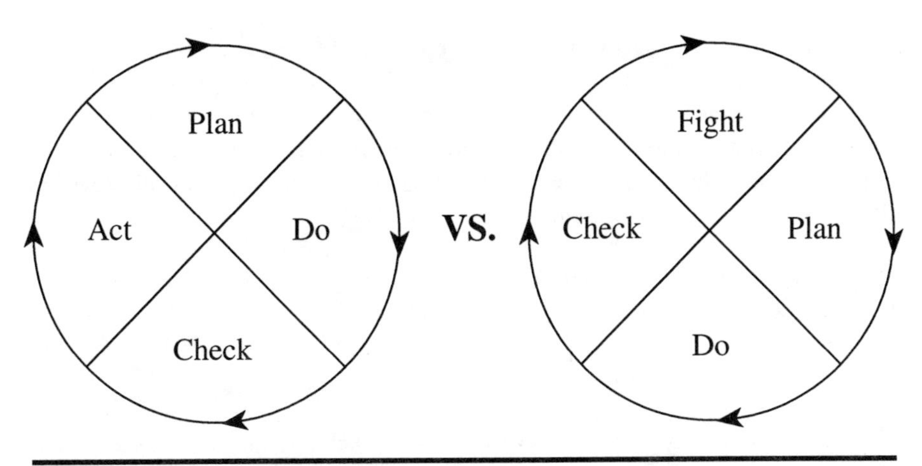


**Figure 1.1** Plan, Do, Check, Act.

It has the overtones of a police force in the industrial engineering setting and is often resented.

In Japan, as pointed by Dr. Noriaki Kano, control means "all necessary activities for achieving objectives in the long term, efficiently and economically. Control, therefore, is doing whatever is needed to accomplish what we want to do as an organization."

The difference can be seen very graphically in the P-D-C-A continuous improvement chart widely used in Japan to describe the cycle of control. A proper control procedure has four stages: planning, doing what is planned, checking the results, and then applying any necessary corrective action. The chart shows these four stages—Plan, Do, Check, Act—arranged in circular fashion to indicate a continuing cycle.

In the United States, where specialization and division of labor are emphasized, the cycle is more likely to look like Fight, Plan, Do, Check (Figure 1.1). Instead of working together to solve any deviations from the plan, employees of American companies often spend time fighting over who is responsible for the deviations.

This sectionalism, as the Japanese refer to it, hinders our collective efforts to improve the way things are done, our national productivity, and our standard of living. *There need be nothing threatening about control if it is perceived as self-imposed and directed at gathering the facts necessary to make plans and take action toward making improvements.*

The quality system includes the control principle as part of the set of philosophies aimed at the efficient achievement of the organization's objectives. Although many of the individual components of the quality system are practiced by American companies, few practice the system as a whole.

## QUALITY AND EXCELLENCE

In common business terminology, the concept of quality is linked to excellence. It is about being the best and at the forefront of one's industry in order to gain and maintain competitive advantage. It is perceived as an absolute, as illustrated in the following sentences:

- We shall strive for quality.
- This company is at the quality end of the market.
- She is a person of quality.
- This product is pure quality.

In this sense, quality is either very difficult to achieve or is relegated to the domain of a select few.

This concept is an integral part of American culture and will remain so. As a business practice, however, it is a hindrance, or, as Karl Albrecht puts it, "Quality is a difficult medicine."[2] Quality in the sense of the best (or excellence) is vague and leads nowhere, for it really does not help to run an organization better. Consider statements that, until 1980, made a lot of sense:

> *"We only wish we could concentrate on better quality goods, but we cannot afford to do this. We would price ourselves out of the market."*

> *"We operate in a commodity market. Everyone's product is the same and quality just does not factor into it."*

According to these comments, quality was either not affordable or not needed.

The following story further illustrates the limitations of a quality concept based exclusively on the principle of best/excellence.

### *Successful Defects*

A brand new shopping mall is clearly struggling. Because of a general business downturn or for other reasons, the anticipated store traffic has not yet materialized. There is one exception: a reject pottery shop selling seconds of famous brands at half price or less. Alone in the mall, this store is clearly thriving.

The pottery manufacturer whose brands make up the stock of the seconds shop is not prospering either. The only part of the output where demand exceeds supply is its rejects (which are, however, plentiful because of the factory's high product quality standards). The managing director is bitter: "This company has been committed to the highest quality for a hundred years, but where is it leading us? Bankruptcy. The customers don't want quality, they just look for bargains. Any old thing which will hold their fancy. Never mind if the color's off and shape's wrong, as long as it is half price. The only thing to do is to increase our reject rate and sell most of our pots as seconds."

The paradox in this story is that the pursuit of quality seems on the surface to be a failure. The shop's customers will overlook many of the characteristics that the manufacturer believes make his products so excellent, provided the price is low enough. Additionally, the one shop in the mall which aggressively eschews a "quality" image alone prospers with a classic "pile them high" display. Back at the plant, the quality standards, so rigorously enforced, lead to mounting stocks of unsold goods. On the other hand, the cut-rate price results in a booming demand for the rejects. All this reflects some major business issues, but the paradoxes themselves are the result of a failure in understanding. A practical and effective notion of quality can help resolve the semantic confusion and may point to some effective business strategies to overcome some of the problems. The most obvious business strategy is to bring out a well-designed, well-crafted, but less expensive line of pottery to accomplish the dual goal of increasing revenues while improving or holding the line on acceptable quality from the customer's point of view. The heart of the issue lies in knowing what the customers really want and need, what they are willing to pay, and what the various trade-offs might be. This point is further discussed in the next section.

In another view of quality, the focus is on the needs of a group on which every business entirely depends—the customer—avoiding the trap of an unattainable excellence. The following is another story that illustrates this concept.

### *A Tale of Two Watches*

Harry and Rod are having a beer after work. It is nearing time to go and Harry is looking at his watch. Rod notices its heavy gold band.

"That's a great-looking watch, Harry."

"Yes, it's a Rolex. I've had it a year or two and it has never let me down. Accurate to a minute a month or less, it shows the date and, of course, it is self-winding and waterproof."

At this point, Harry glances at Rod's watch, a Timex. "How can a heavy hitter like you put up with a watch like that, Rod? I wouldn't be caught dead wearing one."

Rod is not at all ashamed or insulted. "Well, it may not be quite a Rolex but, like yours, it hasn't let me down yet. It is also accurate to a few seconds a year, and you don't need to wind it either. Of course, it shows the date, has an alarm and a stopwatch, and, if I need to, I can check the time in L.A. or London. It cost me all of $30. How much was your Rolex, Harry?"

"Oh, a hundred times more but, of course, it will last me a lifetime."

This left Rod still unimpressed. "Well, that's good but of no use to me. I am absent-minded with things and chances are I will lose my watch in six months, certainly within a year. So the two-year guarantee is more than adequate for me."

Harry snickered into his Mexican beer. "As usual, Rod, you don't see it at all. This watch makes an important statement about me—what I am, and that only the best will do."

"Well, Harry, I hear what you are saying. We all know you need all the help you can get."

The point of this story is that both Harry and Rod are seeking quality in their watches and both feel they have obtained it. In different ways, both the $30 and the $3000 watch meet their individual requirements, whether these are related to function (accuracy), life expectancy, or self-image.

Meeting customer requirements—which differ among customers—is the concept of quality that underlies this book and ISO 9000 in general.

## QUALITY AS MEETING CUSTOMER REQUIREMENTS

Using this definition, quality is the goal of each and every business. No company can regard quality as *not* a central concern and all can and must strive to attain it, maintain it, and constantly improve it.

Although the concept is simple, it is not easy to achieve, and there are quite a few implications to consider. First, there is the focus on *customers,* who are placed right where they belong—at the heart of the business. Businesses vary in every imaginable way, but all depend on customers and their continuing patronage. In a competitive market, how many businesses will keep their customers if they do not meet their requirements? In the long run, none.

No customer group in any market is homogeneous. Customers can be segmented in many ways, for example, into smaller groups with common requirements. Quality, in the sense of meeting customer requirements, therefore entails developing a product for a range of customer groups. In many markets a business will recognize that, practically speaking, it cannot meet the requirements of all possible customers and by deliberate choice will leave some to smaller niche suppliers. Alternatively, the business may itself choose to be highly specialized and cater to the requirements of a selected group of customers. In this case, the pursuit of quality (customer requirements) may overlap with the conventional sense of a quality (excellent) company. However, the larger suppliers focusing on the mass market should be no less committed to quality (meeting requirements). In fact, they cannot be otherwise; a surviving company must be a quality company.

Returning to the story of the pottery shop, using the concept of quality in the sense of meeting customer requirements should point to some solutions. The shop is serving a budget-conscious group (in a recession-hit town) by whom minor defects can be overlooked in an item priced low enough. Indeed it is unlikely that these defects are even a concern. The "pile them high" display gives the comfort of no frills (what the bargain hunter seeks). Thus, the seconds shop is succeeding in meeting its customers' requirements. What about the pottery manufacturer? Here the key may be to recognize the need for a functional range of pots that can be sold at a budget price, perhaps through the regular outlets. It would certainly be better to reduce the supply of expensively produced rejects and direct resources to such a new range. If this strategy succeeds, customer requirements may be even better met with the lower priced but defect-free pots. It is possible that the trade of some of the first-line stores in the mall will improve. The pottery shop will suffer initially as customers find their requirements met in a different way, but it is likely that the redirected retailing focus will eventually be a success, all because of a new understanding of quality.

Customer requirements need to be understood in the widest possible sense. Most customers are looking at more than just the technical features of a product or service. The following story illustrates this point.

### *The Best Boat Water Heater Money Could Buy*

Consultants were brought in to advise a well-established manufacturer of gas water heaters designed for leisure boats. The problems were declining sales and vanishing profits.

A limited investigation into the market confirmed the company's belief that their products were technically the best. Furthermore, engineering analysis proved that they offered both excellent fuel efficiency and real safety features. In a narrow sense, therefore, the products met customer requirements. However, the same investigation of the market demonstrated that in other respects customer requirements were not being met.

In the first place, boat builders (the key customer group) required heaters in a range of colors in order to match cabin decor. The company only offered the product in a white casing. Second, with limited storage space, most boatyards did not want to hold stocks of appliances, but the lack of a water heater at the appropriate stage of production could move back the final schedule. The company had recognized problems in delivery methods. Finally, although customers acknowledged the technical qualities of the heaters, most considered a cheaper but less efficient heater to be more suitable below the luxury end of the boat market. All in all, once customer requirements were viewed in a wider context, the cause of the company's problems, *and* the solution, became apparent.

Requirements comprise *all* the features of a product or service that are of significance to a customer. Some of these may be implicit, rather than requested explicitly by the customer, but are nevertheless vital. For example, when booking a flight, it is not considered necessary to specify that the plane be adequately serviced and maintained; it is an implicit requirement that the airline take steps to eliminate the chances of the wings or the engines falling off. Meeting customer requirements, therefore, also implies ensuring that products and services are *fit for purpose*—another common, practical definition of quality. J. M. Juran calls this "fitness for use."

Whether the requirements are implicit or explicit, meeting them requires identifying and understanding them. Again, the pursuit of quality requires that customers have a central position in the business. Unless suppliers understand customer requirements, it is impossible to satisfy them. In some businesses, this involves discussion of and agreement on the specific needs of individual customers. In off-the-shelf businesses, understanding requirements necessitates continual feedback through monitoring of customer satisfaction, market research programs, or ongoing, day-to-day contact with customers through the marketing and sales personnel.

Meeting customer requirements is a dynamic activity. Both customers and their needs change, and the supplier must recognize this. Unless the company's own program of innovation matches (if not stays ahead of) the pace of change among customers, requirements will cease to be met and setbacks will follow.

## QUALITY IS FREE (OR AT LEAST AFFORDABLE)

Ever since Phil Crosby wrote his seminal work *Quality Is Free,* there has been debate as to just what "free" means. A better word to use may be "affordable." If quality is defined as meeting customer requirements, then not only *must* it be affordable, but it becomes absurd to say that quality *cannot* be affordable. If quality is not affordable, suppliers are by definition not meeting customer requirements and may well face bankruptcy. Organizations must either change production methods so as to be able to afford quality or redirect the business to another group of customers whose requirements can be met.

Although quality must be at the core of a business, ultimately it is one of many steps toward the goal of commercial survival (generating sufficient positive cash flow to provide jobs and remain in business) and profit maximization. Customer requirements are met not out of altruism, but rather because it is an absolute necessity for commercial success. It is, therefore, implicit that requirements be met at the *least cost* (or maximum profit). The pursuit of quality inevitably involves continual design improvement, production innovation, removal of reject and rework, and maximum efficiency and effectiveness. However, the pursuit of least cost does not mean giving the customer less than what is expected, in the hope that the deficiency will not be noticed. In the long run, it will be, and the inevitable consequences of failing to meet requirements will have to be faced. Achieving least cost does not mean compromising quality; it means delivering quality in the most efficient and effective manner possible.

The key to minimizing production and delivery costs is *getting it right the first time, every time.* Failures and rejects are the (high) costs of not getting it right, but these are only the additional costs that arise inside the business. Some of the defects usually go out to customers anyway, and the firm incurs the costs of warranty and recall. Even more serious may be the costs incurred in long-term sales decline due to dissatisfied customers.

It should be clear that in any business there is no option but to pursue quality. If companies fail to meet requirements and provide quality, sooner or later customers will switch their business to competitors. As Dr. Deming has emphasized, "Customers don't complain, they switch. And in most cases, they don't even let you know that they are unhappy." Quality is, therefore, a vital *competitive strategy.* Holding one's own in a market (keeping market share) requires that customer requirements be met at least as well as, if not better than, they are by competitors.

Maximizing the fulfillment of customer requirements through the pursuit of quality is expressed by some as "delighting" customers. Businesses should seek to satisfy not only broad requirements but the more detailed ones as well. When an organization delights customers in this way, it not only keeps their business, but makes it unlikely that they will even consider alternative suppliers. Moreover, they will probably tell other potential customers of their delight.

In many businesses, going the extra mile to meet customer requirements involves an attention to the smallest details:

- The equipment control knobs comfortably fit the hand of the operator.
- The carton can be opened easily, without need of a pair of scissors.
- The consultant's report is titled on the spine (and can, therefore, be quickly located on the client's bookshelf).

These details are, of course, additional to many other and generally more major requirements, but it is the attention to such details that often achieves that edge over competitors.

## QUALITY CAN BE ATTAINED AND MAINTAINED

The traditional approach to quality has focused on the output. This can be described as the "police" method of quality assurance. Sometimes the policeman is assisted by an ally, the "fireman." The limitations of this method and the solution to them are described below.

The role of the quality policeman (quality inspector) is deeply entrenched in American and European management systems. The policing concept works as illustrated in Figure 1.2. The quality policeman's efforts are entirely fo-

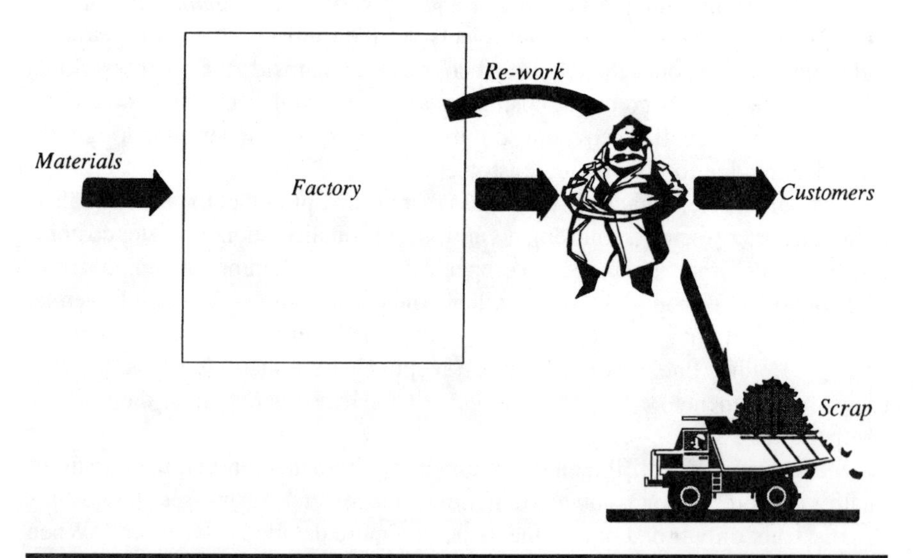


**Figure 1.2** The quality policeman.

cused on the products as they leave the factory (or service business office). Product standards for meeting customer requirements are set, and goods are tested for conformity. Those meeting the standards are shipped to the customers. Those that do not become scrap or are returned for reworking. What happens inside the black box of the factory is of no real concern to the quality policeman.

There are two fundamental problems inherent in this method of quality assurance: (1) waste is institutionalized and (2) in some businesses the product (or service) cannot be effectively tested for conformity to customer requirements until *after* it has been produced. This is especially true of service organizations.

Institutionalized waste is a necessary feature of quality policing: scrap is the quality department's output, and its continued employment depends on a suitable level of waste. If the factory stops sending out faulty products, quality assurance becomes unnecessary. However, this is unlikely because those who identify the product problems remain outside the production process. Without a feedback system, the shop floor has no opportunity to learn from its mistakes. Of course, in practice the quality policeman does not stay rigidly outside the factory; some attempt is usually made to put things right before products go all the way through the system. The later in the production process that defects are identified, the higher the costs, especially if defects are found after shipping. These added costs are the converse of added value.

A modified police approach to quality is represented in Figure 1.3. Here the

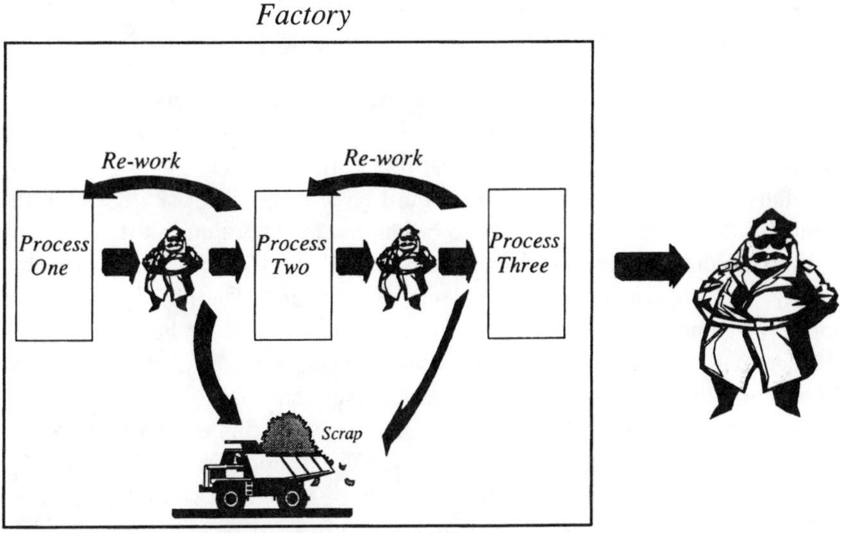

**Figure 1.3** The quality policeman and deputies.

police force has expanded and moved into the factory, which now uses a different production process in which quality inspection is carried out before the product moves onto the next stage. The problem of institutionalized waste remains, however; quality control is still outside the production process.

The second problem with a police-based quality system is that product inspection may not be effective. The tests used may not identify nonconformity to requirements. This may be addressed by continuous review of the testing methods and perhaps testing of the testers. However, in many businesses effective quality assurance through post-production testing is simply not feasible:

- At a restaurant, customer requirements include more than just receiving well-prepared food. Customers also expect the waiter to deal with them in a timely and courteous manner. If the waiter mistreats the customer for any reason, the damage is done. Even if a quality inspector, e.g., the head waiter, attempts to redress the problem after the fact, dissatisfaction still exists.
- Satisfaction with a flight will not be improved by the knowledge that incoming planes are checked to see that they have not crashed or that the cause of a fatal accident is adequately investigated. It is fully expected that adequate safety measures are taken to prevent planes from crashing in the first place.
- The value of professional advice reflects how well the advisor has been trained. It may be that a lawyer's $500 advice is no different from a next-door neighbor's, but whose opinion would it be prudent to trust?

These examples all require quality assurance prior to the testing stage; in these cases, conformity to requirements depends on quality being built into the product or service, because it is too late to test for it after the fact.

Many a management reputation is built on "fire fighting" skills, and in their own way these firemen are likely to be the hardest working, most resourceful, and most valuable members of the company team. The role of the fireman in quality assurance is to solve problems as they are identified by the quality policeman, and the fireman's reputation is built on his or her skill in crisis management. These are the people who always get the mail through, get the product out the door, or fix the problem, come what may.

Without doubt, such heroes are invaluable when things go wrong, as they eventually do. However, much of the energy that goes into such fire fighting would be far better deployed in fire prevention. Moreover, some firefighters so love crisis management that they make no effort to prevent problems from occurring and may even block others' attempts to do so.

### *The $100 Parcel*

Scientos Corporation makes replacement parts for vital medical equipment and has a strong position in this niche market. Although precision manufacture is important, the production skills required are in fact quite low. Scientos' reputation rests wholly on its same-day delivery service.

However, very few new customers were being taken on, and the company was clearly stagnating. A new sales director was appointed and his first task was to find out why so few new accounts had been opened in the past year. The answer was easily found: the salesmen spent virtually no time prospecting for new business. They were called in for a severe reprimand.

Naturally, the accused had some excuses: "We have no time. Not only do we have to see our regular customers frequently, but we often have to deliver the parts to them as well." The sales director checked out this story and found it to be substantially true.

The blame moved upstairs to the board. The managing director was defensive: "I hope this isn't a criticism of Bob in dispatch. Why, this company's success is very much due to him. He always gets the part to the customer by the time promised."

"Yes, he does," said the sales director. "And how he does it is to wait until there is a panic, and then he jumps up and down until one of the sales force gives in and makes the delivery. When that happens, a $10 package delivery really costs us $100 in sales time and expenses. It's no wonder we don't have time to pursue new business opportunities."

"Going by the book" has a dull and boring ring to it. In many situations, however, things work precisely because there is a well-established set of rules designed to prevent problems in the first place. Airplane travel is one example of meticulous procedures designed to ensure that implicit requirements such as safety are met. Passengers expect that the crew knows what to do if anything goes wrong, that there is an effective emergency procedure in place, and that disaster will not just be averted by the last-minute quick thinking of the captain.

The equivalent in business is the *quality system:* an established and proven set of processes and procedures that are continually revised to adapt to a changing environment. Implementing an effective system increases conformity to customer requirements and, therefore, improves quality.

## QUALITY IS A SYSTEM OF IMPROVEMENT

Unlike the police approach to quality assurance, a quality system focuses on documenting and improving the production process itself and not just the output. If companies have the right recipe and the right ingredients and the cook the right training, the meal will be right; some tasting may still be necessary before serving, but this part of quality assurance is now secondary to good cooking. In time, tasting may be discontinued entirely.

ISO 9000 is a standard for such a quality system. Unlike most other quality standards, it is not concerned with a particular product. It is applicable to any situation in which a quality system can be utilized, and, as discussed in later chapters, this can be virtually any business.

A quality system is put in place after the processes making up a business have been analyzed and the correct methods—those that ensure that the product meets customer requirements—have been identified. These methods are then systematized; these form the quality system. Of course, the first attempt will not produce a perfect quality system. Perfection may never be achieved, but improvement will be continuous. Thus, an essential part of the system is learning from mistakes.

At a recent ISO 9000 seminar, the following question was asked of the speaker: "Two weeks ago today we had an urgent order to be sent out to one of our largest customers. At three in the afternoon the Gorman Finisher went down. You know what that meant: we could either get the product off without the final finish and wait for the customer to scream or tell him that we couldn't dispatch until Monday at noon at best, and we knew that wouldn't do either. So what would you do? What use is the quality system in a real crisis?"

The speaker came back without hesitation: "You know your business and your customer. You are the manager, not me. I couldn't possibly advise you on which alternative would leave the customer least dissatisfied. No, what I would do, though, is make sure that you learn from the mistake by investigating why the Gorman went down and what could have been done to lessen that happening. Perhaps you need a back-up finisher or a different maintenance routine. You have to find out. That is the way to use the system to ensure quality in the long term. In other words, have a corrective action procedure in your quality system and use it effectively."

This was a good answer for a number of reasons. An effective quality system is not just a set of rules for quality production. It is recognized that problems will occur. The system is a way to ensure that the same ones do not keep recurring. This is done by establishing procedures for problem identification (e.g., auditing), investigation (e.g., corrective action) and long-term rectification (controlled procedure change).

The quality system approach of ISO 9000 described in this book is formal and documented. Anyone involved in a process can refer to a manual to find out what should be done to ensure conformity (although to do so the worker may need to be trained; the quality system is not a substitute for skills). In very small businesses, high quality is often maintained by an informal, undocumented quality system kept in the head of key staff such as the firm's boss, who is strongly motivated to give customers whatever they require. However, as the business grows, the informal system breaks down, and it becomes more important to document the steps of the quality system. Several key employees may now have responsibilities which affect quality. What happens when the boss is on vacation? As the staff grows, all members need to know how to work in the same way.

### *The Two-Shift Problem*

The new plater had been in place at Smith's Metal Finishing for six months. It looked like a first-rate piece of equipment, and the supplier seemed to have been thorough in the installation. An entire day had been spent training the operators. All was not well, however, judging from the number of customer complaints. The consistency of finish was not as promised; in fact, the old machine had produced a better finish.

A senior engineer from the equipment supplier was asked to investigate. He arrived at 9:00 a.m. on Monday and by 10:30 was confident that the problem could be easily solved: the machine was just out of setting. By the end of the day shift, testing showed that the finish consistency was correct.

However, on Tuesday morning the same problem reappeared, and the engineer recognized that the cause was the same: wrong settings. Again, by the end of the shift the output was near perfect. This time the engineer stayed on for the night shift. He noticed that as soon as the next foreman arrived he reset the machine.

"Why have you changed the setting?" asked the engineer.

"To set it right, of course. I remember that when the machine was put in, the manufacturer's people said it had to be set like this for our material."

The engineer asked to see the page in the procedure manual that detailed the settings for the machine.

"And what manual is that?" said the foreman. "We haven't got one."

The point of the story is that memory is seldom enough. Important operating procedures must be documented and made available to all who need them. Moreover, when procedures are changed, all the manuals in use must reflect the revision. Accurate documentation and control of that documentation are also, therefore, essential aspects of a quality system and requirements of ISO 9000.

An effective quality system should be clear enough that operators know exactly what procedure is to be followed at all times. A business, however, operates in a changing world. As discussed previously, customer requirements are fluid. In part, the activities of competitors change customer expectations. Technological innovation makes it possible to meet requirements in new and more effective ways, and all parties—customers, competitors, and the company— are affected by the macro-economy. Therefore, dynamism must be built into a quality system. Otherwise, the system will become a barrier to adaptation and will ultimately prevent the satisfaction of customer requirements. It will become counterproductive.

The pursuit of quality is continuous. The prime task of any management team is to keep the total quality ball moving up the slope. This concept is illustrated in Figure 1.4. The ISO 9000 quality system is a check that prevents the total quality effort from backsliding, but it must change as the company moves upward.

There is undoubtedly a perceived celebrity status to ISO 9000. Achieving

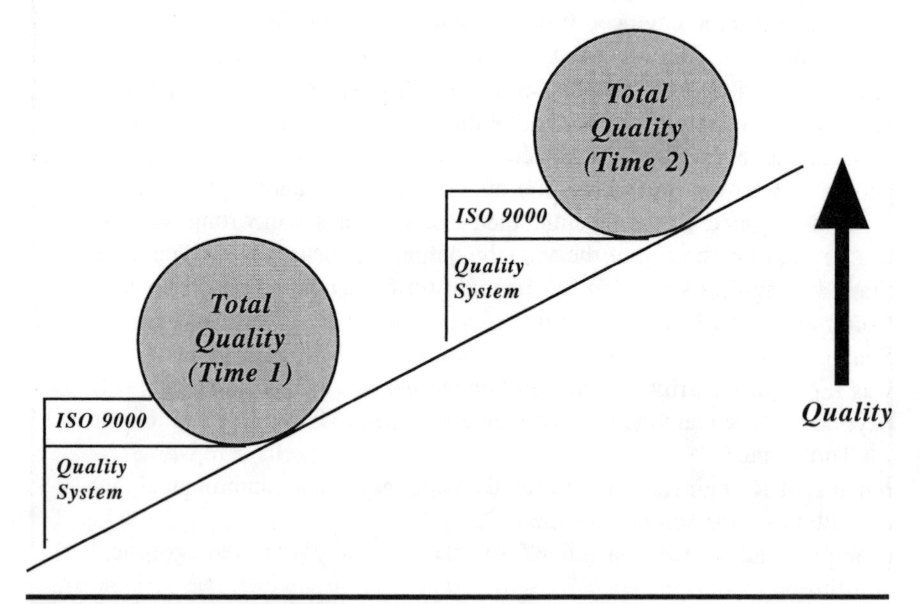


**Figure 1.4** The quality slope.

ISO registration has an importance independent of what lies behind it. However, to implement a quality system merely to pass the ISO 9000 assessment is self-defeating. Without the necessary commitment to quality, the business will not prosper in the long run. ISO 9000 accreditation does not increase the value of a bankrupt firm's assets; failure is the eventual result of a lack of commitment to quality. In the short run, lip service may get past the ISO 9000 assessors upon initial ISO registration, but not during the surveillance visits for recertification. Without real commitment to quality, the system will run down and accreditation will be lost.

Commitment to quality must be company-wide and led from the top. If the directors are not convinced that they should provide quality, the workers cannot be expected to worry about meeting customer requirements. A quality system in an unmotivated organization is like a new car without gasoline: perfect, but immobile. The fuel is staff attitude, motivation, and innovation, and any business has to utilize them to be successful.

This book is about how to assemble a good car—a quality system. A reader should look elsewhere to learn about commitment, motivation and total quality in general, because these aspects of quality are not discussed here.

## QUALITY IS A STANDARD BY WHICH TO MEASURE

Standards imply both specifications (against which a product can be measured to establish if it meets the standard) and commonality. A standard is recognized within a community whether that be a single firm, an industry, a country, or the world. If a product meets a standard of a community, then it conforms to whatever specifications have been determined to be appropriate. Standards also imply some recognized method of assessment. In one way or another, whether or not something meets a standard can be determined.

In the United Kingdom, the standards used in a wide range of industrial, business, and related activities are British Standards (BS) defined by the British Standards Institution (BSI). The BSI originated as the Engineering Standards Committee in 1901. The name was changed in 1918 to the British Engineering Standards Association. The organization received a Royal Charter in 1929 and was renamed the British Standards Institution in 1931 to reflect its expansion beyond engineering. The current ISO 9000 standards are based on BS 5750.

Today, the BSI is involved in a number of activities. Its core work, however, remains the creation and revision of standards. This is done through a process of consultation in the field to which the particular standard applies. BS 5750, for example, was prepared by the Quality, Management and Statistics Committee and through the Technical Committee (QMS/2), in which some 50 industrial, government, and other bodies were represented.

The ISO standards, defined in published documents, number over 8000.[3] The great majority of these standards are product standards; they provide key parameters for a particular product. In a sense, they are recipes for conformity: a particular standard can be used to produce a product whose parameters match those of any other product made to this standard. Nearly all commercial products have a relevant ISO standard.

Such standards have considerable practical value. Buyers and sellers can define a product in a proposal, order, or contract by referring to the standard. Buyers can be confident that a product meeting this standard will conform to a specification that they have decided meets their technical requirements, i.e., their technical *quality* requirements. Suppliers understand the key technical parameters that must be met by the product in order to satisfy customer requirements. Thus, an ISO standard saves both the buyer and the seller considerable work in defining the product and gives both a basis for quality assurance. In many ways, this avoids costly over-inspection.

The buyer and seller of course may, and often do, choose to set additional specifications over and above those covered in the ISO standards. For this reason, the ISO provides a framework within which refinements can be added.[4] To increase confidence that the product fully meets the standard, the buyer usually achieves registration through certification from one of the consulting organizations listed by the Registrar Accreditation Board (see the profile at the end of Chapter 13).

In practice, a product can be checked against a particular ISO standard. The standard will provide technical details sufficient to provide a basis for tests that can establish whether or not the defined characteristics are present. However, this type of standard does not indicate how the product should be crafted to meet the specification. Testing solely for conformity to a standard is, therefore, a suitable role for the quality policeman introduced earlier. Manufacturing a product to conform to a standard may involve a high or low level of efficiency, with consequently high or low levels of scrap. In the end, the product may not meet the customer's requirements, who may need a product that differs in some way from the standard. To meet a different type of requirement, therefore, ISO also has standards for *capabilities* as well as for products.

Product and capability standards are complementary. To ensure road safety, for example, both types of standards are necessary. The design and condition of cars on the road affect safety. Manufacturers of new cars ensure in a myriad of ways that vehicles meet acceptable safety standards: the brakes function, the steering is precise, seat belts are effective, etc. Periodic testing also uses vehicle standards to ensure that the car's key safety features have not fallen below an acceptable level of performance. However, such product standards alone cannot make the streets safe. Drivers must meet capability standards and pass an appropriate testing system (the driving test and licensing process).

ISO 9000 is such a capability standard. It is the standard for quality systems, and it addresses the question of *how* the product or service is produced rather than *what* is produced. Two companies can make similar products to meet a common *product* standard, but under widely different production methods. Two other companies may each produce different output—one a product and one a service, for example—but use similar systems to maximize the quality of their output. ISO 9000 provides a recognized standard for a quality system. Both firms in each example could successfully meet it despite the wide differences in their activities.

As mentioned earlier, any type of standard implies assessment: the process of establishing conformity to the standard. A standard that cannot be assessed is of no use; if there is no way of determining whether or not a standard has been met, there is no need for it in the first place.

There are three types of assessment: first, second, and third (or independent) party. In first-party assessment, the supplier asserts that the product conforms to a published standard. Obviously, there are often concerns as to the value of such an assessment. The buyer may well feel that the assessment lacks objectivity, because it is not in the supplier's interest to admit that a product does not meet the standard. However, first-party assessments are not always worthless. In fact, they are part of trading in good faith; buyers often count on a supplier's honesty. Moreover, the supplier's claims may be legally enforceable through the purchase contract.

In second-party assessment, the customer establishes, through appropriate means, that the supplier's product meets the standards that the customer requires. The customer, therefore, tests the products or, in the case of a capability standard, assesses the procedures used within the supplier's organization. Such assessment is effective because the two parties to the transaction (buyer and seller) are involved and satisfied.

Second-party assessment can, however, be costly and inconvenient. If a factory supplies a number of customers with the same product and all wish to be assured that the standard claimed is being met, then the same tests will be duplicated with the costs multiplied by the number of customers concerned. If a capability standard is involved, the process of assessing the factory will be duplicated. The supplier's assessors may be on the premises so often that the production costs significantly increase due to disruption of existing or employment of additional staff to deal with less-than-welcome visitors.

Third-party, or independent, assessment is carried out by an outside organization that customers recognize as authoritative. For example, because a product has been assessed by ISO or a similar body, its adherence to the relevant standards will be accepted. Furthermore, if a company has undergone third-party assessment, it is likely that new customers will consider it as a supplier. Third-party assessment is, therefore, commercially valuable to a company as well as to the consultants involved.

All standards, including ISO 9000, can be assessed by a third party. An organization attains ISO 9000 registration through evaluation by a recognized assessor and agreement to regular inspection/surveillance by this same body. If the organization passes, it is then qualified for inclusion in the *Register of Quality Assessed Companies* (published in various countries by a designated group or a government department; see the profile at the end of Chapter 13 for details). In the United Kingdom, for example, the National Accreditation Council for Certification Bodies in turn assesses and accredits assessor/certification bodies.

The subject of choosing an assessor is critical and is discussed in some detail in a later chapter.

## ENDNOTES

1. C. D. Whethan, *A History of Science,* 4th ed., Macmillan, New York, 1980.
2. *Quality Digest,* Oct. 1993.
3. "ISO in Brief," *ISO 9000 News,* Vol. 1, p. 7, 1992.
4. Theodore Kinni, "The Fast Track to ISO Certification," *Quality Digest,* pp. 30–35, Oct. 1993.

# A BRIEF DESCRIPTION OF ISO

## Overview

ISO (the International Organization for Standardization) is a worldwide federation of national standards bodies representing 90 countries. It promotes the development of standardization and related activities to facilitate the interna-

---

*Source: ISO 9000 News,* Vol. 1, 1992. Notes and remarks from an interview with Frank Voehl after a speech by Dr. Eicher at the ISO 9000 Forum Application Symposium, Washington, D.C., October 8, 1993.

tional exchange of goods and services and develop intellectual, scientific, technological, and economic cooperation.

## Budget

ISO's budget totals approximately 94 million CHF per annum.

## Personnel

The Central Secretariat in Geneva employs 146 full-time staff members from 27 countries.

## Structure

ISO is made up of some 173 technical committees, 631 subcommittees, 1830 working groups, and 18 ad hoc study groups. These represent the viewpoints of manufacturers, vendors and users, engineering professions, testing laboratories, public services, governments, consumer groups, and research organizations in each of the 90 member countries.

## International Standards

Over 8000 international standards and technical reports have been published by ISO, representing almost 70,000 pages (as of 1991/1992) of technical text in one language. Coverage includes information processing, graphic industry and photography (19,800 pages), mechanical engineering (17,000), basic chemicals (5200), and nonmetallic materials (4700).

## International Relations

Approximately 450 international organizations are in liaison with ISO technical committees and subcommittees.

## Secretary-General

ISO's current secretary-general is Dr. Lawrence D. Eicher, who has said about the ISO 9000 "phenomena," "I choose to use the plural "phenomena," because I see the ISO 9000 standards as having made their mark in distinctly several different ways." It became apparent soon after the institution of the ISO 9000 standards that they would enjoy the most widespread recognition in industry, the most rapid adoption by the international standards community, and the greatest sales of any ISO standard in existence." This surprised many experts, even though the ISO 9000 standards were recognized from the beginning as being significantly different from what might be called "normal" engineering standards, such as those for units of measurement, terminology, test methods, product specifications, etc. The ISO 9000 concept is that certain generic characteristics of management practice could be usefully standardized, mutually benefiting producers and users alike. A report originating in France went so far as to call this new concept "standardization of the third kind."

## President

John Hinds (United States) says that quality is a competitive necessity in today's global markets. Citing his experience at AT&T, Mr. Hinds states that businesses are convinced that they must improve and enhance quality efforts. Thus, it seems certain that ISO 9000 will continue to grow in importance.

## Mailing Address

ISO Central Secretariat, 1 Rue de Varembe, Case Postale 56, Ch-1211 Geneva 20, Switzerland. Phone: +41 22 749 01 11. Fax +41 22 733 34 30.

2

# WHAT IS ISO 9000?

## INTRODUCTION

A deliberate modification of the acronym for the International Organization for Standardization (ISO), according to Sprow,[1] sounds like *isos,* the Greek word for equal, homogeneous, or uniform. This was done because IOS sounds too much like chaos, and the word order inevitably changes with different languages. One observer has quipped that ISO 9000 could also stand for International Strategic Opportunity for the '90s, which it certainly might be.

The intent of the ISO standard is to clarify and standardize terms as they apply to the field of quality management. Many common words are used in the quality field in a specific or restricted sense due to the adoption of quality terminology by different sectors of business and industry to suit their specific needs. For example, much confusion has arisen in the understanding of the terms *quality control, quality assurance, quality management,* and *total quality management.* The introduction of a multiplicity of terms by quality professionals in different industrial sectors has also caused confusion. The approach taken by ISO 9000 to solve this is to provide many concepts translated into terms and definitions for the development and application of the ISO 9000 standards[2] (and 10000 series of standards for auditing).

*Quality control* concerns the operational means to fulfill quality requirements. *Quality assurance* aims at providing confidence in this fulfillment, both within the organization and externally to customers and authorities.[3] (In the context of the standards, the English terms "ensure" and "assure" are used as follows: "ensure" means to make sure or certain, and "assure" means to give confidence to oneself or to others). *Quality management* includes both quality control and quality assurance, as well as the additional concepts of *quality policy, quality planning,* and *quality improvement.* Quality management operates throughout the *quality system.* These three concepts—quality control, quality assurance, and quality management—can be applied in all parts of an organization.

*Total quality management* brings to these concepts a long-term global management strategy and the participation of all members of the organization for the benefit of the organization itself, its members, its customers, and society as a whole.[4]

The terms defined in this international standard have direct application to the following series of international standards on quality and the related series of international standards:

- **ISO 9000:** Quality management and quality assurance standards (guidelines for selection and use)
- **ISO 9001:** Quality systems (model for quality assurance in design/development, production, installation, and servicing)
- **ISO 9002:** Quality systems (model for quality assurance in production and installation)
- **ISO 9003:** Quality systems (model for quality assurance in final inspection and test)
- **ISO 9004:** Quality management and quality system elements (guidelines)
- **ISO 10011:** Guidelines for auditing quality systems
- **ISO 10012:** Quality assurance requirements for measuring equipment

Other pertinent standards can be obtained from the ISO 9000 Forum (see the profile at the end of Chapter 5). Special attention should be paid to vocabulary standards in the statistics field (ISO 3534: Statistics—Vocabulary and Symbols):

- **Part 1:** Probability and general statistical terms
- **Part 2:** Statistical quality control
- **Part 3:** Design of experiments[4]

## THE ORIGINS OF ISO 9000

ISO 9000 began in 1979 when the British Standards Technical Committee 176 was launched to set forth generic quality principles to satisfy the need for an international minimum standard for how manufacturing companies establish quality control methods. This included not only control of product quality, but maintaining uniformity and predictability as well. Consumers wanted assurance that in the new world market—whether buying telephones, bread, wheat, or widgets—they would be getting quality and reliability for their money, today, tomorrow, or next year.

To accomplish this, 20 actively participating countries and 10 additional observer countries met and created, by consensus, a series of quality-system management standards called ISO 9000, which was finally issued in 1987. The standards were based in large part on the 1979 British quality standard BS 5750, as well on as the Canadian standard CSA Z299, the American ASQC Z1.15 standard, MIL Q 9858A, and to a limited degree the Union of Japanese Scientists and Engineers (JUSE)-based Deming prize guidelines.[4]

ISO 9000 was a great success from the start. It was the first ISO standard to go beyond nuts and bolts and attempt to address management practices. It quickly became the most widely known, widely adopted ISO standard and has sold more copies than any standard ISO has ever published. Although it is voluntary so far, over 50 countries have adopted it as a national standard. According to a recent survey, 82% of European blue-chip companies are familiar with its content and 64% have initiated action to become registered with ISO. Although the numbers on this side of the Atlantic may not be as high, interest in it is exploding.[4]

These standards for quality systems, ISO 9000 and its forerunner, had their origins in the military. Because of the critical nature of military products and the practical problems of investigating faulty products used in action, emphasis was placed on the manufacturing procedures and quality systems of the suppliers. Standards for appropriate quality systems were set. These included both international standards through NATO and national standards for cooperating and allied governments.

As such standards became established and known throughout industry, demand grew for something comparable outside the defense field. Eventually, in 1979, this led to BS 5750 and later to ISO 9000. The revised 1987 version of ISO 9000 was more comprehensive in scope and remains the recognized and accepted standard for quality systems today.

ISO 9000 was drafted not only to cover activities outside the military, but to be universally applicable. ISO 9000 can be applied to the quality systems of all commercial organizations and some noncommercial ones as well. This means that it is not just relevant to manufacturers; it is equally relevant to suppliers of services. However, a service provider is unlikely to be encouraged by a reading of the ISO 9000 standard. The language, terminology, and apparent assumptions are clearly targeted more to the manufacturer than to the service provider. (Even manufacturers outside the engineering field may feel that the standard is not written with their businesses in mind.) Despite this, ISO 9000 is intended to have universal application, and in fact the manufacturing elements of the standard can in all cases be adapted to even the most service-based business. By 1995, however, there should be a comparable ISO 9000 standard designed specifically for the service industries.

**Table 2.1** Relationship of the BS 5750 and ISO 9000 Series

| | BS 5750 | ISO 9000 Series |
|---|---|---|
| Guide to selection and use of appropriate part of the standard | Part 0/0.1 | 9000 |
| Guide to overall quality management and system elements | Part 0/0.2 | 9004 |
| Quality specifications for: | | |
| Design/development, production, installation, and servicing | Part 1 | 9001 |
| Producing to a customer's specification (or published specification) | Part 2 | 9002 |
| Final inspection and testing | Part 3 | 9003 |
| Scheme for stockists (equivalent to Part 2) | Registered stockists scheme—Levels A and B | — |
| Guide to use of Parts 1, 2, and 3 | Part 4 | — |
| Guide to quality management and quality elements for services | Part 8 | 9004-2 |
| Guide to the application of BS 5750 Part I in the development, supply, and maintenance of software | Part 13 (TickIT Initiative) | — |

*Note:* Further guideline parts to the standard are planned: Parts 7, 9, 10, 11, and 12.

Although BS 5750 and its ISO 9000 counterpart have been referred to here as one standard, they are in fact a series, and each was originally published in separate documents. BS 5750 is made of Parts 0 to 4, 8, and 13. (Parts 5 and 6 are no longer current.) These are listed in Table 2.1 along with the corresponding ISO 9000 documents.

Except for some minor syntactic differences, the content of the ISO 9000 Series is the same as BS 5750, with the key parts having an ISO 9000 Series equivalent. The ISO 9000 Series was modeled on BS 5750 because that was the international pioneering standard for quality systems. A company meeting the requirements of BS 5750 (whichever part is relevant) also meets the requirements of the equivalent in the ISO 9000 Series. If assessment and registration are obtained for BS 5750 Part 1, this is accepted as a satisfactory assessment for ISO 9001.

The practical value of the equivalence of BS 5750 and ISO 9000 lies in the ability to conduct business throughout the single market of the European Community (EC). As indicated in Table 2.2, all industrialized countries have a

**Table 2.2** International Quality System Standards

| Country | Specification for design/development, production, installation, and servicing | Specification for production and installation | Specification for final inspection and test |
|---|---|---|---|
| **International** | **ISO 9001: 1987** | **ISO 9002: 1987** | **ISO 9003: 1987** |
| Australia | AS 3901 | AS 3902 | AS 3903 |
| Austria | OE NORM-PREN 29001 | OE NORM-PREN 29002 | OE NORM-PREN 29003 |
| Belgium | NBN X 50-003 | NBN X 50-004 | NBN X 50-005 |
| China | GB/T 10300.2-88 | GB/T 10300.3-88 | GB/T 10300.4-88 |
| Denmark | DS/EN 29001 | DS/EN 29002 | DS/EN 29003 |
| Finland | SFS-ISO 9001 | SFS-ISO 9002 | SFS-ISO 9003 |
| France | NF X 50-131 | NF X 50-132 | NF X 50-133 |
| Germany | DIN ISO 9001 | DIN ISO 9002 | DIN ISO 9003 |
| Holland | NEN-ISO 9001 | NEN-ISO 9002 | NEN-ISO 9003 |
| Hungary | MI 18991–1988 | MI 18992–1988 | MI 18993–1988 |
| India | IS: 10201 Part 4 | IS: 10201 Part 5 | IS 10201 Part 6 |
| Ireland | IS 300 Part 1/ISO 9001 | IS 300 Part 2/ISO 9002 | IS 300 Part 3/ISO 9003 |
| Italy | UNI/EN 29001–1987 | UNI/EN 29002–1987 | UNI/EN 29003–1987 |
| Malaysia | MS 985/ISO 9001–1987 | MS 985/ISO 9002–1987 | MS 985/ISO 9003–1987 |
| New Zealand | NZS 5601–1987 | NZS 5602–1987 | NZS 5603–1987 |
| Norway | NS-EN 29001: 1986 | NS-ISO 9002 | NS-ISO 9003 |
| South Africa | SABS 0157: Part 1 | SABS 0157: Part II | SABS 0157: Part III |
| Spain | UNE 66 901 | UNE 66 902 | UNE 66 903 |
| Sweden | SS-ISO 9001: 1988 | SS-ISO 9002: 1988 | SS-ISO 9003: 1988 |
| Switzerland | SN-ISO 9001 | SN-ISO 9002 | SN-ISO 9003 |
| Tunisia | NT 110.19–1987 | NT 110.20–1987 | NT 110.21–1987 |
| **United Kingdom** | **BS 5750: Part 1:** | **BS 5750: 1987: Part 2:** | **BS 5750: 1987: Part 3:** |
| U.S. | ANSI/ASQC 091 | ANSI/ASQC 092 | ANSI/ASQC 093 |
| U.S.S.R. | 40.9001–88 | 40.9002–88 | — |
| Yugoslavia | JUS A.K. 1.012 | JUS A.K. 1.013 | JUS A.K. 1.014 |
| European Community (CEN) | EN 29001 | EN 29002 | EN 29003 |

national standard for quality systems compatible with ISO 9000; therefore, assessment and registration have worldwide recognition and commercial value.

ISO 9001 defines the standard for and requirements of a quality system under 20 main headings in Section 4, numbered 4.1 to 4.20 (Sections 0 to 3 are essentially introductory). The two requirements of 9001 that distinguish it from 9002 and 9003 are *Design Control (4.4)* and *Servicing (4.19)*. Of these, Design Control is arguably the more important, if only because servicing is regarded as necessitated by design. In other words, servicing may be needed because of a particular design activity, but not vice versa.

## THE EXISTING STRUCTURE OF ISO 9000 AND RELATED STANDARDS

The parts of the ISO standard fall into two groups: (1) the quality system requirements themselves (ISO 9001, 9002, 9003, and 9004) and the audit series (10011 and 10012) and (2) the guidelines to the standard itself. A company seeking registration under the standard opts to be assessed under only one of these parts, e.g., 9001 or 9002 (although it is possible for different sites, branches, or departments of the same company to seek registration under different parts). When an assessment is made, it is done based on one of these parts. A company's success or failure depends on its demonstrating that the quality requirements have been met.

As indicated earlier, there are five main parts in the series, from ISO 9000 to ISO 9004. To avoid misunderstandings and misinterpretations, ISO 8402 gives precise and detailed definitions of essential terms used in the quality area.

ISO 9000 itself is sometimes described as the road map of the system. Its guidelines help both suppliers and customers to obtain an understanding of what the ISO 9000 Series is really about. ISO 9000 elaborates on the general philosophy of quality system standards, their characteristics, the existing types, and where and when they are best used and describes what elements quality assurance models should incorporate. It also discusses demonstration and documentation requirements, pre-contract assessment, and contract preparation.[5]

If ISO 9000 is the road map of the quality system, ISO 9004 is the set of building blocks that make it possible to customize quality standards so that they conform to real-life situations. Using ISO 9004, a quality system can be adapted for specific situations. As a tool in internal quality management, ISO 9004 can be a link to total quality management programs based on continuous improvement.

A chemical company may decide to implement an ISO 9000 quality system. It will look through all the elements in ISO 9004 and decide which ones it will retain and which ones it can do without. The company must be sure, however, that it includes everything it needs for incorporation into its own quality management specifications. Another chemical company will probably compile a similar list. A watchmaker, however, will come up with a different list, as will a garage or a hotel.[6]

ISO 9004 is a comprehensive collection of quality objectives from which any company may select what its activities require. No one company needs everything on the list, because requirements and production processes differ from one organization or industry to another. There is, of course, a minimum list of topics that must be part of any system that deserves the quality label.

ISO 9004 has 20 detailed chapters that cover risks, cost and benefits, management responsibility, quality system principles, system documentation and auditing, economics, quality in marketing, quality in specification and design, quality in procurement, quality in production, control of production, product verification, control of measuring and test equipment, nonconformity, corrective action, handling and post-production action, quality documentation and records, personnel, product safety and liability, and statistical methods.[6] Of all the ISO 9000 standards, 9004 is the one that seems ideally suited for suppliers to large organizations, as well as a logical starting point for most small business operations.

The ISO 9001, 9002, and 9003 quality assurance systems are the basic requirements for a supplier's quality management system. They are the standards against which the quality management system will be assessed.

ISO 9001 covers the areas of design and development, production, installation, and servicing of products or services.

ISO 9002 addresses quality management in production and installation. Both phases require contract review, document control, purchasing, process control, handling, storage, packaging and delivery, training, and internal quality audits.

ISO 9003 covers quality assurance obligations of the supplier in the areas of final inspection and testing.[6]

## Description of ISO 9001

In ISO 9001 the meaning of "design" is much the same as in normal language. A firm carrying out design is expected to generate a product that meets a defined customer requirement:

- An architect designs a building to meet the space requirements of his clients.
- A software house writes a system to fulfill a specific information requirement.
- A crane maker manufactures a specially designed overhead crane for a particular factory.
- A management consultant designs a consultancy program to solve defined problems of a client company.

In these examples, a particular customer's requirements are defined and then a product or service is designed to match. Frequently, however, products or services are designed for customers who are unknown until a sale is made from stock. Volvo did not design the 850 series specifically to meet a particular individual's personal requirements; a buyer of a Volvo 850 merely falls within the segment of the car-buying population whose requirements are met by such a car. Design of this type is obviously very common throughout the manufacturing industry. However, in such cases the design process is not part of the contract with the customer; the customer only agrees to buy because the off-the-shelf product meets his or her needs. For this reason companies involved in supply from stock will normally seek ISO 9002 rather than 9001. Similarly, 9002 is appropriate where there is no design activity involved because the customer has provided a precise product or service specification. A jobbing engineering shop is, for example, provided with detailed drawings of the component to be produced, together with a material and manufacturing specification. The customer expects the product to be the same as might be made in-house or by an alternative supplier. In this case ISO 9002 rather than 9001 is appropriate.

## The Three Components of ISO 9000

In Figure 2.1, the twenty subclauses of the quality requirements for ISO 9001–9004 are shown in italics and arranged in three major blocks. The central block of nine clauses is considered the core of the requirements, because these concern what happens in the operating process itself. Very broadly, this term covers input, what is done with this input, (i.e., the process), and the output (i.e., what goes out to the customer). The sections in the left and right blocks have a supporting rather than core role, but are just as essential as those in the central Operating Process block. To meet the standard a quality system must be shown to fulfill the requirements under Quality System Control and Support Activities as fully as those included in Operating Process.

### *Operating Process*

The requirements included under Operating Process are described briefly here. Any reader who intends to design a quality system to meet ISO 9001, however, should obtain and read the actual standard.

#### Contract Review

One of the fundamental aspects of quality is meeting the customer's requirements. Clearly, to meet these requirements a supplier must know what they are.

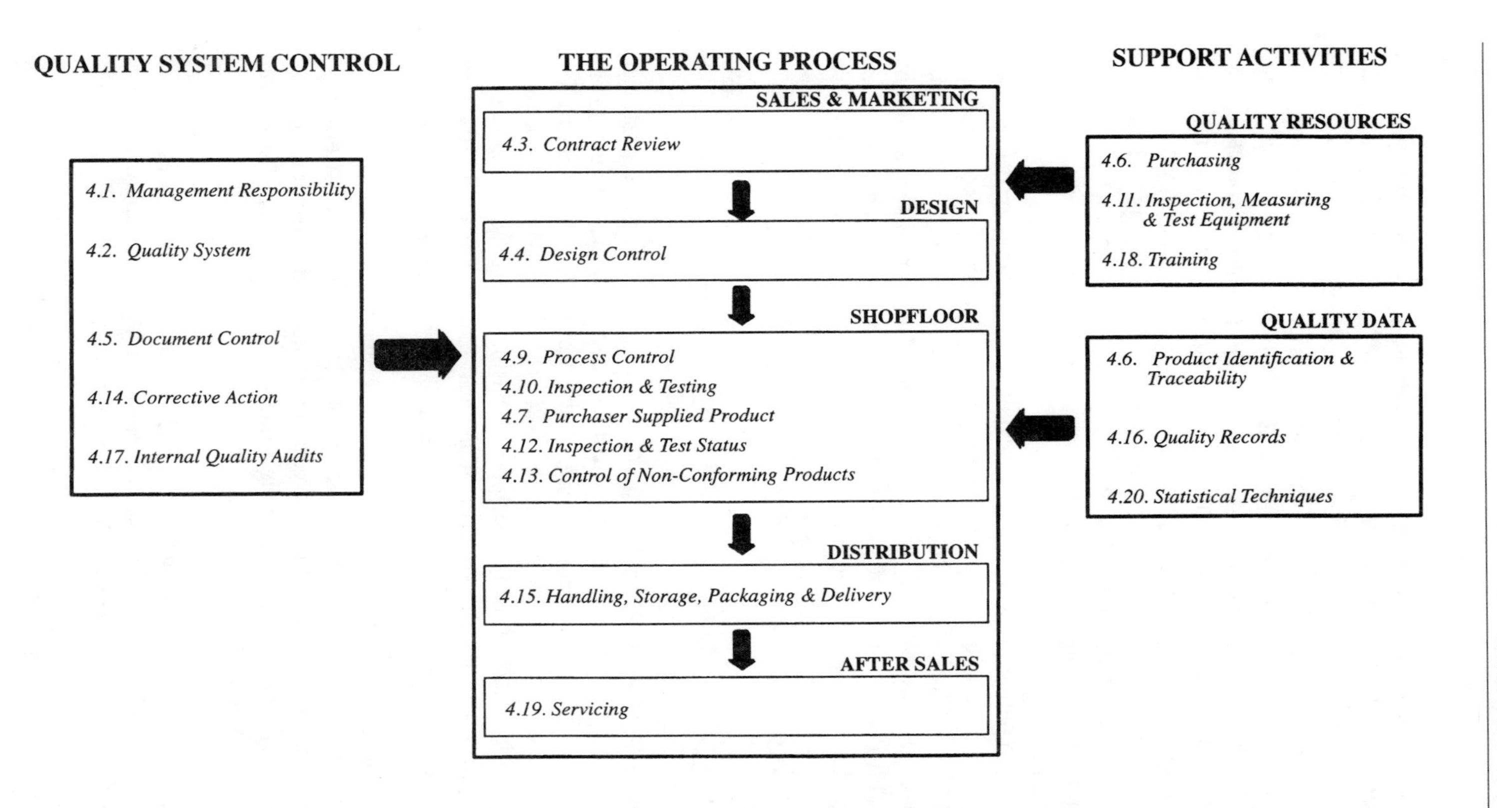


**Figure 2.1** ISO 9000.

Contract review is concerned with adequately defining and documenting these requirements and establishing that the resources needed to meet them are available. What should be covered in such a record of requirements and how it should be documented will vary from business to business.

In an industry in which subcontracting is the norm (e.g., printing, construction, many services), the contract review appropriately precedes any design or production activities and, therefore, fits logically as shown in Figure 2.1. However, in businesses supplying from stock, contract review would *follow* production of the product or service and would determine whether the available products met requirements. In Figure 2.1, therefore the Contract Review inner box would be shown between *4.15 Handling,* etc. and *4.19 Servicing.*

Obviously, contract review follows drawing up the contract or offering and in effect, therefore, follows the marketing process, an activity not explicitly covered in ISO 9000. Similarly, certain other activities vital to the survival of any business are also not covered. The most obvious omission is the accounting function. This does not mean that functions such as marketing and accounting have no quality dimension—clearly they have—but they are not formally addressed by the standard. In the assessment process for ISO 9000 a company is not evaluated in these areas.

## Design Control

Starting with an adequate definition of the requirements of the customer, design work must be carried out by qualified staff who are equipped with appropriate resources to produce a design that matches the requirements. The specific activities involved here will, as with all requirements of the standard, vary widely according to the type of business. The qualifications required to carry out design work on a nuclear reactor are obviously very different from the skills required to prepare a questionnaire in a market research company.

Design control requirements also cover the need to verify designs, establish criteria for verification, and control the output documents. Once a design is established, it is essential that this specific design be used and not an earlier, superseded draft. Ensuring this involves some form of document control and identification procedure.

The next four requirements are concerned with what happens at the service center or shop floor and cover the actual steps taken while making the product or providing the service to ensure that it meets requirements.

## Process Control

This requires that the work process be carried out in a controlled way. Included are documenting how the process is to be carried out, providing suitable written instructions for those doing so, and monitoring what happens during the process. For example, is the operating temperature of the furnace within the correct limits? Have the fire sensors been installed in the positions specified in the drawings? By what criteria is the output acceptable?

Special mention is made of the requirements of processes whose output cannot be adequately tested after manufacture and prior to customer delivery. Many service activities fall into this category.

## Inspection and Testing

Inspection and testing is concerned with establishing whether the input into the work process, the output, and the work at various stages in between meet defined requirements. The input may be third-party materials.

A special type of input is customer-supplied product, e.g., a component that is to be finished in some way in the supplier's factory. This is covered in *Purchaser Supplied Product (4.7)*. In this case the requirement includes appropriate inspection, but also addresses the need to look after the customer's product, to make sure the correct one is processed, and that its condition does not deteriorate while at the supplier. (In the wording of the standard, a "supplier" is the company registered for ISO 9000 and the "purchaser" is the customer.)

It is worth noting that inspection and testing of output is an explicit requirement of the standard, even though an effective system should not depend only on inspection and testing. The better the system, the less need for post-production inspection. The quality policeman should have a diminishing role and, in an ideal world, be eliminated.

## Inspection and Test Status/Control of Nonconformity

If testing is used to verify quality, it is essential to know which inputs, outputs, and in-process product have been tested and which tests and inspections have been applied. It must be established that the final product is up to standard prior to forwarding it to the customer and that the appropriate tests have been carried out. Stamps, labeling, location in the process area, and a variety of records are all suitable methods for meeting this requirement.

If, when testing products, some are identified that do not meet requirements, these should be separated from satisfactory products by, for example, marking and moving them to a special area prior to reworking or scrapping.

The last two requirements included under Operating Process concern the treatment of the product after it has been made.

### Handling, Storage, Packaging, and Delivery

This requirement addresses the need to keep the product in good condition after it leaves the shop floor and before it reaches the customer. It must be handled (moved within the manufacturer's premises), stored prior to forwarding, packed for delivery, and delivered so as to prevent either damage or deterioration. The latter may limit the shelf-life of the product.

Appropriate methods to meet this requirement obviously depend on the product involved. Lifting by mechanical shovel is appropriate for builders' sand, but not for a mainframe computer. In the case of some services, certain requirements may not be applicable. Although *all* the requirements of the standard should be carefully considered in the context of a particular business, there may be a few that do not apply.

### Servicing

This is explicitly applicable in only some situations, despite the fact that one of the clauses that distinguishes ISO 9001 from 9002 is, "where servicing is specified in the contract." If such servicing is specified, procedures are required to make sure that servicing work is carried out as required. If the contract with the customer does not specify servicing, then there is no requirement to meet. Some businesses may, however, choose to include in their quality system some form of servicing, even if it is not a contractual requirement. This may include various forms of customer follow-up. In addition to any formal requirements of ISO 9000, a company seeking registration should consider including in its quality system some safeguard for long-term customer satisfaction.

## *Support Activities*

The various requirements of the standard grouped as Support Activities are not integral to the production process, but they are needed if the quality system is to be successfully implemented. They fall into two subgroups: Quality Resources and Quality Data.

### Quality Resources

Three requirements—clauses *4.6, 4.11,* and *4.18*—ensure that the resources available within production are appropriate to quality needs. *Purchasing (4.6)* covers the development of procedures to ensure that supplies brought into the production process meet requirements. Specifics mentioned in this clause concern the selection and assessment of suppliers (the term "subcontractor" is used), documenting the supply process so that suppliers know precisely what is necessary to meet requirements, and verifying that what is supplied is what is required.

It is worth noting that the requirements of implementing a purchasing system do not require that previously satisfactory suppliers be minutely scrutinized. Those that have worked out well in the past should more than qualify for inclusion on an approved supplier list (which is commonly one element of an appropriate purchasing procedure). Nor do suppliers have to be ISO 9000-registered themselves. However, to ensure that their supplies are up to standard, suppliers may need to provide assurance of *their* quality systems, and ISO 9000 may be the most practical means for them to do this.

If inspection and testing are carried out within the production process, any instruments or equipment used in this activity must be capable of providing appropriate results, e.g., the micrometer is accurate enough to determine if the component is within the required range of tolerance. *Inspection, Measuring and Test Equipment (4.11)* is the requirement of the standard that meets this need. It covers procedures for selecting appropriate equipment for the test, calibrating and checking its accuracy, and ensuring that it is kept up to an appropriate standard. The application of this requirement in some service businesses may present problems.

The third class of quality resource included is people—*Training (4.18)*. Even the most automated plant is dependent on staff being trained to meet the needs of the job. In some businesses quality output is almost totally dependent on the skills of the people involved. Any business committed to quality must address and plan training needs.

## Quality Data

ISO 9000 requires records to demonstrate that quality activities are carried out. Throughout the clauses of the standard discussed above, the need for records is specifically mentioned. There are also requirements for quality data: identifying products and thereby tracing them through the production process, keeping records, and using statistical techniques to evaluate quality data.

There can only be quality records on a specific product (or product batch or, in the case of some services, project) if it can be identified. The requirements of *Product Identification and Traceability (4.8)* can certainly be met by physically labeling products, e.g., stamping the machine with a unique number. The quality records related to this specific product can then be examined. Other products, e.g., bulk deliveries of four, cannot be labeled in this way, but a batch of the product can nevertheless be linked, through records, to the specific processes carried out. For example, it can be determined that the flour delivered to the bakery on March 1 was part of a batch from a particular silo and was milled on February 12 during the third shift.

To be of use, quality records must be filed systematically, retained for an appropriate time (product life may be the criterion here), kept up to date, and maintained in a usable form. They do not have to be on paper; electronic data is an alternative. These requirements are specified in *Quality Records (4.16).*

## Quality System Control

A quality system includes the procedures carried out within and in support of the production processes. From another perspective, however, a quality system must be documented, reviewed, and updated in line with changes in the environment. Mechanisms are also needed to identify deficiencies in either the operation or the content of the system. This aspect of a quality system is covered in ISO 9000 Part 1 through five clauses that are grouped together under Quality System Control.

A quality system does not just happen. It is a major management task to both introduce an effective system and to maintain it. At the top level a policy decision must be made in relation to quality, a *quality policy.* Typically, this is a one-page statement from which the system follows. The responsibilities for implementing each part of the quality system also must be defined. Usually one person is put in charge of coordinating them (the management representative). Special attention must also be given to responsibility for inspection and testing. Finally, the working of a quality system must be periodically considered and decisions made about necessary changes. All these requirements are covered in ISO 9000 Part 1 in *Management Responsibility (4.1).*

The clause of the standard *Quality System (4.2)* (so called even though the whole is a standard for quality systems) might be better titled if it included "documented." The requirement in this respect is two-fold: the system must be documented and must describe how the system is to be implemented. Typically, *how* is covered by a procedure manual.

The document containing the quality system is also required to be controlled—*Document Control (4.5).* This includes an approval process for the contents, the availability of up-to-date copies to all concerned, and procedures for changing/updating the documents or parts of it as changes in the system are agreed upon (again by some controlled method).

Unavoidably, things go wrong. No matter how rigorous the quality system, the standard of the plant, and the training and motivation of the work force, problems will occur. Such problems are reflected in the output: products do not conform to quality requirements. The standard's requirements for *Corrective Action (4.14)* cover procedures for the identification of such deficiencies, the actions taken to investigate their cause, and the prevention of recurrence. The latter may lead to a need for a change in the quality system, which might have to be considered by a management review *(4.1)* and brought about through the provisions for document control *(4.5)*.

Lastly, it is a requirement that deficiencies identified are not only dealt with but are also actively sought through *Internal Quality Audits (4.17)*. Such audits must be carried out systematically (to a schedule and method) and may lead to corrective actions and again to review and change. Internal audits mirror the work carried out by external assessors (the bodies whose reports lead to ISO 9000 registration) and are therefore essential as part of the process of approval. However, and more importantly, they can be a vital tool in quality enhancement and, consequently, commercial success.

## Quality Improvement

Standards such as ISO 9000 have been criticized for being static. It is said that they ensure adherence to a given standard of quality and in effect inhibit the dynamic process of quality enhancement. Such a problem usually only arises through poor implementation of a quality system. An effective quality system builds in dynamic quality improvement. The triad shown in Figure 2.2 provides an effective quality improvement model. Internal quality

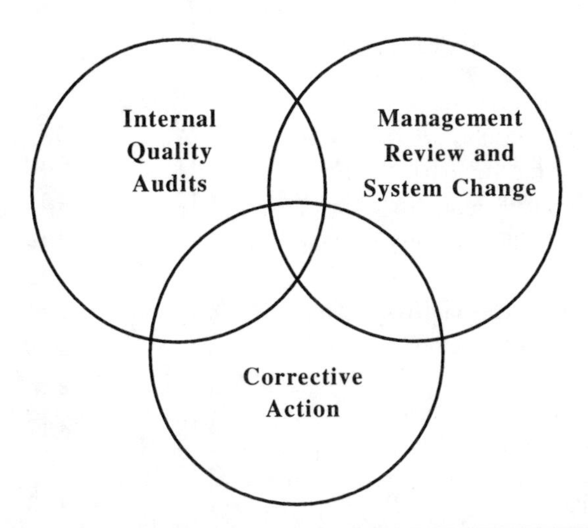


**Figure 2.2** The ISO quality triad.

audits identify deficiencies that are investigated through corrective action with recommendations made for change. These are considered at a management review, and change in the quality system is agreed upon and implemented. In turn, the revised procedures are audited, and if deficiencies are still found, the process is repeated.

All the requirements of ISO 9001 have not been covered here. It should be clear that the standard itself is general and can be applied to all businesses with a design element (this is described elsewhere), but it must be interpreted and implemented to meet the needs and circumstances of a particular firm. The standard defines what must be included in an effective quality system, but it cannot *itself* be followed. Most of the remainder of this book covers the devel-

**Table 2.3** ISO 9001, 9002, and 9003

| | Clause nomenclature | | |
|---|---|---|---|
| Requirement | ISO 9001 | ISO 9002 | ISO 9003 |
| Management responsibility | 4.1 | 4.1 | 4.1 |
| Quality system | 4.2 | 4.2 | 4.2 |
| Contract review | 4.3 | 4.3 | |
| Design control | 4.4 | | |
| Document control | 4.5 | 4.4 | 4.3 |
| Purchasing | 4.6 | 4.5 | |
| Purchaser-supplied products | 4.7 | 4.6 | |
| Product identification and traceability | 4.8 | 4.7 | 4.4 |
| Process control | 4.9 | 4.8 | |
| Inspection and testing | 4.10 | 4.9 | 4.5 |
| Inspection measuring and test equipment | 4.11 | 4.10 | 4.6 |
| Inspection and test status | 4.12 | 4.11 | 4.7 |
| Control of nonconforming products | 4.13 | 4.12 | 4.8 |
| Corrective action | 4.14 | 4.13 | |
| Handling, storaging, packaging, and delivery | 4.15 | 4.14 | 4.9 |
| Quality records | 4.16 | 4.15 | 4.10 |
| Internal quality audits | 4.17 | 4.16 | |
| Training | 4.18 | 4.17 | 4.11 |
| Servicing | 4.19 | | |
| Statistical techniques | 4.20 | 4.18 | 4.12 |

opment of an appropriate quality system, one that meets the requirements of the standard. Before the end of this chapter, however, the parts of ISO 9000 that meet the circumstances of organizations without a design element should be briefly considered.

## ISO 9002 and 9003

The clauses of ISO 9001, 9002, and 9003 and their respective numbering are provided in Table 2.3. Neither 9002 nor 9003 has any requirements that are *not* in 9001. They do, however, omit some of the requirements of 9001 (with more omissions in 9003 than 9002).

As previously discussed, the differences between 9001 and 9002 lie in only two areas, of which the critical one is design control. ISO 9002 is for organizations that either lack design function or have a design function but choose to exclude the design process and seek registration for ISO 9002. This book deals mostly with 9001 and 9002, but for brevity we will often simply refer to ISO 9000, except where it is necessary to discuss the different requirements of organizations with or without a design element.

ISO 9003 has a fairly specialized application and is appropriate for a limited range of businesses (comparatively few are registered for 9003 as compared with 9001 and 9002). Therefore, 9003 will not be discussed in detail.

## ENDNOTES

1. Eugene Sprow, "Insights into ISO 9000," *Manufacturing Engineering,* p. 73, Sep. 1992.
2. *ISO 9000: International Standards for Quality Management,* 3rd ed., International Organization for Standardization, Geneva, 1993, p. 29.
3. *ISO 9000: International Standards for Quality Management,* 3rd ed., International Organization for Standardization, Geneva, 1993, p. 30.
4. *ISO 9000: International Standards for Quality Management,* 3rd ed., International Organization for Standardization, Geneva, 1993, p. 31.
5. *ISO 9000 News,* Vol. 1, No. 1, Jan. 1992, p. 5.
6. *ISO 9000 News,* Vol. 1, No. 1, Jan. 1992, p. 6.

# ISO/TC 176: THE CHANGE MASTERS AT WORK

## Overview

Reg Shaughnessy and Peter Ford are the Chairman and Secretary of the ISO Technical Committee 176 (ISO/TC 176), which is in charge—with the help of hundreds of experts from across the world—of finalizing quality assurance requirements in a wide international consensus. The committee was formed in 1979 and completed the ISO 9000 standards in 1986 (published in 1987). A total of 63 countries are currently involved with this committee.

## The Role of TC 176

Over the past 13 years, ISO/TC 176 has conceived, developed, prepared, and continuously improved upon the core ISO 9000 standards. Beyond that basic mission, the committee has worked with other technical committees in ISO or in the International Electrotechnical Committee (IEC/TC 56) to develop supplementary standards that became useful as development work on the main standards progressed.

## The Mission of TC 176

The mission has been from the outset to achieve standardization in the field of generic quality management. This definition covers quality systems, quality assurance, and generic supporting technologies, which include standards providing guidance on the selection and use of the core standards. This very broad mission excludes, however, the preparation of technical standards related to specific products or services. The committee is strictly concerned with quality and leave the preparation of product or service standards to other technical committees (TCs) in ISO.

*Source: ISO 9000 News,* Vol. 1, 1992.

## The Three Subcommittees

Three subcommittees (SCs) deal with specific areas. They are assisted in their work by several working groups to which specific topics are assigned.

SC 1, the first of these subcommittees, deals with concepts and terminology and has produced the ISO 8402 Standard on Terminology. The French standards organization, AFNOR, runs the secretariat of this subcommittee and one of its working groups. The other two working groups in SC 1 have conveners from the British Standards Institution (BSI) and the American National Standards Institute (ANSI).

SC 2 deals with developing quality systems, specifically the ISO 9000 series of standards. It is run by BSI and comprises nine working groups. Convener responsibilities for one or more of these working groups are shared between experts appointed by national standards associations of the United Kingdom (BSI), the USA (ANSI), Canada (SCC), and Germany (DIN).

SC 3 is responsible for supporting technology and the development of the tools needed to implement the Quality Programme Standards, e.g., metrology and test equipment. The Dutch standards organization (NNI) runs the secretariat of this subcommittee. The secretariat for its three working groups is handled by experts from BSI, ANSI, and DIN.

## Coordination with Other Committees

Coordination with other committees is the responsibility of the joint QDS (Quality, Dependability, Statistics) group that brings together officers of ISO/TC 176, IEC/TC 56 (Dependability) and ISO/TC 69 (Statistical Methods). One of the topics in which the QDS group is involved is terminology, because different language practices have developed in isolation over the years in sectors drawn closer by the quality revolution. The QDS group identifies problems and needs and provides direction to the appropriate groups for action or resolution. They do not, for example, develop definitions or provide drafts.

The fact that standards result from a wide international consensus, brought about in TC 176 and its subcommittees, clearly indicates that the standards meet universal needs.

## U.S. Delegation to TC 176

The U.S. delegation to TC 176 is headed by Don Marquand, who is a well-known quality assurance professional.

3

# WHY DO IT? (WIFM: WHAT'S IN IT FOR ME?)

## INTRODUCTION

This chapter is intended to help the reader decide whether ISO 9000 is worthwhile for his or her organization. In addition to the benefits and drawbacks of ISO 9000, its relevance is also discussed: to which types of companies and organizations can it be effectively applied?

## THE BENEFITS OF ISO 9000 REGISTRATION

In Chapter 1, the general benefits of quality and quality systems were covered. A company can realize these general benefits without ISO 9000 registration, and many do so. ISO 9000 offers, however, specific advantages beyond such general advantages of a quality system and also improves the effectiveness of the system. It is these specific benefits of ISO 9000, both external and internal, that are the focus here.

### Survival

One of the strongest arguments for a company adopting ISO 9000 is that it may become necessary to keep major customers, as illustrated in the following scenario.

### *We Can't Deal with You Any More, Joe*

Joe Burns had always been committed to quality and over the years this had paid off well. Burns Technics produced highly specialized components, and the investment he put into both equipment and people made Burns the leader in a niche market. The largest customer by far was a public utility with whom Burns had sole supplier status.

Joe had been asked to visit Tom Howell, the engineering buyer of the utility. As far as he knew, there was no problem with the products or the delivery. In fact, only last month a technical manager had gone out of his way to commend Burns to his counterpart in another major utility. Still Joe was uneasy. Tom had not seemed his normal, affable self, and there had been those letters asking for details of Burns' quality systems. If he had a weakness, Joe knew that it was his paperwork, but why ask about the quality system when the excellent quality of Burns was a byword in the industry? Perhaps the letters were just leftovers from the bad old bureaucratic days before he had come along.

The meeting with Tom started off well; the usual pleasantries about wives, children, dogs, and golf. Inquiries about the latest delivery from Burns suggested that there was no problem in this area. Then Tom got to the point of the meeting.

"I will be blunt, Joe. As things stand, we won't be able to place any more orders with you after July."

"But I have had no complaints from you about the products. I am sure we can discuss the money side of things if you have had other quotes."

"Well, Queros, Inc. is very eager to do business with us and can supply all our requirements, but I have doubts about them. However, I will have no choice. Look at this memo from top management."

Tom passed across a memo headed "Technical Suppliers and ISO 9000."

"In six months' time I can only buy from suppliers who are registered for ISO 9000. The only exception is if no available source has ISO 9000. Queros has. I understand from our quality department that you have not replied at all to their inquiries."

The strongest case for seeking ISO 9000 registration, therefore, is that without it a company will no longer be able to supply some of its major customers. ISO 9000 may be the price that has to be paid to keep a substantial slice of business. It may be a condition of survival. As in the story of Joe Burns, a supplier usually has fair warning of what is coming. However, it generally takes about a year from start to finish for a company to obtain ISO 9000 registration, and that assumes everything goes well. The timetable imposed by a major customer may not be long enough. Moreover, it is better to work to one's own timetable than to someone else's. Also, there are definite marketing benefits to taking the initiative.

Clearly, the reader must consider what is happening in his or her own industry when weighing the likelihood that ISO 9000 will be a formal prerequisite even to quote for business. It appears that few industries are untouched by ISO 9000. A limitation on even the largest customers, however, is that they cannot require ISO 9000 approval of their suppliers if none of them has it. An assessment of the potential requirement for ISO 9000, therefore, should consider both customers' indications and whether or not competitors are going down this road. Once started, however, the momentum can rapidly build up. In the management consultancy business, for example, the situation has changed dramatically in only two years. Instead of having *no* interest in obtaining ISO 9000 approval for themselves (although consultants often recommended ISO 9000 to their clients), many consultancies are now scrambling for registration as fast as possible.

Seeking ISO 9000 out of necessity is bound to be viewed negatively. If a company adopts the standard reluctantly, because customers demand it, chances are that the full benefits of a quality system will not be obtained. However, the coin is two-sided; if existing customers demand ISO 9000, it is very likely that new business will come in as a result of successful registration. At its simplest, this will mean orders from customers who have already adopted an ISO 9000-only supplier policy; this may enable a small company to make the leap from supplying only correspondingly small customers to blue-chip business. ISO 9000 may bring in not only more, but a different class of business and herald a period of rapid growth. As an example, a furniture manufacturer had for years tried to supply products to a certain government agency, but without success. With ISO 9000 approval, the company was accepted on the approved supplier list and within a year obtained orders which doubled revenue. The costs of ISO 9000, therefore, in this case were demonstrably recovered in less than a year. This is by no means unusual.

Extra business through ISO 9000 does not just come from large customers with a formal requirement that suppliers be approved by the standard. ISO 9000 almost always enhances the quality standing of company. Because all buyers seek quality, there is a positive business gain. If few competitors in an industry have (as yet) sought ISO 9000, those that have will be distinguished as quality leaders. To be the first in an industry to be registered offers a major marketing opportunity, but one that should be rapidly exploited because others will soon catch up. In general, the benefits of ISO 9000 will only be reaped if a company actively promotes its new status. Gaining ISO 9000 will take money and effort; once gained, it should be made a central part of the marketing effort—including mentions in public relations, advertising, and direct mail to customers—and should be built into proposals and quotes.

Another source of additional business through ISO 9000 registration is from companies in the European market and overseas in general. An internationally recognized quality standard reduces barriers. When buying from a distant supplier, quality can be an especially serious concern. Often, much depends on perceptions of the ability of a supplier to meet requirements, and this is inevitably uncertain when the supplier is from another country. Adherence to a known quality standard helps to reduce these concerns. Also, although some countries are behind the United Kingdom in terms of the number of companies registered to a national standard, the momentum is increasing. Just as large companies in the United Kingdom are starting to adopt a BS 5750-only supply policy, their counterparts in Germany, France, Italy, Japan, and the United States are likewise insisting that suppliers demonstrate an effective quality system. Assessment via parallel national standards (see Table 2.2) automatically confers approval through the international ISO series of standards, which in all countries is a recognized equivalent of the local national standard for quality systems. ISO 9000, therefore, potentially offers increased international business.

As stated earlier, this chapter covers the specific benefits of ISO 9000 rather than quality systems in general. The external benefits of ISO 9000 cannot be practically separated, however, from the general benefits of a quality system. As will be shown, ISO 9000 helps cement a quality system; it helps to ensure that the system works well. An effective quality system will produce quality improvements, and improved quality will bring in business. In the end, this is by far the most important long-term external benefit of ISO 9000.

In a business environment in which the number of suppliers and vendors to any given organization is being reduced, those that have achieved ISO 9000 registration will clearly be in an advantageous position. As Dr. Deming has said, reducing the number of suppliers, based upon objective criteria, is a key to survival.

Before moving to the internal benefits, one last point to must be made: ISO 9000 can only bring external benefits if customers understand what the standard means. By and large, in business-to-business markets (where the customer is another company or organization rather than a private individual), ISO 9000 is understood even if only vaguely. Outside business-to-business markets, among the general public, ISO 9000 is not known, and in such retail-level markets the external benefits of having the standard may be slight. A grocer does not need to worry that customers will stop dealing with him if he cannot display an ISO 9000 certificate at the front of the store. Similarly, if he does display it, the extra customer impact will probably be insignificant. However, the range of retail-only businesses that have chosen to seek ISO 9000 is surprising, e.g., doctors, dentists, and schools. Generally, it will probably be the internal rather than the external benefits that are sought, but even when customers have a low awareness of ISO 9000 as such, attainment of registration can be communicated and understood as a symbol of commitment to quality, similar to the implied excellence behind the Malcolm Baldrige Award. The ordinary consumer is as much concerned with quality as the most technical of industrial buyers.

The general *internal* benefits of a quality system all relate to getting it right the first time—fewer supplier-related rejects and errors, scrap, and reworking, less downtime in tight schedules, and less frustration because someone else did not meet requirements. Such savings can be a massive benefit to a business, but can only be obtained if the quality system is effective. ISO 9000 is a standard for effective systems.

## Symbol of Commitment

ISO 9000 registration is also a symbol of commitment. Preparing a company for ISO 9000 is not a trivial matter, as will be demonstrated in the remainder of this book. It inevitably has a significant cost. ISO 9000 involves having outside assessors visit the company to establish that the quality system is being followed in full. A company seeking ISO 9000, therefore, cannot just pay lip service to quality; those that do will fail the assessment. Also, the assessment for ISO 9000 involves registering the entire company or site and all employees. Of necessity, therefore, the process of seeking ISO 9000 implies important messages for all:

- Quality is the concern of every employee.
- All employees are committed to the quality system.
- If it does not work, it will be fixed—not ignored.

This applies not only to the factory, but also to managers—right up to the top. It also applies to the public sector, such as federal, state, and local government agencies. This is important, because in some small companies quality problems can arise as much through the boss ignoring procedures as through employees doing so.

### *Fine, But I Wanted It Green...*

Tideswell Controls produces customized air conditioning units. With so many possible permutations in design, it is vital that customer requirements be precisely defined. The owner of the company, Paul, had designed a detailed checklist to make sure that every possible requirement was covered and specified. This was filled in by the salesman, sent to the design room, and was used as a check on the factory. Paul was no tyrant, but a salesman only forgot to complete the customer requirement form once. It usually did not happen twice.

Paul was usually involved in larger orders, and a few were handled only by him. He was very pleased when he won an order for a major new factory in Oshkosh. With 33 units, it was the largest single order ever. Paul discussed all the details with the customer and personally briefed both the design team and the production managers. Of course, he did not complete a customer design form; he never did. There was no need: after all, he had designed the form and knew its contents by heart.

When the order was nearly ready, the customer was invited to visit Tideswell to see some of the equipment. The first five units were displayed in reception, with the dark blue stove enamel mirror-polished.

After a brief glance, the customer frowned. "Yes, they seem fine, Paul, but you must know I wanted them green. You have been to our other factory and seen that all our gear is a standard green. No way can we have just the control boxes blue."

Repainting was not a simple matter. At the very least, all the units would have to be disassembled. "Well, don't look at me, Paul," said the finishing room manager. "Blue is our standard, and blue it is unless something different is specified on the form."

With ISO 9000 everyone, including Paul, would be required to follow the contract review part of the quality system. Just because he is the boss and designed the system, Paul is not excused from following the procedures. Similarly, all other members of the staff are expected to follow the system. It is not just the boss that insists; it is the system.

### *Telling the Shop Floor*

Andrew was seen as the rising star of the business. Single-handedly, he not only brought in the best business, but his design work was first-class. His shortcomings? Like many really bright people, he could be a bit arrogant, or perhaps he just didn't realize that not everyone was as quick on the uptake as he was. The quality system required that written job instructions, be passed to the workroom. Andrew prepared instructions, but they were a bit short on detail and he could be curt if asked to explain more fully. "Just get on with it, Anne," he would tell the workroom manager. Sometime this led to problems, but Anne, who held the designers in awe, just stayed behind and put things right.

Because the quality system had been developed to ISO 9000, internal quality audits were routine. An instance of Andrew's curt instructions leading to problems was identified and reported to the quality manager (who was also a senior director). A corrective action was duly issued, and Andrew was given the task of investigating the problem. He was forced to recognize that the deficiency was his and owned up to the mistake in his report. However, the quality manager was not satisfied and called Andrew in.

"You have identified the problem, Andrew, but in honesty I am sure that Anne had recognized this already. The question is, how do we stop it from happening again? And don't tell me you will just try harder next time."

Eventually it was agreed that the quality system should be changed and any deficient work instructions returned to the author for amendment before work started.

Andrew, even with the best of intentions, soon lapsed and again sent instructions lacking clear details. Anne now returned them for correction. Andrew hated it, but could not blame Anne.

"It's this ISO 9000. You can't get away with any shortcuts now," he complained as he sat down to a late dinner at home. "In the future, I will just have to spend more time on these silly instructions and get them right."

The depersonalization aspect of ISO 9000 also alleviates other personnel problems. Problems in performance can be judged not only in the opinion of a manager, but against a standard that is seen to be impartial and objective and based upon fact rather than innuendo. Performance problems can also be taken out of a formal hierarchy and addressed across the board.

Incidentally, the quality system would have allowed Anne to raise a corrective action to deal with the problem; the system provides a mechanism for real problems to be addressed without their becoming personal issues, thus removing personalities from the matter.

## Management Control Tool

A quality system is also a tool of management control. Without a formalized set of procedures, management control is just a matter of bosses demanding and workers jumping. At worst, requirements are viewed as personal whims imposed from above without any known reason. They may be followed, but reluctantly. More often, time is spent in sabotaging a tyrannical regime. A formalized system is a great improvement. Things are done because they are in the book, and everyone knows what is required of him or her and why. Still, some of the requirements are felt to be onerous and at management's whim rather than existing for good reason. Arbitrariness is reduced, but is still present.

A quality system assessed to ISO 9000 is, however, legitimized. The requirements of the system are now seen not as managers' whims, but as necessary to comply with a recognized standard. Who can argue against the system? Furthermore, although an ISO 9000 system is a tool of management control, it encourages a rational and benign system. In particular, active and positive participation is encouraged through the requirements for controlled change procedures. If the system is to work, all must understand its purpose of maximizing quality and be encouraged to participate fully in making changes to solve problems.

## Corrective Action Feature

An ISO 9000 system must incorporate the trilogy of audit, corrective action, and management review discussed in Chapter 2. This is a powerful problem-solving tool. A further internal benefit of ISO 9000 is, therefore, that problems must be faced up to and solved. In any business or organization there is a tendency to patch or make do and concentrate on the short term. Come what may, the product must get out and the money in (or the equivalent in a nonbusiness environment). Keeping one's nose to the grindstone reduces vision to the short term. By never lifting up one's heads and taking a longer term view, suddenly twenty years of experience is twenty years of repeating the same mistakes. A quality system designed to meet the requirements of ISO 9000 enforces this longer term view through the need to identify problems and solve them—and keep on solving them until everything is almost perfect. In a perfect system, problems are predicted, published, and ultimately prevented from occurring in the first place.

### Framework for Growth

Finally, a further internal benefit is that an ISO 9000 quality system is a framework for the successful growth of a small company. A company may start as little more than a one-man band. Quality is high because the owner is committed to his or her success and not only oversees everything but pretty much *does* everything, including staying close to the customers. As success comes, staff are brought in, but initially they are just helpers working under the constant personal supervision of the owner. However, even with the greatest commitment and the longest of days, the owner starts to find that he or she cannot physically be everywhere at once. If the owner is out getting orders, the workers at home are left to their own devices. Sooner or later this leads to a crisis. Quality slips, and the workers are blamed for a lack of commitment. Perhaps the answer is to bring in better qualified staff, but who wants to work for someone who is never satisfied?

At the appropriate time, the answer to controlling growth is to set up a quality system. ISO 9000 provides a standard which, if met, will ensure that the system is effective and can grow with the business. The company is still individual, with the stamp of the founder, but staff now have greater independence within the guidelines of the system. Their participation makes quality a company-wide concern and no longer dependent only on the owner's driving energy. With everyone working from the same blueprint, the owner can afford to focus energy where his or her interests and skills really lie. Furthermore, the system allows new staff to join in, work to the best of their talents, and commit to quality. In turn, this attracts a higher quality of staff. All of these factors come together both to allow and stimulate successful growth. Of course, over time the quality system must change in order to meet the new circumstances and conditions of the company, but in a system designed to meet ISO 9000, this dynamic element can be built in.

## THE DRAWBACKS OF ISO 9000

There are potential drawbacks to ISO 9000 that should be considered before any decision is made to implement a system. First and foremost is cost. However, cost must be weighed against benefit. Some financial considerations are outlined at the end of this chapter.

## Culture Shock

A company moving from a situation with no formal quality system to one that meets ISO 9000 will face a culture shock, and this will be particularly acute in small companies where management issues are largely the domain of the owner. As discussed, a major internal benefit of ISO 9000 is that everyone, from the top down, has to be committed to the system and willing to follow the procedures even when it feels uncomfortable. The greatest change may be faced by the boss; he or she perhaps must change from being an absolute ruler to a constitutional monarch. The boss is bound by the same rules as the office junior. In a larger organization the same problem may be faced by the entire management layer. They can no longer be sovereign in their own areas. If you the reader, as is likely, are the owner of a small to mid-size company and are used to having everything your own way, how will you cope when the foreman raises a corrective action that points out a problem that originates from your desk? Can you handle this? If not, ISO 9000 is not for you.

## Bureaucracy

Bureaucracy is often seen as the major drawback to ISO 9000. Some, wrongly, see an ISO 9000 system as the sum of its forms and nothing more. It must be acknowledged that there is some truth in this charge. A requirement of the standard is keeping records, e.g., *Quality Records (4.16),* and generally this involves forms. However, it is difficult to imagine an operating process producing consistently high quality without records of some sort being kept. Often these are kept accurately, but in little black books known to only a few people; if these people are away, the records lapse. Worse, the record-keeping is spasmodic and haphazard.

If records are needed, they should be accurate and complete. This will be best achieved if the forms are well designed and an auditing system is in place to check that recording is done. If the records serve no useful purpose, they should be neither made nor kept. The process of designing a quality system for ISO 9000 involves a critical review of existing records. Quite likely, some records will be scrapped as new ones are introduced. It is even possible that the total record-keeping activity will decline. Certainly an ISO 9000 system can cause a massive increase in forms, but this usually results from problems in the system design. The standard does not require that any specific forms be kept as part of the system; it cannot do so, because it is only a standard against which individual systems are measured.

The forms (or other equivalent records such as computer files) in each employee's system should be essential to the successful operation of his or her own process; if not, they should be scrapped. Arguably, periodic critical review of all forms should be built into the system.

## Compliance vs. Excellence

Another possible drawback of ISO 9000 is that it can degenerate into a legalistic game. At worst, the quality system can be designed merely to get through ISO 9000 without any regard for a real improvement in quality.

### *The Fourth Copy*

The consultant was reviewing the working of the company's purchasing system and asked to see the current order forms. They came in pads of four: a top sheet and three carbonless copies.

"How is each copy used?" asked the consultant.

"The top copy goes to the supplier, of course. The second goes to the department which will receive the order, and the third goes in the ordering file."

"And the fourth copy?"

"Oh it goes to Pat."

A little later, the consultant asked Pat where she kept her copy of the order form.

"Well I haven't any room to file my copy. When they start to build up, I throw them away."

## The Tail Wagging the Dog

Much ingenuity is devoted to fitting the operating process to the system rather than vice versa: this job is a one-time thing and requires methods that are outside the system, but with a bit of tweaking it will look right in the records. These problems only arise because either the motive for seeking ISO 9000 is wrong or insufficient thought or time has been allocated to designing the system. Maybe the impetus to ISO 9000 was the insistence of a major customer, but it is better (and probably not much more expensive) to go the whole way and design an effective system—and reap all the benefits. Turn lemons into lemonade: turn an imposed burden into a real vehicle for positive change.

If the system does not match the needs of the business, as represented by constantly bending the rules, the system was badly designed in the first place. The blame for this cannot be placed on ISO. The standard allows enormous flexibility for designing a system to match almost any situation. Some of the blame may be placed on the consultant who designed large portions of the system, but who left the consultant to his or her own devices in the first place? Consultants can play an invaluable role, but it is a supportive one. It is the owner's responsibility to match an ISO 9000 system to his or her individual needs. If it does not work, change it. If this is not done, most of the benefits and, in the long run, ISO 9000 approval will be lost. A poorly designed system cannot command adherence, and the independent assessors will find so many noncompliances that registration will be withdrawn anyway.

This introduces a final consideration. Outside assessors can be a real nuisance. They take up time, frighten the staff, and generally poke their noses into the business. Worse still, they get paid for it. However, a system such as ISO 9000 requires independent third-party assessment. If this is not feasible, neither is ISO 9000. Also, inspection by an independent third-party assessor may be preferable to successive waves of customers examining the procedures (and perhaps also looking for ways of lowering the price). Finally, why should anything be hidden from the assessor? The company chose the firm to act as an assessor, and the quality system belongs to the company. The assessor is only checking that the things that should be done are being done. True, the assessor has to make sure that the company's system matches the requirements of the standard, but once over that hurdle the only yardsticks the accessor can measure with are the company's own.

## THE RELEVANCE OF ISO 9000

A common view of ISO 9000 is that it is a good thing in general and for other companies. Some organizations find it very good for their suppliers, but not for themselves. Other businesses believe that they are unique and that ISO 9000 was not written to meet the needs of their very specialized operation. Perhaps a company feels too far removed from the type of engineering operation that ISO appears to have had in mind.

The fact is that *all* businesses, at least according to their owners or managers, are unique, special, and completely unintelligible to anyone who has not spent a lifetime of initiation into the mysteries of the craft. ("You mean to say that you have no experience in making burnished left-hand gimlets with eccentric grommets...?") Granted, but all businesses are also the same. At the very least, they all take input, do something with it, and provide output to customers whose needs must be satisfied if the business is to thrive.

As previously shown in Figure 2.1, the core of the ISO 9000 requirements concern the operating process, and any other requirements have a supportive (but vital) role. Any operating process can be characterized as a sequence of input–process–output (Figure 3.1). Implementation of a quality system to meet ISO

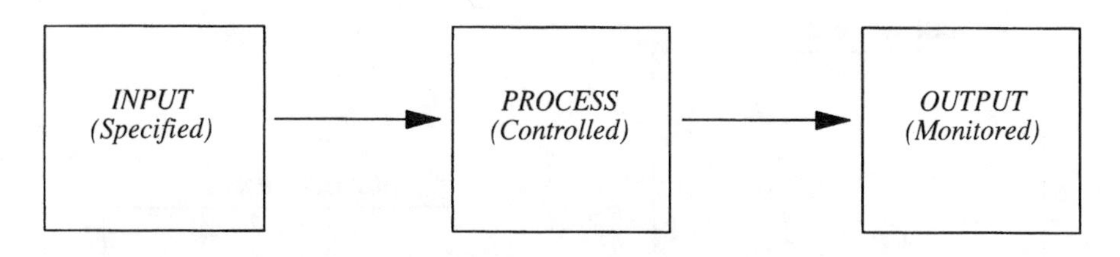


**Figure 3.1** The operating process.

9000 standards seeks to ensure that the input is to a specified standard (e.g., through the purchasing process), that the process itself is controlled, and that the output is monitored for conformity to requirements.

It is difficult to think of a business that does not fit the pattern of input–process–output. Figure 3.2 provides three examples of this pattern with the particular inputs, processes, and outputs described. The examples progress from

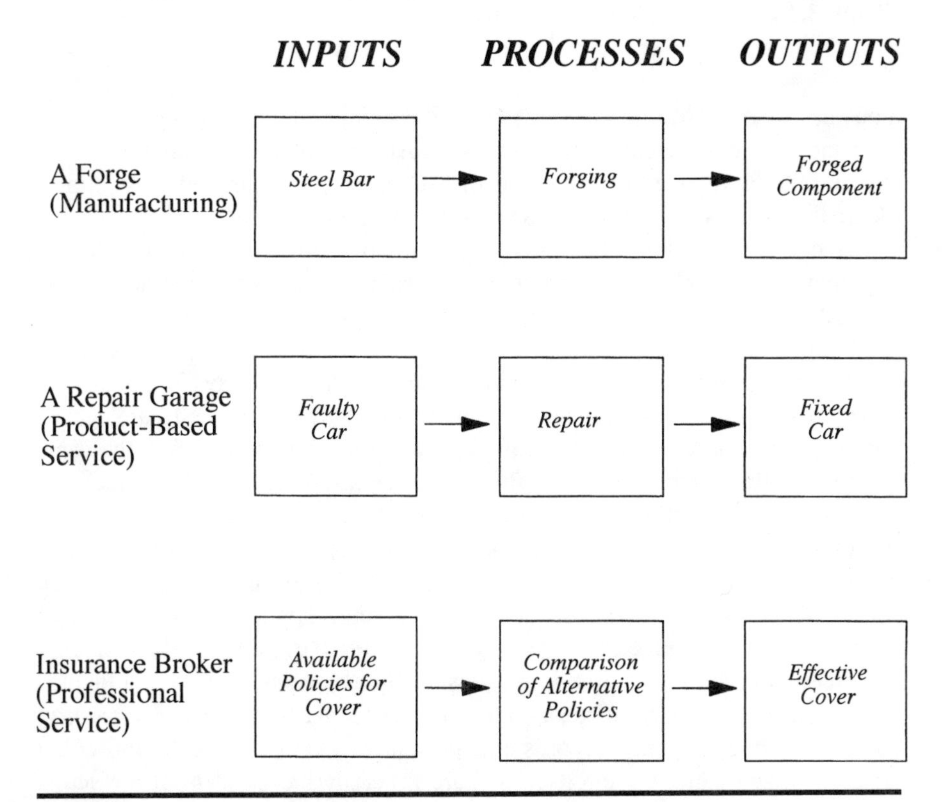


**Figure 3.2** Operating processes.

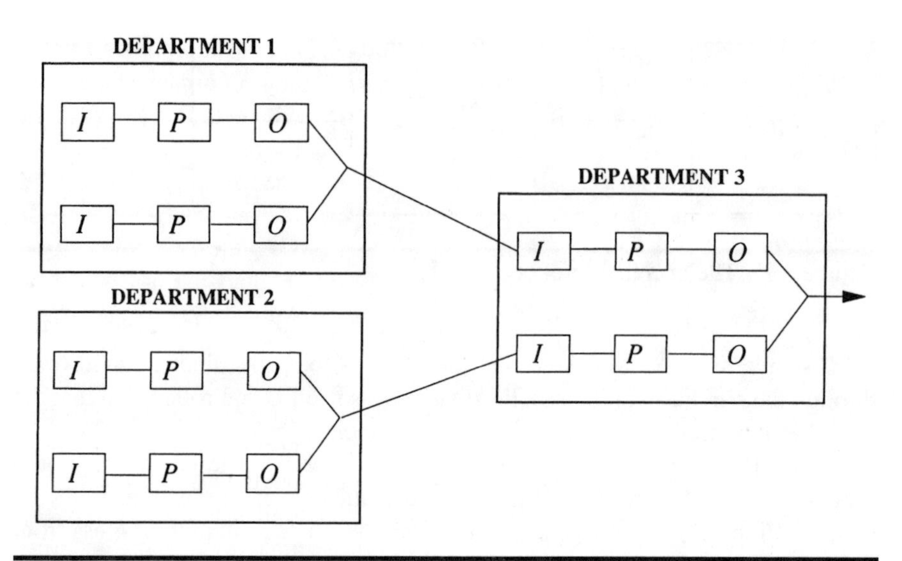


**Figure 3.3** Complex operating process.

a business that might find the language of the standard familiar (forging) to one far removed from the engineering industry. All, however, have input–process–output, and the relevant requirements of ISO 9000 can be applied to maximize the quality in each of the three stages of the operating process.

Of course, complex businesses have a multitude of input–process–output sequences (Figure 3.3), but given analysis time this complexity can be adequately represented, and the application of ISO 9000 will become easier to grasp.

As noted earlier, all businesses are unique, and therefore their quality systems will be unique. Even within a particular industry, the quality systems will vary widely to account for differences in the inputs, the way the processes are carried out, and the variety of outputs. However, all companies will pursue the same quality goal through implementing their own systems, the adequacy of which can be measured against the requirements of ISO 9000.

Returning again to Figure 2.1, the requirements of the standard contained within the Operating Process box can be applied to all businesses because they address input–process–output sequence; the universal application of the support activities is then even easier to recognize. At least two of the three quality resources—purchasing and training—exist in all businesses, and in most there is a need to control inspection, measuring, and monitoring equipment. The requirements classified as quality records and as quality system control are those that arise from the quality system itself and are generally independent of the actual business activity.

All this is a theoretical argument for the universal application of ISO 9000. In addition, empirical evidence indicates a very wide range of organizations now registered for the standard. In fact, it is now difficult to find any group of businesses that does not include ISO 9000 firms. Moreover, interest is not confined to commercial businesses. Other types of organizations known to be either registered or, at the time of this writing, considering ISO 9000 include central and local government departments, doctors and healthcare organizations, schools, and a British police department (the Notting Hill station of the Metropolitan Police was reported in the *Independent* (9 April 1992) to be asking Scotland Yard for approval to seek BS 5750).

A final point before moving from the relevance of ISO 9000 is that whereas in principle any organization can realistically seek to be ISO 9000 approved, some will find the process easier than others. Particular problems may be faced in very small companies (one-man bands cannot carry out their own auditing, but might consider setting up cooperative schemes with similar but complementary businesses), very large companies (because of the complexity), or any business in which management lacks the time for strategic planning.

## THE COSTS OF ISO 9000

Because variations are likely to be so large between organizations, no general figures can be given for the net cost of ISO 9000. In addition, any figures estimated soon become outdated. Estimates must be made in each and every specific case. The costing framework provided in Table 3.1 takes into account the value of the gains from ISO 9000 as well as the costs entailed. Clearly, it is necessary to decide in any such costing exercise the time period to be considered. Some of the associated costs are one-time (e.g., consultancy and initial assessment) and others are ongoing. The gains are all generally ongoing.

**Table 3.1** Costing ISO 9000

| Costs | $ | Gains | $ |
|---|---|---|---|
| Assessment | ___ | Value of retained business | ___ |
| Consultancy and training | ___ | Value of additional business | ___ |
| Staff time | ___ | Value added to products | ___ |
| Marketing and related expenses | ___ | Efficiency savings | ___ |
| | | Government grants | ___ |

# SPIKE AND THE POLARIS SUBMARINE

## Overview

Generic quality management standards can be seen as a tool originally invented for the convenience of big buyers and their suppliers. Large companies and government procurement agencies were, in fact, the first to stipulate in contracts that their suppliers operate specific types of quality assurance programs. In the early days, each big buyer had its own set of requirements, which had to be verified by inspection or audit teams. Over time it became apparent to suppliers with more than one big buyer client that something should be done to reduce the variety and number of audit inspections they had to endure for more or less the same reasons. What was needed was a single, common standard for quality assurance management which, if implemented and verified by periodic audit inspections, would satisfy most of the needs of all of their clients.

## Royal Navy Ship Production

Rear Admiral D. G. Spickernell—Spike to those who know him—first became involved in quality assurance management in the United Kingdom as Deputy Director of the Royal Navy's Ship Production Department in the early 1960s. Later he became Director-General of the British Standards Institution (BSI) and subsequently Vice President of ISO. Admiral Spickernell is now retired, at least from his ISO, BSI, and Navy posts, but his contributions to the promotion of BS 5750 and ISO 9000 are legendary.

## Quality Assurance and the Polaris

Spike asserts that the major advances in quality assurance management came to the United Kingdom in the early 1960s with the Polaris program, which introduced a new contract philosophy and document: General Requirements for the Assurance of Quality in Submarines (GRAQS). This was a quality control

*Source:* Interview with Frank Voehl along with excerpts from a speech by Dr. Lawrence Eicher at the ISO 9000 Forum Application Symposium, Washington, D.C., October 8, 1993.

system document that defined the role of the British Navy as a purchaser and described the functions carried out by its suppliers.

Subsequently the Royal Navy's Ship Production Department was reorganized and the GRAQS was joined by another quality control system document, the SCIT (Standard Conditions of Inspection and Tests). Along with these and similar developments in the army and air force came a significant misstep: the number of inspectors covering all defense purchases quickly grew to some 16,500. The program, according to Spike, had gone too far. He recounts a visit to Harland and Wolff, the shipbuilding company in Belfast, during which he was convinced that something had gone seriously wrong. "We not only told the contractors what was wanted, but we also told them how to do it. As a consequence, suppliers were having to do things that were both unnecessary and uneconomical."

## The Winds of Change

A major change in approach was needed, and to achieve it a common quality assurance standard, one that told industry what was expected but not how to do it, would have to be used by all major purchasing organizations in the United Kingdom. Defining this standard had to be a joint effort between the governmental and commercial sectors. This was eventually realized in BS 5750 in the United Kingdom and later in ISO 9000 at the international level.

In the United Kingdom alone there were stunning savings to be realized. A training program was devised for BS 5750 assessors in the defense department. Teams were assembled with sufficient technical expertise to be able to relate quality requirements to each sector, and 3000 companies had been approved by 1979. The ability to invite only those companies to tender for defense work whose quality was assured in accordance with BS 5750 meant that the 16,500 inspectors could be reduced to 3000.

# 4

# WHEN, WHERE, AND WHO: RELATIONSHIPS BETWEEN ISO 9000 AND CLASSIC QUALITY ASSURANCE

## INTRODUCTION

The following is an adaptation of the classic Japanese quality assurance system to the ISO 9000 environment. The purpose is to demonstrate the compatibility of this system in answering the *where, when,* and *who* issues involved in ISO 9000 certification (registration). Although these questions are answered in detail in Chapters 5 to 13, they are summarized here to provide a deeper understanding of Japanese quality assurance systems and ISO 9000.

The principles contained in this chapter are based on the work of Tetsuichi Asaka and Kazuo Ozeki,[1] as originally documented in the research materials and writings of the Union of Japanese Scientists and Engineers (JUSE).[2]

## MAKE QUALITY TOP PRIORITY NOW

Putting quality first is fundamental to the long-term survival of every organization. Organizations that neglect quality assurance in favor of delivering a product first in a competitive market later discover defects and suffer for it in the long run. Many companies have failed for this reason. In the 21st century, the same will be said of those organizations that choose not to implement ISO 9000.

## BUILD IN QUALITY EVERYWHERE

It should be understood that inspections and examinations do not create quality; quality is built in during the product development process. ISO 9000 administrators need to create improvement targets to build quality into the process. The administrator might set the target at 133% or more of the current process capability, and then work with management and employees to create and implement a quality improvement plan on a quarter-by-quarter basis.

## PROBLEMS ARE OPPORTUNITIES TO IMPROVE THE QUALITY ASSURANCE SYSTEM

Administrators should view claims and quality problems as opportunities to improve the organization and attitudes and to implement reforms. The fundamental principle of quality control is to identify the root cause of a problem so that it will not recur. If the administrator does not search for the root cause and strive to prevent the recurrence of the problem, his or her work becomes haphazard.[2]

## QUALITY ASSURANCE CHECKPOINTS FOR THE ORGANIZATION

**Motivating for quality consciousness:**

- Are the philosophy and general policies of top management easy to understand and have they been thoroughly implemented?
- Have employees been made aware of the damages the organization suffers due to poorly prepared workers, which resulted in customer complaints (loss of customer confidence, loss of image, and so on)?
- Have concrete examples been provided to staff to show the importance of quality as a shortcut to lower costs, higher customer confidence, and a greater sense of achievement in working?

- Have managers and employees been provided assistance in understanding the role that quality plays in their work?

**Objectives and planning:**
- Are quality targets clear and well understood?
- Has the quality assurance improvement theme been clearly communicated?
- Is each individual given instructions on his or her part in the plan for carrying out the improvement themes that will achieve these targets?
- Are the plans related to these targets and improvement themes clear?

**Education:**
- Are the chances for achieving the goals and plans improved through education, exchanges with other organizations, and participation in events outside the organization?
- Have the functions that make the offerings useful to the market been explained, and has the current extent of the product's use in the market been identified?
- If a problem arises, who takes charge, gives proper instructions for solving the problem, and directs the improvement activities?

**Practical work and its improvement:**
- Are tasks related to the quality characteristics carried out thoroughly?
- Does a handbook exist summarizing work procedures to teach employees how to do their jobs?
- Have workers been taught how to use computers, instruments, and tools and to make revisions and adjustments?
- Is an audit in place to check that the work methods are performed properly?
- Are workers encouraged to upgrade their technical knowledge and skills? How much time is spent each year per employee?

**Problem solving and team activities:**
- When problems or accidents occur, are workers guided in solving the problem?
- When on-the-spot emergency fire fighting must be done, is the root cause of the problem identified to make sure that it does not recur?
- Is the project team directed to work together to solve a problem?
- Are effective and rational problem-solving methods used, such as the seven quality control tools?
- If improvements and reforms are needed in the organization, systems, or standards to prevent a problem from recurring, are the people involved a part of the necessary actions?
- Is careful consideration given to whether the workplace culture is the problem and are appropriate measures taken to change the situation?[3]

The ISO 9000 guidelines (ISO 9000: 1987[E]) offer the following summary comments on the ISO 9000/quality assurance relationships—all those planned and systematic actions necessary to provide adequate confidence that a product or service will satisfy given requirements for quality:

- Unless given requirements fully reflect the needs of the user, quality assurance will not be complete.
- For effectiveness, quality assurance usually requires a continuing evaluation of factors that affect the adequacy of the design or specification for intended applications, as well as verifications and audits of production, installation, and inspection operations. Providing confidence may involve producing evidence.
- Within an organization, quality assurance serves as a management tool. In contractual situations, quality assurance also serves to provide confidence in the supplier.

Providing user-based requirements, providing evidence, and providing confidence are the three key aspects that link ISO 9000-style with Japanese quality assurance systems.

## ENDNOTES

1. Kazuo Ozeki and Tetsuichi Asaka, *Handbook of Quality Tools: The Japanese Approach,* Productivity Press, Cambridge, Mass., 1990.
2. In 1991, Productivity Press, under the leadership and direction of Norman Bodek, published a two-volume complement to the *Handbook of Quality Tools* called *TQC Solutions.* This was based upon material originally published in Japan by JUSE and subsequently edited and translated for the American market.
3. According to Dr. Asaka of JUSE, most problems can be classified as follows: (1) problems related to worker skills or attitudes: pure mistake, not following the operating procedure, skills not yet adequate, concern for quality not strong enough; (2) problems related to the workplace quality assurance system: the quality characteristic to be assured not well defined, operating standards incomplete, management points unclear, casual attitude about quality assurance methods, quality control process chart not yet complete; (3) lack of motivation to solve the administrator's problem: no desire to delve deeply into the problem and solve it, administrator's leadership in setting improvement goals and in making improvements inadequate; (4) problems in the workplace culture: never delving deeply into problems, blaming the workplace custom; (5) problems originating in another department: design error, error in determining customer specifications. Asaka believes that if problems are solved in a haphazard manner, a problem might be mistaken

for a recurring worker error when the true cause is the daily training and quality control education being provided to the students and workers. Try to create an atmosphere that motivates everyone to build quality into their courses and seminars.

An administrator should look for the root cause of any problem that occurs, consider whether he or she—and not others—is causing the problem, and implement the basic policies needed to correct it.

## HIGHLIGHTS: A FIVE-YEAR REVIEW OF ISO 9000 (1987–1992/93)

- The ISO 9000 standards have been directly adopted, without change, as national standards in some 58 countries, including all of the European Community and other countries, such as Japan and the United States.
- A 1991 survey of 2500 blue-chip companies in Western Europe showed that awareness of ISO 9000 is high; 82% claimed familiarity with the standards, with 64% seeking audit and registration. Awareness and registration are highest in the Netherlands and Switzerland.
- Third-party assessment and registration services exist for recognizing conformance to ISO 9000 standards in at least 32 countries. The number of companies on the waiting list to be registered is so long in some countries that the delay for assessment service is from 9 to 15 months.
- The ISO 9000 standards have been cited as a basic building block for the development and operation of the European Organization for Testing and Certification (EOTC). In certain fields, such as medical devices, legislation will call for ISO 9000 registration by suppliers. Whether or not this materializes, many companies have come to the conclusion that doing business in the newly forming integrated market of Europe will necessitate being recognized as meeting the requirements of ISO 9000, or better.

*Source:* ISO 9000 Forum, 1993.

- Many nationally and internationally recognized product certification systems (e.g. the British Standards Institution [BSI] Kitemark in the United Kingdom and the JIS mark in Japan) have incorporated the ISO 9000 standards as a first-phase qualification for approval to use their marks in specific product certification schemes.

- A great number of large industrial companies, particularly those with operations in many countries, have initiated vigorous programs to implement the ISO 9000 standards at their operation sites. One list includes Volkswagen, Du Pont, Renault, Corning, Exxon Chemicals, Sandoz, Rank Xerox, and many more.

- Numerous large governmental purchasers, including the Ministries of Defence in the United Kingdom and Singapore and the Department of the Navy in the United States, have made ISO 9000 registration (or its equivalent) a requirement for their large contract suppliers.

5

# HOW TO IMPLEMENT ISO 9000: AN OVERVIEW

## INTRODUCTION

The only steps necessary for achieving ISO 9000 certification are (1) design and implementation of a quality system that meets the requirements of the standard and (2) a successful assessment completed by a suitable assessor body. An overview of the major steps involved in the process is provided in this chapter. Full details are covered in Chapters 6 to 13, which provide a detailed action plan for an organization to implement ISO 9000 entirely through its own resources. However, few businesses are likely to carry out all the work themselves. The possible role of consultants and other forms of outside assistance is covered in the latter part of this chapter.

## CHOOSING YOUR PATH TO ISO 9000: THE MAJOR ACTIVITIES

There are nine major activities involved in ISO 9000 certification, as represented in Figure 5.1 Reference to other chapters is indicated in Figure 5.1; project planning, for example, is covered in detail in Chapter 6. The activities in the

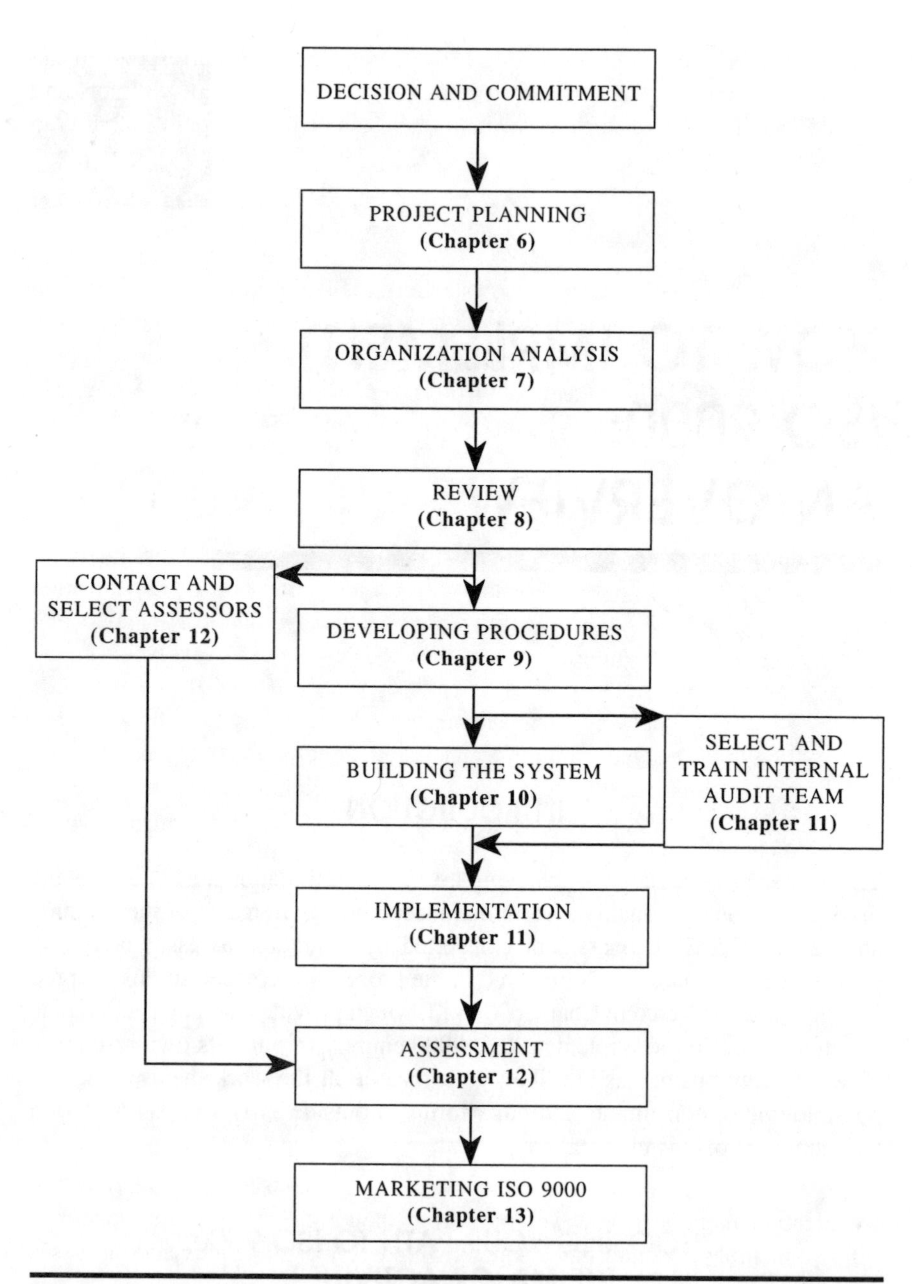


**Figure 5.1** ISO 9000: the major building blocks.

center block of the figure follow logically in sequence and correspond to the remaining chapters in this book. Two steps, however, selection of assessors and selection and training of the internal audit team, can be taken at points other than as illustrated in the figure.

## The Path Less Traveled

The first decision should be which standard to obtain. In Europe, it has been most common to apply for ISO 9001 or 9002. ISO 9003 is viewed as too narrow for most organizations and ISO 9004 as too general. There has recently been a strong push from TC 176, for organizations to consider the value of using ISO 9004 as the first phase before getting involved in ISO 9001 or 9002.

## Decision and Commitment

Whatever else is needed to implement the ISO 9000 standard chosen, commitment must come first. At least the senior management of the organization must believe that ISO 9000 is a worthwhile goal and should clearly understand both the major benefits and the extent of the considerable work involved. If there are any major doubts, the project is better postponed until they have been resolved. Not only the senior management should be committed, however; all staff will be involved and should understand the benefits for both the company and themselves individually. Also, they should be briefed on how they will be involved in setting up a quality system and executing it. A bridge between the commitment of senior management and the rest of the staff is a formal *quality policy*. As will be described later, the formal documentation requirements of ISO 9000 include this quality policy. Typically, it is a short statement that commits the organization to implementing a quality system to meet the requirements of ISO 9000 and requires the involvement of all staff in the system. An example of a quality policy is provided in Figure 5.2; the wording can be adapted to meet the needs and internal style of a particular organization.

In a company managed through regular board meetings, the quality policy may be formally adopted by resolution and then suitably displayed. However, it is essential that all staff be told at this point what the policy means and how they will be involved. How this is done will depend on the size and structure of the organization. Generally, however, the best method is one or more short meetings led by a member of senior management, who describes the policy and discusses why it has been adopted and what will happen next.

The decision to apply for ISO 9000 also involves a choice of which part—in most cases either 9001 (including design) or 9002 or 9003 (excluding design). (Some organizations may prefer to begin with 9004 in order to understand the

**SPECIMEN QUALITY POLICY**

## *COMPANY QUALITY POLICY*

It is the policy of Business & Market Research plc to provide the highest quality of service to clients.

The Company is a commercial business operating in a competitive market. The pursuit of the highest quality of service to clients is as essential to the long term growth and survival of the business as cost control and optimum pricing.

In order to ensure that all work is carried out in a manner which provides the highest quality of service to clients, the Company has put into effect the Quality System. This complies with the requirements of BS 5750 Part 1: 1987/ISO 9001. The Quality Manual defines this system and the work procedures entailed.

***All staff are required:***

To be completely familiar with and understand all procedures of the Quality System relevant to their own work for the Company.

To follow and comply with the requirements of all such procedures.

This policy statement has been adopted by a resolution of the Board of Directors dated October 7th 1991.

Peter Jackson

**Peter Jackson, Director**

**Figure 5.2** Specimen quality policy.

main building blocks of the quality system.) Generally, the choice will be clear-cut; the business either involves a design element as part of its contracts or it does not, and the choice will be made accordingly. In theory, a business with a design function may tactically choose to exclude this activity and register for 9002 only, but some key marketing advantages of ISO 9000 could be lost (see Chapter 13 for further discussion of this point). Moreover, in most situations the extra effort required to achieve 9001 rather than 9002 will not be very great, and in either case ISO 9000 will be a major project.

In a few cases, the choice between 9001 and 9002 will be uncertain at the outset. In this situation, either the decision can be deferred until the organization analysis has been completed or 9004 can be chosen so as to get up and running quickly.

A related decision will be whether to seek ISO 9000 registration for the entire organization or for only some departments, branches, or units. This book is written primarily with the smaller company in mind, and in most cases the organization will not be complex enough for this question to arise. In larger businesses there may be an argument for introducing ISO 9000 in part of the organization as a pilot and then phasing it in throughout. Unless, however, the pilot department is relatively self-contained, many of the external and marketing advantages of registration will not be gained immediately.

## Project Planning

In virtually all companies the process of gaining ISO 9000 will be a major project, possibly the largest ever undertaken. Much will depend on the choice of an effective project leader and supporting team. A timetable is needed as part of the plan; otherwise there will be a tendency for completion to be delayed. Significant costs will be incurred, which must be budgeted for. All these and other elements of project planning are discussed in Chapter 6. Another aspect of project planning is the use of outside assistance—consultants or others—which is discussed later in this chapter.

## Organization Analysis

A manager of a smaller company may be surprised that he or she needs to carry out an analysis of the organization because a hierarchical diagram of the company is usually available. However, a more fundamental analysis than this is needed, one that probably involves looking at the business in a new way. Chapter 7 describes in detail what is required and shows how this type of analysis is necessary to relate the particular organization to the requirements of ISO 9000.

## Review

The most fundamental part of an effective quality system is the *quality procedures:* the working methods to be followed in order to maximize quality. Once the organization analysis is complete, the review (Chapter 8) is undertaken to determine what procedures are required. In at least some areas of the business, it is likely that adequate procedures are already in place and being used, although they may not be recognized as procedures. It is unlikely, however, that they will be sufficiently documented to meet the requirements of the standard, but the work involved in documenting an effective and adequate existing procedure is fairly simple. In other areas, a review will show that adequate procedures are not in place. The outcome of the review will be a list of required procedures, including both new ones and those that are in place but need documentation. Another outcome of the review will be a set of policy statements on how each separate clause of ISO 9000 will be implemented in the particular company. These eventually form the core of the *quality manual.*

## Selection of Assessors

ISO 9000 registration requires the assessment of a quality system and its implementation by third-party assessors. Some experts and practitioners have argued that this is the most critical step in the entire registration and certification process. The British Standardization Institution (BSI) is the best-known accredited assessor body; however, there are many others, although several specialize in particular types of businesses. In practice, most businesses seeking ISO 9000 will be able to choose from among at least three potential assessors; they should regard this choice as if they were choosing suppliers and apply normal commercial judgments. The assessment process is not a one-time event; after a company has been successfully assessed initially, follow-up surveillance visits are carried out by the assessor body to make sure that the quality system continues to be followed, with a further full assessment often carried out after three years. There is, therefore, a continuing relationship with the assessor, which emphasizes the importance of the choice.

There is some lead time both during the selection process and from signing up to the actual assessment. The process of selection, therefore, is usually started at about the time of the review. The details are discussed in Chapter 12.

## Developing Procedures

Developing the required procedures is one of the most important and yet most time-consuming parts of an ISO 9000 project. A wide range of staff, not just the project team, should be involved. This part of the process is described in detail in Chapter 9, which includes some illustrative sample procedures.

## Internal Audit Team

An essential part of implementing a successful quality policy is internal auditing. The team that will carry out this work should be selected and trained well before the new quality system is implemented. This is discussed in Chapter 11 (Implementation).

## Building the System

The most visible part of a quality system is its documentation. In Figure 5.3 the required documentation is represented as four distinct levels, the most critical being the procedure manual. The policy statement (one page at most) should be written at the outset of the project. The quality manual is also fairly short; its purpose is to relate a company's quality system to the requirements of the standard. Most of the work required will arise out of the review (Chapter 8). The bottom layer of documentation is the records kept on the operation of the system. The master copies of any forms or other recording media should be included in the procedure manual.

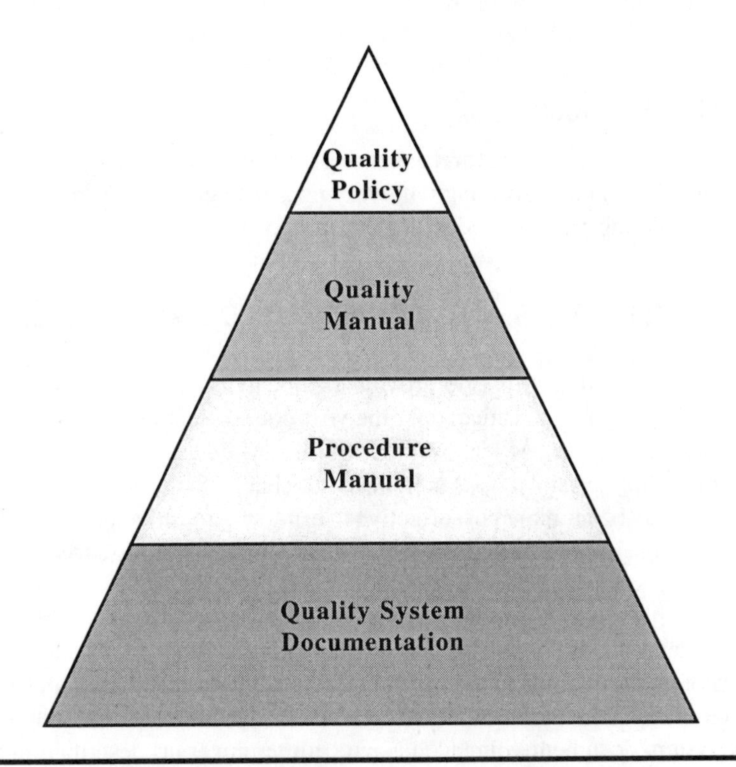


**Figure 5.3** ISO 9000: documentation.

Chapter 10, which describes how a complete quality system can be set up and suggests appropriate formats, also discusses an important aspect of documentation: meeting the requirements of the standard for document control.

### Implementation

Once documented, the system has to be successfully implemented and operated for a period of time before an external assessment can be considered. Implementation can be either a one-time "big bang" throughout the organization or can be phased in department by department. There are good arguments for both approaches; these as well as other aspects of implementation are covered in Chapter 11.

### Assessment

The culmination of the project will be a successful first assessment. Chapter 12 describes what happens during an assessment; it is much less stressful if an organization knows what to expect and on what basis the assessment will be judged favorably or otherwise. As previously indicated, assessment is not a one-time affair. Chapter 12 also covers follow-up surveillance visits.

### Marketing ISO 9000

Having gone to the trouble and expense of becoming registered for ISO 9000, a company should take advantage of every possible benefit. This necessitates a positive marketing program, which is the subject of Chapter 13.

## CONSULTANTS AND OTHER OUTSIDE ASSISTANCE

The purpose of this book is to provide a guide to in-house implementation of ISO 9000. However, in practice, only the very confident are likely to rely solely on their own resources. At least some form of outside assistance will probably be sought. This certainly does not have to entail a large-scale consultancy program; it may be far more cost effective to bring in a consultant to guide critical stages of the project. There are also other forms of outside assistance that can be considered. The role and choice of consultants is discussed first, and this chapter concludes with suggestions about other possible sources of outside assistance.

Consultants should not be used as an alternative to the work of internal staff. The role of a consultant is to advise and facilitate, not to substitute. A consultant might be asked to prepare first drafts of some of the more standard parts of the quality system documentation (such as procedures covering the requirements of the standard shown under Quality System Control in Figure 2.2 of Chapter 2) and perhaps the quality manual, because these are somewhat similar across companies. For the critical procedures of the operating process and support activities (shown in Figure 2.2), as well as the analysis and review underlying them, it is vital that the client organization's own staff have the primary input. The reason for this is that a consultant's work will be limited in duration; in all probability it will be finished well before the assessment. In any case, it is not the consultant who must use the procedures. If the staff of a company substantially design their own system, they will truly own it and be responsible for its successful implementation. They can never blame anyone but themselves for the parts of the procedures that do not work (and some will not work the first time, however carefully they have been planned). Unfortunately, some consultants may offer to "sit in a corner and write you a quality system," and they should be rejected.

The arguments for and against using consultants in setting up a quality system to meet ISO 9000 are summarized in Table 5.1. The main argument for using consultants is that they offer an expertise that few organizations seeking ISO 9000 are likely to have in house. If they are good, they will know the requirements of the standard inside and out and have a broad base of experience in implementing it across a range of businesses. This is important, because the requirements of the standard must be interpreted in the context of a particular business. As mentioned earlier, the standard is not written in language that nonengineering businesses will find user-friendly. Particularly in the case of service activities, considerable creativity may be needed to find ways in which the business can conform to some of the requirements. On the other hand, some find that it is not essential for the consultant to have specific experience in a particular business, because one of the benefits a consultant can bring is the cross-fertilization of ideas from different businesses that have been past clients. One last advantage is the fact that an experienced consultant can draw on available field-tested quality system documentation. However, for both ethical and practical reasons, a consultant should not be expected to provide sets of

**Table 5.1** For and Against Using Consultants

| For consultants | Against consultants |
|---|---|
| They know ISO 9000 requirements. | They charge high rates. |
| They have expertise in implementation. | They are paid to learn the business the client already understands. |
| They bring cross-fertilization of ideas from other clients. | They can take over the project so that the client loses ownership. |
| They have available material from other quality systems. | |

manuals that require the name of a company to be inserted. At best, some sample documents may be adapted, but no more.

The disadvantages to using consultants have to do mainly with cost. Consultants have nothing to sell but their time and experience. At the time of this writing, the charge basis may range from $100 per hour/$800 per day for a one-man consultancy firm up to $250 per hour/$2000 per day for a senior member of staff from a large practice. Such rates may seem expensive, but they usually cover all the consultant's non-travel-related costs, not just wages, and are probably not much more than the *full* cost of the time of senior in-house staff. Also, a good consultant should save the client considerable time that would otherwise be wasted in confusion and mistakes. The old saying that a consultant is "someone who borrows your watch to tell you the time" has some truth in it. Consultants inevitably charge for the time they spend understanding a business, but in return they offer the advantage of a fresh perspective on what to the client are over-familiar activities. Furthermore, how many clients would even bother to "check the time" on their own?

A consultant who takes the right approach encourages the in-house quality team to set and meet deadlines for each step in the project. Too often, internal projects are repeatedly postponed because of the pressure of day-to-day business. This can result in the consultant's doing all the work, without the essential internal involvement. In practice, even a half-competent consultant will not let this happen, but this illustrates the importance of selecting a good consultant. The choice of the wrong one can be disastrous, especially in terms of momentum and time lost.

Consultants generally offer full ISO 9000 packages involving 10, 15, 20, or more days of work designed to guide the client from ground zero to an implemented quality system. The U.K.-based scheme is around 15 days. However, consultants can certainly be used more sparingly, and most are willing to sell their time in units of single days. A consultant working on this basis might, for example, be asked to give initial overall guidance (one day), participate in the organization analysis and review (three days), and review the system immediately prior to implementation (one day). In this way, at a cost of five consulting days, an outside perspective is brought in and an independent judgment made of the match between the system and the standard before formal assessment. Mixing and matching the input of consultants with other forms of outside assistance can also be considered. For example, in Europe, local Training and Enterprise Councils (TECs) have sponsored self-help clubs for local small businesses seeking registration, with the costs of consultants shared by the group. In the United States, it is anticipated that local Quality Councils, such as one in Erie, Pennsylvania, will fill this particular role.

Consultants come in various forms. The only important difference is between good ones and bad ones; unfortunately, this aspect is the most difficult to judge beforehand. Some suggestions for minimizing a poor choice are provided here. The size of consultancy firms can range from one-man bands (which are numerous) to medium-sized practices up to multinational groups. Undoubtedly, one-man bands can offer excellent and cost-effective service. Moreover, there is no chance of a glib front man beginning the process but leaving the actual work to less experienced associates, which can happen with larger practices. Unfortunately, the quality of one-man bands varies enormously. Although some are excellent, others range from the barely competent to the outright fraudulent. Therefore, the risks of poor service are higher than with a larger consultancy. Another problem with one-man bands is that they have no additional resources to draw on; the consultant may be first-class, but the company is in trouble if he or she is sidelined with an illness. Also, they cannot easily bring in additional advice. Although even with a larger consultancy the work may be largely carried out by a single individual, other staff are available for support and final appraisal of the completed quality system before implementation.

Another difference among consultancies is specialization. Some specialize in quality or even ISO 9000 implementation, whereas others generalize. The largest practices may offer a quality team or unit as part of a range of specializations. On the whole, the specialists may have more to offer. After all, what a client needs is expertise in ISO 9000. However, there is one good argument for a generalist: with broad experience the consultant may be able to diagnose business problems outside of a strict quality approach and therefore make a greater overall contribution to the business.

The process of selecting a consultant starts with drawing up a short list of available consultants who apparently have something useful to offer.

## Trade Associations

A company should always seek the advice of the trade association for its own type of business. Formally or otherwise, the association may be able to provide the names of quality consultants with experience in that particular business. Moreover, for other reasons, it is worth learning at an early stage what involvement, if any, the trade association has had with ISO 9000 (see Chapter 6). Similarly, the trade press may well mention firms in the particular industry that have recently gained ISO 9000 and could be asked about their experience with consultants. Local chambers of commerce may be a similar potential source.

## ISO 9000 Forum

The Forum has access to a vast database of certifying bodies and boards on a worldwide basis. A listing can be obtained from the Forum by contacting Sahri Tasser (phone: 011-41-22-749-01-11). See the profile at the end of this chapter.

## Making the Right Choice

Having identified potentially suitable consultants, a company should ask no more than two or three to bid on the project. To ask more would be a waste of time for both the consultants and the company. The consultant will hold an initial meeting with the company before preparing a formal proposal document. Each proposal should be read carefully to ascertain the following:

- Does the consultant demonstrate an understanding of the nature of your business and why it is pursuing ISO 9000? A competent consultant should understand this at the initial meeting.
- Exactly what work does the consultant propose to carry out? Will he or she guide the company through the process from start to finish or concentrate on specific activities?
- How does the consultant intend to carry out the project? A recognized method is to carry out an initial audit (essentially, the review covered in Chapter 8), identify where work is required, and, after this is complete, carry out a final audit to establish that the new quality system meets the standard.
- Has the consultant specified a firm timetable and a fixed cost for the project, or at least decided how the company will be charged?

If not already covered in the written proposal, it should be established who specifically will carry out the consultancy (assuming the firm is not a one-man band). Also, a representative (or representatives) of the company should insist on meeting the individual consultant who will work on the project. This is crucial. Whether the consultancy firm is large or small, most of the work will depend on one individual, and the members of the company must feel comfortable working with him or her. It is not necessary to become friends, but it is necessary for the client to have confidence in the personal skills of the consultant and be able to communicate with him or her.

Undoubtedly, when considering a possible consultancy a company will consider the experience such a firm can offer in its own or a related business. In most cases, experience in a specific business is not essential, but there should be some knowledge of the general type of business. A consultancy with experience only in heavy engineering is unlikely to be the best choice for a service operation. Also, references from past clients should be requested. Of course, these will reflect the better rather than the worse examples of the consultancy's work, but they will at least indicate that some clients, at some time, have been satisfied. Finally, a company should establish the consultancy's own position on ISO 9000. Has it taken (or is it at least planning to take) its own medicine?

## Training Courses

The major form of outside assistance apart from consultants is training courses. These include open courses for anyone interested and courses tailored to meet the needs of a particular business. The latter are essentially another type of consultancy and will not be discussed further.

Many companies offer as their core business seminars on a range of business subjects, including quality and ISO 9000. At the time of this writing, charges typically range from $200 to $400 per delegate day, with one- or two-day courses common (the total amount at risk is, therefore, fairly modest). The more expensive courses do not necessarily offer better information, but the seminar groups may be smaller and individual attention greater. Companies marketing this type of training usually advertise by direct mail, and many businesses may already have received the necessary literature whether they realize it or not.

Training courses in quality subjects are also organized through local quality councils, and these bodies should certainly be approached to learn what is locally available. Grants or subsidized courses may also be offered through these councils, which is another good reason for making contact.

Finally, trade associations should be contacted for details on training specific to a particular industry.

# ISO 9000 FORUM: A COMMUNICATIONS SUPPORT FOR ISO 9000 USERS

## Overview

Companies and organizations embarking on quality management and quality assurance programs can make use of the necessary guidelines in the ISO 9000 series of international standards. When it comes to implementing and operat-

*Source:* ISO 9000 Forum, April 1993/CS93U970063. Interview by Frank Voehl of ISO 9000 Forum Leaders, Washington, D.C., October 8, 1993.

ing the standards, however, practical assistance is needed. This assistance is provided by director Juichi Nagano, who is also involved in the ISO Central Secretariat. Sahri Tasser provides facilitator support out of Switzerland. The four part-time members are Jacques Olliver Chabot, Neil Cook, Roger Frost, and Anke Varcin.

## Key Issues Addressed

Straight answers are provided to dozens of specific questions, such as:

- Where can I find more information about certification and conformity assessment?
- Where can I obtain a list of assessment bodies recognized in a particular country?
- Will there be a large number of sector-specific versions of the ISO 9000 standards?

Answers can be provided by several sources, but these sources must first be identified. A central clearinghouse for information helps save precious time, either by providing answers directly or by indicating the most qualified relevant source. This is part of what ISO has done in creating the ISO 9000 Forum. This service is an international communication facilitator created to support the implementation of the ISO 9000 series of standards.

## Forum Services

The ISO Forum provides users and potential users of ISO 9000 standards access to information from experts and problem-solvers. By subscribing to the Forum, members are entitled to a range of services, including:

- *ISO 9000 News,* a newsletter on quality management standards, published six times a year
- Discounts on new and revised editions of the ISO 9000 series
- Reviews of topical books and articles on quality management and quality assurance
- Listings of third-party registrars of quality systems and of auditor accreditation bodies
- Information on sources of training materials
- The opportunity to attend ISO 9000 Forum Application Symposia at a reduced charge

## Forum Activities

The Forum is intended to answer the numerous requests from companies on how they can qualify for ISO 9000 status. The aim is to compile the answers to the basic questions into one package so that businesses can find what they need to know about the ISO 9000 standards as quickly and inexpensively as possible.

Because it is published by the ISO Central Secretariat, *ISO 9000 News* has close links with national member bodies of the ISO worldwide network and can thus provide readers with a direct line to new international developments, such as the efforts by the ISO Council Committee on conformity assessment to promote mutual recognition of ISO 9000 certificates.

In recognition of the learning needs of many readers, particular attention is given to reporting on training materials as they become available, as well as special features on particular issues, such as Memoranda of Understanding between quality system registrars.

## ISO 9000 Publications

The Forum provides publications on quality management and quality assurance to its subscribers either free or at reduced rates.. Publications of the ISO 9000 Forum library include a list of relevant ISO/IEC (International Electrotechnical Commission) guides and associated documents and a worldwide directory of national third-party registration bodies, of which the second edition will soon be available.

The ISO 9000 Forum aims to facilitate communications between newcomers to quality standardization and those who already have experience to draw on and advice to share. Regular news on ISO 9000 implementation in companies and organizations in sectors as varied as those of land mobile radio communications and the leisure industry contributes to this aim.

The future direction of the ISO 9000 Forum will depend on the interaction generated by ISO 9000 users and those who wish to join their ranks. One potential development has been identified by Reg Shaughnessy, who has made the following comments on the launching of the Forum initiative:

> Initially, this initiative was envisaged as a "think tank" educational network. As the issues associated with global quality systems become clearer, it is possible that a network for consensus and debate by the parties of direct interest will be essential. The ISO 9000 Forum could provide such a vehicle.

## Information

Anke Varcin and Roger Frost, Promotion and Press Services, ISO Central Secretariat, 1, rue de Varembe, Case postale 56, CH-1211 Geneve 20. Phone: +41 22 749 01 11. Fax: +41 22 733 34 30.

6

# PROJECT PLANNING: THE FOUNDATION OF IMPLEMENTATION

## INTRODUCTION

Introducing ISO 9000 is a major project. This chapter, the first of the "how to do it" chapters, shows how the project can be planned effectively. Topics covered include the project leader and the team, resources, initial research activities, scheduling, and budgeting.

## THE PROJECT LEADER AND THE TEAM

The project leader's key task is to ensure that everything that has to happen between the formal start of the project and a successful assessment actually happens on time. In addition, the project manager will often carry out many of the tasks required as part of the project, although ideally most of them will be delegated, leaving the project leader to concentrate on managing. However, in most smaller businesses and organizations, the project leader is inevitably involved in doing much of the detailed work. In a larger company, the project leader may not have to be involved in managing the quality system once it is up and running; he or she does not have to become the management representative, in the terminology of the standard. Again, however, in most smaller organizations, the chief designer of the quality system has a continuing role in its operation, becoming, in many cases, the in-house quality guru. In some organizations, the designer of the system reports to the Director of Quality, who only indirectly heads up the project.

## The Choice of a Leader

Although many organizations do not have the luxury of choosing from among possible candidates for project leader (because there is only one in the running), it is desirable that the project leader chosen have at least some of the following strengths:

- **Authority:** In order to keep the project on schedule, the project leader needs the authority to coordinate, if not command, staff and other resources. While the project is under way, business will undoubtedly have to be carried on as normal. When the involvement of staff is required in the project, some will plead the pressures of normal work as a reason for delay or sidestepping. The project leader needs the authority, as necessary, to demand the necessary input into the project, whatever the excuses. (He or she also needs the experience and wisdom to recognize when the project really must be put aside to avoid real damage to the business.) In a smaller or medium-sized company, the project leader, therefore, needs to be either at the director level or only one step down. At this level, the project leader will have the necessary authority, and the rest of the staff will understand his or her position.
- **Understanding of the business:** The foundation of a successful ISO 9000 project is applying the requirements of the standard to the particular business. This book and other sources will provide knowledge of the requirements, but the leader must bring to the project an understanding of the particular business: how it is structured and organized, what is produced in the core processes, and how these work. If the project leader is chosen on the basis of authority, he or she will most likely have the necessary understanding of the business and will probably have managed some of the critical functions for some time. Incidentally, this need for an understanding of the core processes of the business may be a factor against choosing a project leader from the service-oriented or more specialized departments, including accounting and finance. The financial director may be, on other grounds, the ideal candidate for the project, but may face practical problems if he or she is relatively remote from the work of the core processes. The need for a close understanding of the business is also a very good reason for not allowing an outside consultant to take on the role of project manager. Even

if a large-scale consultancy involvement is anticipated, project management should remain firmly with internal staff. In fact, one of the project leader's key roles is choice of and close liaison with consultants.

- **Project management experience:** The project leader should have a track record of managing projects, preferably ones outside the day-to-day operation of the business. Such experience might include buying and commissioning major equipment for the company, reorganizing the company structure, or implementing a new computer system. In such projects the leader will have learned how to rapidly acquire expertise in a new field, how to coordinate others, how to improvise, what to do when things start going wrong, and how to prevent a setback from becoming a catastrophe.
- **Adequate knowledge of and commitment to ISO 9000:** In very few businesses will the project leader have this knowledge at the start of the project. What he or she needs is the drive and enthusiasm to learn as much as necessary about the standard. Such knowledge may be obtained from reading this book or attending training seminars, working with consultants, or discussing the requirements with other businesses who have either gone through the process of gaining ISO 9000 or are currently doing so.
- **Sufficient available time:** Finally, the project manager must have sufficient available time to carry out the work. Since he or she will almost certainly have an existing and important role within the business, some functions may have to be reassigned (delegation of routine tasks may have long-term benefits to both the individual concerned and the company) or the individual may simply have to find the extra time needed to manage the project. He or she may even have to do both. However it is done, the leader's commitment to the project will require a portion of his or her time. How much time depends on the situation within the company—how much work is required to develop and implement a quality system and the extent to which tasks can be delegated.

This covers the key elements of an ideal project leader for ISO 9000. The other question is who should *not* be given the job? It has been found that the source of many problems experienced in gaining ISO 9000 can be traced to making the wrong people project leaders. Two poor choices are the "dead elephant" and the "playful pup."

A typical dead elephant is one of the founders of a business, but perhaps the one who was always "Number Two." This person has attained a certain status and is paid accordingly, but no one is quite sure what his or her responsibilities are. Such dead elephants may have an apparent authority because of their seniority within an organization. However, they are no longer used to exercising it at a practical level. They may claim to have considerable knowledge of the business, but perhaps this is based on involvement ten years ago; they are now rather isolated from the day-to-day work of the business. They are also unused to new challenges and may find it very difficult to understand the concepts of a quality system and the standard itself. Above all, dead elephants have lost any capacity for urgency and action. Unfortunately, they often have something that no one else has: time. Dead elephants are often selected just because no one else can be spared from day-to-day activities. The example of the dead elephant might, therefore, be restated: whoever has the time available to be project manager is unqualified for the job.

Playful pups have a lot of enthusiasm, quite different from dead elephants. In fact, they demonstrate that the most dangerous people within an organization are not the ignorant and idle but the ignorant and industrious. Typically, they are "pups" in the sense of being young and new to the organization and very eager to prove their worth by master-minding ISO 9000. However, they have a limited understanding of the organization's core processes and, even worse, fail to recognize their limitations. Although they have as yet no real authority, they may have the arrogance to alienate other staff from the idea of a quality system. In addition, playful pups have probably only ever played; they have no real experience in managing projects.

The project leader is not the only in-house member who needs to be involved. As a general rule, the wider the involvement of staff throughout the organization, the more effective the new quality system will be. Although in many organizations the project leader may be the only permanent member of the project team, other staff should be involved, as necessary, to carry out or advise on specific tasks. This is particularly the case with documentation and writing procedures. Beyond a certain point, the delegation of project tasks to ad hoc groups of staff increases rather than diminishes the demands put on the project leader; he or she has to spend time chasing down everyone involved and making sure that their work both meets the schedule and covers the requirement. The consultation process is, however, vital. One effective strategy has been to have a one-point contact within each department, who is responsible for coordinating data gathering and documentation at the local level.

A few organizations may have an ideal potential project manager with adequate time available. This is fortunate, but there is a danger of the project becoming a private affair. This must be resisted, because even though the project manager might be technically capable of developing an effective quality system, it will then belong to the individual rather than to the company. This will lead to acute problems at the implementation stage. Consultation throughout the organization is needed not only to provide input into the design of the system, but, just as critically, to ensure that it is truly owned and felt to be so by the entire company. A department will not resent following a set of procedures if it has been closely involved in developing them. There is a good chance that a department will resent procedures that were designed without its consultation.

At the project planning stage, therefore, it is essential to consider how consultation will be handled. This might be at several levels. In a company managed through regular board meetings, the project manager could be asked to present a progress report, followed by a discussion, at each meeting. This would ensure that all the functional heads are involved in the project. An ad hoc group of managers below board level might meet weekly to discuss specific problems and progress. Additionally, staff from all levels might be extensively involved for a shorter period as procedures are developed for particular departments or functional areas. Some of these staff (and not necessarily the most senior in the hierarchy) may be asked to work together to write procedures once this stage of the project is reached.

## RESOURCES

Apart from staff time, an ISO 9000 project is unlikely to require extensive resources. Records will have to be filed adequately, and documents and forms will eventually need printing, but these are unlikely to involve much more than a limited amount of additional stationery. More substantial expenditures could be involved if the review stage suggests an additional need for processing (or associated measuring) equipment or inspection, but often core activities are only formalized rather than changed as a result of ISO 9000.

One resource, however, that should be seriously considered, if it is not already in use, is a word processor. The documentation required for ISO 9000 can be produced without a word processor, but the work is more difficult and mistakes in the final documentation are more likely, which can be expensive in the long run. Many drafts of the documentation are likely to be needed before finalization, and without a word processor several drafts will have to be completely retyped. Furthermore, once ISO 9000 is implemented, changes will need to be made to the documentation, both to correct deficiencies that can only be identified through operating the system and to take account of changing circumstances (changes to the quality system will be ongoing). Again, a word processor is not essential, but it is a tremendous help. The equipment is no longer expensive; prices have fallen drastically over the last few years. Currently, a complete package including a printer can be purchased for around $1000, and even the non-technical employee can learn enough of a word-processing package to be able to use it with only a few hours of initial instruction. Moreover, most organizations will gain some additional benefits from word processing over and above its application in ISO 9000.

## ISO 9000 ROLLOUT PLAN

One of the first functions of the project leader and the team is to prepare an ISO 9000 rollout plan covering the critical activities involved in planning, organizing, implementing, and controlling the project. An outline of a sample ISO 9000 rollout plan, along with key questions to ask, is provided in the profile at the end of this chapter.

## INITIAL RESEARCH

An early task of the project manager should be to carry out some initial research. Some of this may already have been done before the commitment to ISO 9000 was made. Areas that should be investigated in this initial research are as follows.

### What Is Happening in the Industry?

Other organizations in the same industry or field of activity as the company seeking registration will almost certainly be involved in ISO 9000, either considering it or already registered. Although each company's quality system is and should be unique, businesses involved in similar types of activities will face similar problems in applying ISO 9000 (e.g., how to apply *4.11 Inspection, Measuring and Test Equipment* to an employment bureau). The particular industry's response to ISO 9000 may be minimal, consistent but informal, or formalized through trade association recommendations (e.g., *Quality Assurance—Guidelines for Management Consultancy: The Management Consultancies Association*). In some industries there are sector schemes: common approaches to ISO 9000 implementation developed by the consultancy arm of organizations such as the British Standardization Institution (BSI). An understanding of such industry approaches should be gained before starting an ISO 9000 project, and the implications for each stage of the work should be considered. However, companies considering ISO 9000 should bear in mind that trade association guides and even BSI sector schemes are not mandatory. Although it may be wise to follow the rest of the industry in applying the standard, it is not necessary. Moreover, the assessment does not measure the company against what is set out in such guides; the assessment is against the standard and the standard alone.

Methods of learning about what is happening in a particular industry include contact with the relevant trade associations, reading the trade press, and even direct contact with similar businesses. Such research requires little effort or time. In addition to providing information on how ISO 9000 is applied in a particular industry, effective research can produce much other useful information, such as names of consultants with relevant experience.

### What Are Other Local Companies Doing about ISO 9000?

In addition to watching what is happening within an industry, it is important to develop local contacts. It is possible that other local firms will either have just gone through the process or be at the same stage, and even an informal chat on the phone could yield useful tips and insights. Local chambers of commerce can be an excellent method of making contacts. Unfortunately, not all advice can be trusted. One company was said to have failed because it bought envelopes from a supplier that was not ISO 9000 registered. Another was said to be in serious trouble because its broom closets were not labeled. These examples are simply not believable at face value, although they may be distorted versions of some actual problems (i.e., an inadequate purchasing system and a lack of quality documentation). The moral is to listen but not to use such unsubstantiated stories, however convincingly told, as a basis for decisions.

### Initial Contact with Assessors

Although the selection of an assessor can be left until later in the project, there is no harm in obtaining literature packs from assessors at an early stage. If a written request for such material includes a very short description of the organization and its activity, the assessment firm may let the organization know if it is interested in working in that particular industry. Some firms will carry out assessments of any types of business, but others choose not to be involved in particular areas.

## THE TIMETABLE

It is essential to set an initial timetable for the project. It will probably have to be modified several times, but without some key target dates the project will drag on and on. It is vital to spend adequate time on the process, but the quicker the new quality system is implemented, the sooner internal benefits will be realized. Moreover, the external benefits (and payback) cannot accrue until assessment and registration are complete.

How long will, or should, the whole process take? This varies significantly among organizations. Each project leader must make his or her own judgment based on an estimate of the activities involved and the resources available. The overall timetable is comprised of two major stages: from design to implementation and from implementation to successful assessment.

The design to implementation stage is likely to take at least two to three months from scratch, but in most cases it should be completed in well under a year. The determining factors include the complexity of the organization and the availability of staff time (including the project leader) to carry out the necessary work. If consultants are involved, their availability may be a factor, but there would have to be some very strong arguments for using a consultancy whose work plan would delay the timetable.

The period from implementation on is again likely to be at least two to three months, but in most cases should be no longer than nine. Once implemented, the company must be wholeheartedly committed to the operation of the quality system. Unavailability of staff time to operate the system should never be a reason for delay, although it might have been a reason for delaying implementation. However, the process cycle time of a particular businesses does affect the post-implementation period. The assessors will expect to find evidence that at least the procedures covering most of the activities are being applied. In a business making large-scale capital equipment, each project may span several months, and the quality system cannot be assessed until a number of projects have been completed. In such a case, the process cycle time will be important. In other businesses, however, this will not be significant; in catering, for example, the core process cycle is only a matter of hours.

Another concern affecting the implementation to assessment period is the handling of nonconformities. The issue is not so much that mistakes in operating the system will be more common in the early day (this is inevitable) but that the experience necessary for handling the problems through the quality triad of internal audit, corrective action, and management review (see Chapter 2) must be acquired. This process will require a minimum amount of time, depending on how the triad is set up to work.

Finally, the unavailability of assessor time may be a limiting factor. Most assessor bodies require two to four months notice to carry out an assessment, the starting point of the period usually being the date of application and payment of at least some of the fees. However, if the process of selecting the assessor is carried out concurrently with other activities, it is unlikely that the assessor's immediate unavailability will lengthen the overall timetable.

Taking into account the periods required up to and after implementation, it is very unlikely that the entire project will be carried out in less than six months, but it should be complete within twelve or eighteen months at most.

One of the first tasks of the project manager should be to prepare an initial timetable of major activities. A Gantt chart, as illustrated in Figure 6.1, is an effective tool. The chart is divided into weekly columns (the example has 27), with the major project activities written down the side. Strips or lines are used to show the planned timing of each activity, perhaps with the names of the staff

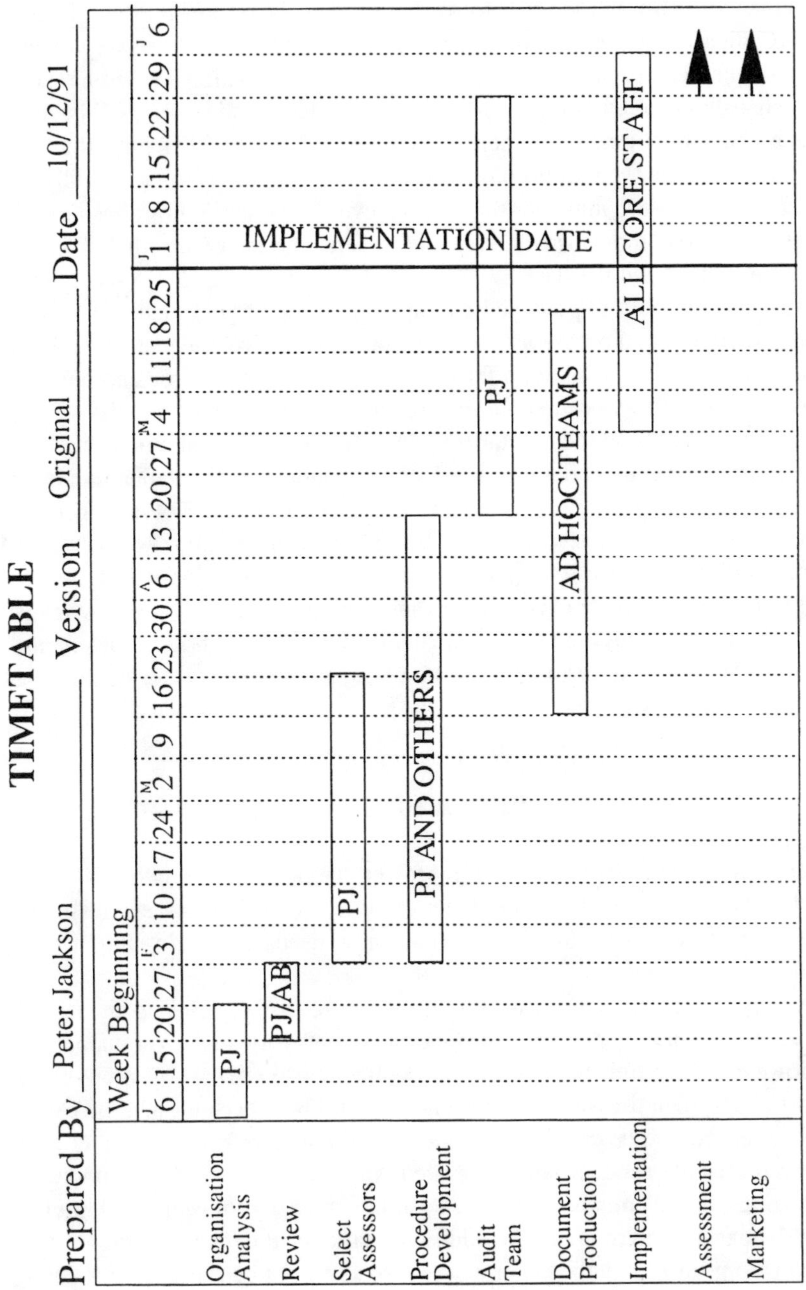

**TIMETABLE**

Prepared By Peter Jackson Version Original Date 10/12/91

Week Beginning

J 6 15 20 27 F 3 10 17 24 M 2 9 16 23 30 A 6 13 20 27 M 4 11 18 25 J 1 8 15 22 29 J 6

Organisation Analysis — PJ

Review — PJ/AB

Select Assessors — PJ

Procedure Development — PJ AND OTHERS

Audit Team — PJ

Document Production — AD HOC TEAMS

Implementation — ALL CORE STAFF

Assessment

Marketing

IMPLEMENTATION DATE

**Figure 6.1** ABC, Inc. ISO 9000 project timetable.

principally involved written in. In the example, Procedure Development is planned to span the weeks from February 3 to April 13 and be the responsibility of PJ and Others. Critical dates, e.g., the implementation date (June 1 in the example) and the assessment, can be shown as vertical lines (which can also be used to show gaps such as holidays). In preparing the initial timetable, judgments will have to be made about how long each major activity should take. Inevitably, the first version of the timetable will need subsequent amendment, and this will only be the first of several revisions. For this reason, even if the initial draft has limited circulation, it is recommended that it include a version number (original, revision 1, revision 2, etc.) and the date.

Once the timetable is produced and approved, the project manager should regularly review actual progress against the plan. Of course, the plan should not be changed every time an activity falls behind schedule, but there is no point in displaying a beautifully drafted but unrealistic chart. A balance must be struck, therefore, between using the timetable to control the project and modifying it to adjust to reality. It is essential to restrict who can authorize timetable revisions; generally it is best to reserve this authority strictly for the project manager.

The Gantt chart can also be used for more detailed sub-timetables. For example, it might be wise to prepare a timetable for each major activity represented in Figure 5.1 of Chapter 5. Such charts can be drawn up as each stage is reached. When revisions are made to the main chart, corresponding adjustments will be needed in the sub-charts, and vice versa, another reason for controlling the authority to revise.

## BUDGETING

The final aspect to be considered in project planning is making funds available when they are needed. Before committing to the project, some assessment of overall costs was probably made, which now needs translating into a cash flow plan.

The largest cost in most ISO 9000 projects is usually management and employee time, but only rarely do accounting systems formally cover budget for this. However, if the time put into the project by factory workers results in extra working hours, then a cash flow projection should take account of this. Other staff time that should be considered is the cost of any additional personnel who may be required to operate the quality system. In most smaller and medium-sized organizations, this is probably not the case, although it may show up as additional general labor required to cover the additional tasks of the quality team.

Apart from staff time, the major external costs are for consultants or training courses, if used, and the charges made by the assessment bodies. Before any

**BUDGET ($)**

Prepared By Peter Jackson Version Original Date 10/12/91

| | Week Beginning | | | | | | |
|---|---|---|---|---|---|---|---|
| | J 6 | F 3 | M 2 | A 6 | M 4 | J 1 | TOTAL |
| Consultant | | 1,600 | | 1,600 | | 1,600 | 4,800 |
| Training Course | 800 | | | | 1,600 | | 2,400 |
| Assessors | | | | 4,000 | | | 4,000 |
| Word Processor | | 2,000 | | | | | 2,000 |
| Other Materials | | | | 1,000 | | | 1,000 |
| Additional Staff Costs | | | 1,000 | 1,000 | 5,000 | 2,500 | 9,500 |
| TOTAL | 800 | 3,600 | 1,000 | 7,600 | 6,600 | 4,100 | 23,700 |

**Figure 6.2** ABC, Inc. ISO 9000 project budget.

commitment, firm price quotes should be obtained. The previous chapter gave some guidance on consultant and training costs, and Chapter 12 discusses the sums likely to be incurred in assessment. Other costs associated with the project might be the purchase of a word processor and the expenses involved in printing and stationery, which will probably be minimal. The only other major costs might be those that arise from any changes in the core process itself. Clearly, these cannot be anticipated in this book, if they arise at all.

The Gantt chart approach can be adapted to show the outlay of the budget over time. An example is provided in Figure 6.2: consultant costs are shown to total $4800 and appear as three equal payments in February, April, and June. Again, some revision may become necessary as the project develops, and the cash flow plan should be kept in step with the timetable, because when payments have to be made is often as critical as the amount involved.

# ISO 9000 PROJECT ROLLOUT PLAN

## Introduction

The focus of the ISO 9000 implementation team during the initial planning review should be on the critical items that the team has been working on to implement the ISO 9000 system and achieve certification, along with other items to be included in the master plan. To assist the Implementation Team with their evaluation, a checklist of twenty items and associated questions have been grouped into four categories: planning, organizing, implementing, and controlling. These categories can then be charted and progress tracked for the entire ISO 9000 project implementation in order to ensure success.

## Scoring the Questions

Each question can receive a maximum score of five points and a minimum score of zero. In order to obtain a perfect score of five in a category, the team must be able to provide substantial documentation to support that score. A score of three would indicate average performance. A score of zero would indicate no evidence at all. As there are 20 questions, an overall score of 100 points would indicate a perfect project; 70 to 90 points would indicate an excellent score, 50 to 69 would indicate a good score, 30 to 49 would indicate a fair score, and 10 to 29 would indicate a poor score. Below ten would indicate a very poor score. Keep in mind that a low score at the beginning of the ISO 9000 project is natural. It is the progress throughout that counts—up to the final ISO 9000 project item in the last phase.

## Narrative Descriptions of the Twenty Questions According to Category

- **ISO 9000 Project Planning** *(35 points):* The ISO 9000 project planning category contains seven questions which can result in a maximum score of 35 points as follows:
  1. Describe how your ISO 9000 project team has gathered and analyzed the facts of the situation(s) for improvement. To what degree has the situation analysis been performed? Describe how the fact finding or awareness of the opportunity, situation, or problem was undertaken as the first step in building an ISO 9000 project plan. *(5 points)*
  2. How have the ISO 9000 project objectives been established? Describe how the planning objectives for the entire ISO 9000 project were outlined to indicate what had to be done, where the primary emphasis needed to be placed, and what was to be accomplished at the end of the 100-day period. Were the minimum results and maximum results identified? Are the objectives in writing and were they measurable? Was it specified what was to be measured and when it was to be measured, i.e., weekly, monthly? Were the objectives realistic and achievable? *(5 points)*
  3. Were possible alternative courses of action determined? How much emphasis was placed on searching for and examining alternatives? Were the advantages of each alternative explored in detail? Were the benefits provided by each alternative identified in relation to the minimum and maximum results to be achieved? *(5 points)*
  4. Were the negative consequences of each course of action determined? Were the negative variables, limitations, and their consequences used to simplify the decision and narrow the choices? Was a rating system used for weighing alternatives? *(5 points)*
  5. How was the decision reached on the basic course of action to follow? Was this the point in the planning process when the ISO project plan was formally adopted? Were the people who would be affected by the decisions consulted and their input obtained on how to best implement the ISO 9000 project? *(5 points)*

6. How were strategies developed and priorities, sequencing, and timing of major steps determined? Was a strategic plan developed to execute the ISO 9000 project? *(5 points)*

7. Was a determination made as to how and when the overall ISO 9000 project implementation results were to be measured? Were specific standards and objectives established against which progress was to be checked? Did the checkpoints meet the following criteria: Were they written, specific, realistic, and measurable? Were the sources of information identified? *(5 points)*

- **ISO 9000 Project Organizing** *(20 points):* This category contains four questions which can yield a maximum total of twenty points as follows:

8. Were the job tasks needed to implement the ISO 9000 project identified and analyzed in detail? How did the organization determine what work had to be performed, which activities belonged together, and how each was emphasized? *(5 points)*

9. How was the scope of relationships, responsibility, and authority for the ISO 9000 project determined? How were determinations made on what kind of decisions were needed, which part of the organization should carry them out, and how each manager was to be involved? *(5 points)*

10. How were qualifications for the positions determined? How were people trained to carry out the ISO 9000 project objectives? How were people found either within the organization or from the outside to meet the ISO 9000 project objectives? *(5 points)*

11. Describe how the necessary resources were allocated. How was information provided to make this activity realistic? Did allocations include budgets for people and materials, space utilization, scheduling, and so forth? *(5 points)*

- **ISO 9000 Project Implementing** *(25 points):* This category contains five questions which can yield a maximum total of twenty-five points as follows:

12. Describe how qualified people were found to implement the ISO 9000 project. Were the skills needed to implement the ISO 9000 project identified and matched to the people selected? *(5 points)*

13. Describe how the people were trained and developed to implement the ISO 9000 project activities. Was a training plan developed prior to beginning the implementation? Were the people told what was expected of them and given the resources to carry out their ISO 9000 project tasks? *(5 points)*

14. How were individual performance objectives determined? Were these performance objectives mutually agreed upon by the individual and his/her manager? Were these performance objectives used as a training and coaching device? Were they later used to make an evaluation of the overall effectiveness of the ISO 9000 project? Do these individual performance objectives reflect the overall ISO 9000 project objectives as a whole? Were these objectives measured throughout the ISO 9000 project life cycle? Did the people involved monitor their own performance in relation to the objectives? Were the routine duties, problems, and innovative performance well documented? *(5 points)*

15. How were responsibility, accountability, and authority assigned? Once objectives were agreed upon, were people given the necessary authority to carry out their roles? Were delegation and participative management used to spread and decentralize authority? How was delegation of responsibility carried out and control exercised over the work to be performed? How were the people motivated internally to carry out the ISO 9000 project objectives? *(5 points)*

16. How were day-to-day activities coordinated? How did management integrate the efforts of the people to coincide with the ISO 9000 project objectives? How were employees encouraged to accomplish their tasks? How were differences managed, conflict dealt with, and performance coached? How were problems identified and anticipated? *(5 points)*

- **ISO 9000 Project Controlling** *(20 points)*: This category contains four questions which can result in a maximum of twenty points as follows:

17. How was progress measured and deviation from the ISO 9000 project goals documented? Describe how control of the ISO 9000 project helped verify whether everything was happening in conformity with the plans. How was the determination made that the ISO 9000 project objectives were being met? How was control used to measure progress? Were checkpoints set up to identify key control points to be measured along the way? *(5 points)*

18. Describe how individual performance was measured. Was the measurement made against performance objectives? Was the measurement done on a regular predetermined basis? Were obstacles and problems documented and corrected? *(5 points)*

19. How was corrective action taken as the ISO 9000 project progressed? How were deviations from standards and the work plan monitored? Were corrections made in a timely manner? Did management modify the goals, redraw the plans, reassign individuals, and add new duties?

Describe whatever corrective action was taken to get the ISO 9000 project back on track. *(5 points)*

20. How were recognition and rewards provided for individual performance? Were individual performance problems acknowledged and corrections made in a timely manner? Were new skills acquired and self-development obtained via this ISO 9000 project? How were workers motivated and a high level of effectiveness demonstrated throughout the ISO 9000 project life cycle? *(5 points)*

7

# ORGANIZATION ANALYSIS

## INTRODUCTION

The first task in designing a quality system to meet ISO 9000 is to analyze the organization. This provides a tool for identifying the procedures that will be required and planning how they will be related to build a coherent system.

Most companies have an organizational chart showing how departments and individuals relate in the hierarchy. This type of analysis is not irrelevant to developing a quality system, but neither is it sufficient. It is not what it meant by organization analysis. Instead, the focus needs to be on the activities of the organization: what happens, for example, to turn an order into a customer delivery?

This chapter shows how to carry out an appropriate analysis for almost any type of organization. The point of the analysis—why it should be carried out at all—will become clearer in later chapters.

## OPERATING PROCESSES AND SUPPORT ACTIVITIES

The most basic analytical division of an organization is shown in Figure 7.1. Any organization can be split into two parts: the operating process and the support activities.

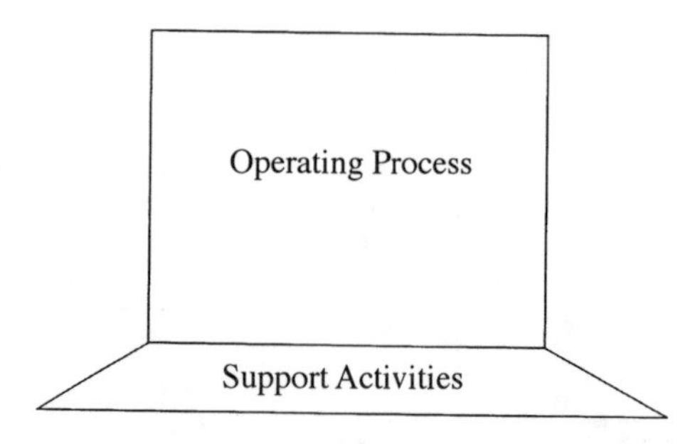


**Figure 7.1** Organizational activities.

The operating process is what the organization does to achieve its objectives (profits, growth, survival, etc.). It consists of its core activities and in a commercial business covers all the activities which directly turn a customer inquiry into a revenue-earning delivery. Typically this covers sales and marketing, design work, producing the product or service, delivering it, and, where required, providing after-sales support.

The support activities, on the other hand, provide the environment in which the operating process can be carried out. These activities include purchasing, financial information, management, personnel, building and plant maintenance, and similar activities. Such support activities may be centralized within the organization, but this need not be the case. Purchasing, for example, may be carried out by several groups, each linked to a particular part of the operating process. Support activities are represented in Figure 7.1 as the base supporting the operating process.

## THE OPERATING PROCESS

Most organizations have operating processes represented by either Figure 7.2 or Figure 7.3. Some may have a combination of both basic structures (Figure 7.4).

Organization A in Figure 7.2 is typical of made-to-order businesses. Sales and marketing activities generate orders. Design work then produces a shop floor (or factory) specification, shop floor activities turn out the product (which may be a service rather than physical goods), and distribution ensures that it is delivered to a customer, who is then supported by after-sales services. In some businesses, design and after-sales service may not be a requirement of the process, i.e., they are not part of the contract between supplier and customer. These businesses should clearly seek ISO 9002 rather than 9001. Even when

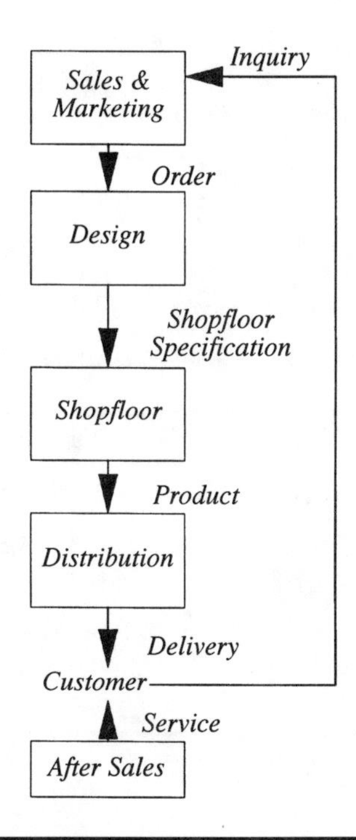


**Figure 7.2** Organization A operating process.

design and after-sales service are in the contract, the decision may be made to exclude the activity from ISO 9000— again, such businesses should seek 9002 rather than 9001.

Figure 7.3 shows the operating process of another type of organization (B). The difference here is that orders are met from stock, and if the customer requirement cannot be met by the range of products available (or sales cannot persuade the customer that it can), the customer will go elsewhere. In this case, the shop floor feeds products into stocks held in distribution (instead of producing to specific orders as in organization A), and deliveries are made from these stocks. This type of organization usually involves a physical product. Services can rarely be held in stock.

Organizations such as B do not have design as part of the operating process, because design work is not carried out to meet the requirements of any particular customer (although, through market research, it may be planned to meet the needs of typical customers). Rather, in these businesses, design is concerned with developing a standard product range, and the work is probably best considered as being part of support activities. Design activities in this type of structure may

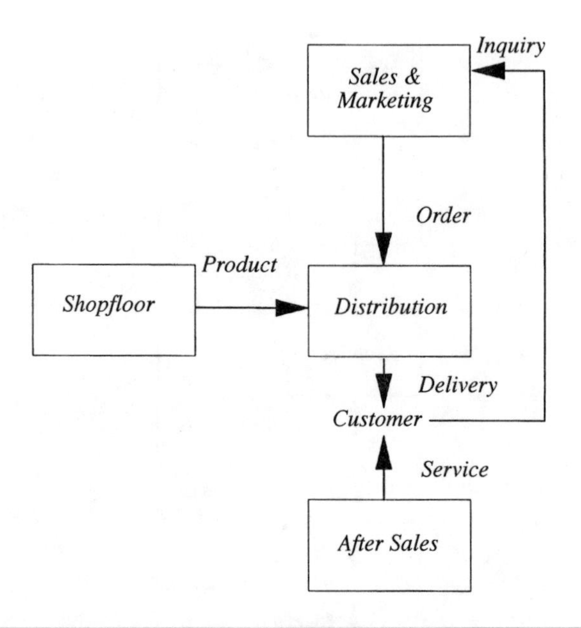


**Figure 7.3** Organization B operating process.

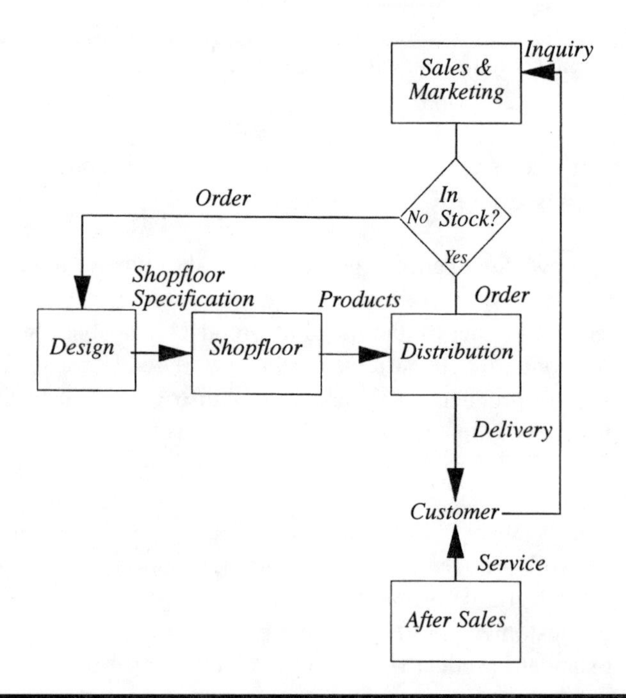


**Figure 7.4** Organization C operating process.

or may not be included in the scope of registration sought for ISO 9000. The company may choose either 9001 or 9002.

Figure 7.4 represents a combination organization, in which some orders are met from stock and others are made to meet specific customer requirements.

Each major part of the operating process is discussed below, starting with the most complex.

## THE PRODUCTION WORK AREA

It should be stated at the outset that although a shop floor (or production work area) may be a specific area where manufacturing processes are carried out, in the context of this book the term is used to refer to any activity involved in turning out a product or service; the activity need not be carried out in a factory or office area. The work, for example, may even be undertaken at the customer's site.

What happens in a production work area varies considerably in different types of businesses. For example, the activities within an attorney's office are quite unlike those in a chemical plant. However, all work areas, without exception, are made up of interconnected chains of input–process–output.

Figure 7.5 shows a very simple work area (A). It could represent a business making wire coat hangers, for instance. A1 shows one input, one process, and one output. In the coat hanger example, the input is wire coils, and the process includes straightening and cutting the wire, forming it to shape, and twisting it to produce the final coat hanger—the output. The process in the box in the figure is, however, simplified and represented as only one process. In A2 of Figure 7.5 the process is analyzed in more detail and represented as a chain of input–

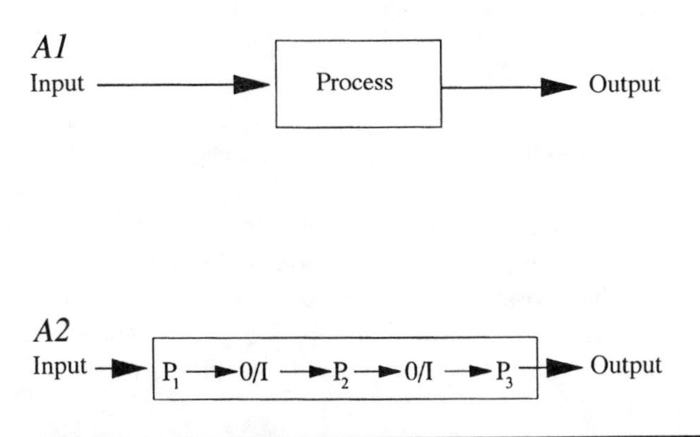


**Figure 7.5** Production work area A.

process–output, where the output from one process becomes the input to another (shown as O/I). In the case of the coat hanger, the sequence might be as follows: straightening and cutting the wire P1, with the straightened and cut output fed in as an input to P2, bending the wire to shape, and the bent wire being fed as an input to P3, the final twisting.

One very important point is that in Figure 7.5, A1 and A2 are from the very same production work area. The only difference is that A1 does not describe the process in detail (i.e., it is left at a major process level, or low level, of detail), whereas A2 provides more detail. It is possible with some processes that a third level of detail could be represented. Neither A1 nor A2 is a true model of the actual production; the level of detail needed in organization analysis is determined solely by how the resulting analysis is used in the review or procedure design stages of developing a quality system. In practice, therefore, a judgment about the level of detail required must be made when analyzing the production work area. The level of detail required is the minimum level of detail necessary to carry out the review and design procedures. The best practical advice is to stay initially at the fairly general level and, if necessary, break down elements into more detail later.

The chain of input–process–output should be thought of in a very broad sense and is certainly not confined to physical input, process, and output. For an insurance broker, for example, choosing a policy from those available on the market in order to best match the client's needs is as much a process as machining a lock assembly. A common type of process relevant in most businesses and usually vital to quality is testing. Obviously the forms of testing vary. In the coat hanger example, the final process might be testing the hangers against a standard shape and rejecting any that do not conform. A process might also be passive, e.g., keeping a store of materials required in the active process. Similarly, input does not have to be tangible. It can consist of various types of information, for example, the range of available policies on the market. One type of information, however, that is not regarded as production input is the specification of what is to be produced, because this is what connects production to design or sales and marketing (refer to Figure 7.2).

A special type of input is that supplied by a customer for incorporation into the final product, referred to as purchaser-supplied product in ISO 9000. This can pertain to made-to-order businesses as well. An example is a casting that an engineering shop machines as a final component: the casting is returned to the customer with further work done to it. Examples of this type of arrangement can also be found in services: information supplied by a client to a management consultancy can be regarded as incorporated into the final product, the written recommendations.

Work area A represented in Figure 7.5 showed only one straight line of

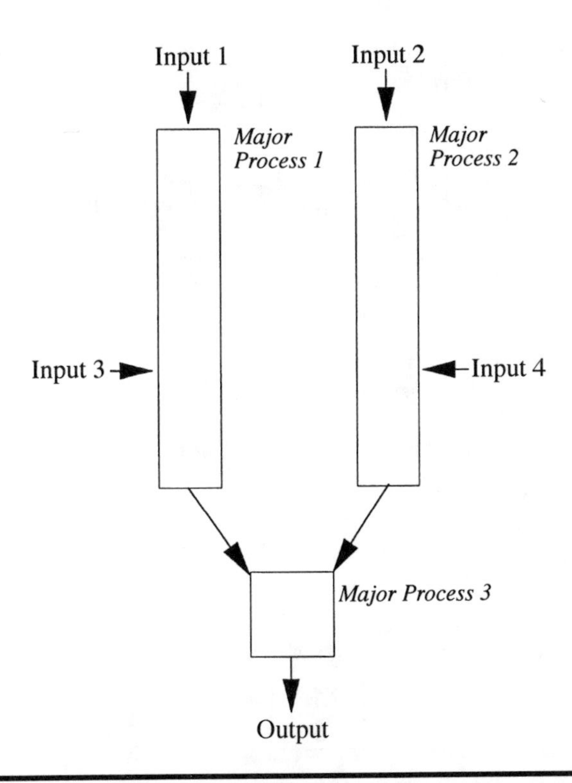


**Figure 7.6** Production work area B.

input–process–output. Usually, the situation is more complex. Figure 7.6 represents work area B in which two separate processes converge. Continuing with the coat hanger image, the input on the left-hand side of the figure could be wire, processed in major process 1 into the final wire hanger. However, in this case a different hanger is being produced, one that has a plastic strip covering the rail of the hanger. The input on the right of Figure 7.6 is, therefore, a plastic strip, which in major process 2 is cut and shaped. Major process 3 brings the two lines together: the finished hanger is assembled complete with rail cover.

Note that in Figure 7.6 the processes have been left at a general level of detail. They could be broken down to show the more specific processes in the same way that A1 was broken down as A2 in Figure 7.5. Also, additional input is shown entering the processes. (In the processing of the plastic strip, the additional input 4 could perhaps be gold paint to add some decoration.)

Another type of production work area is represented in Figure 7.7. Here, the two major processes do not converge at all; they could be the processing of two quite distinct product lines. However, it is not uncommon for such parallel

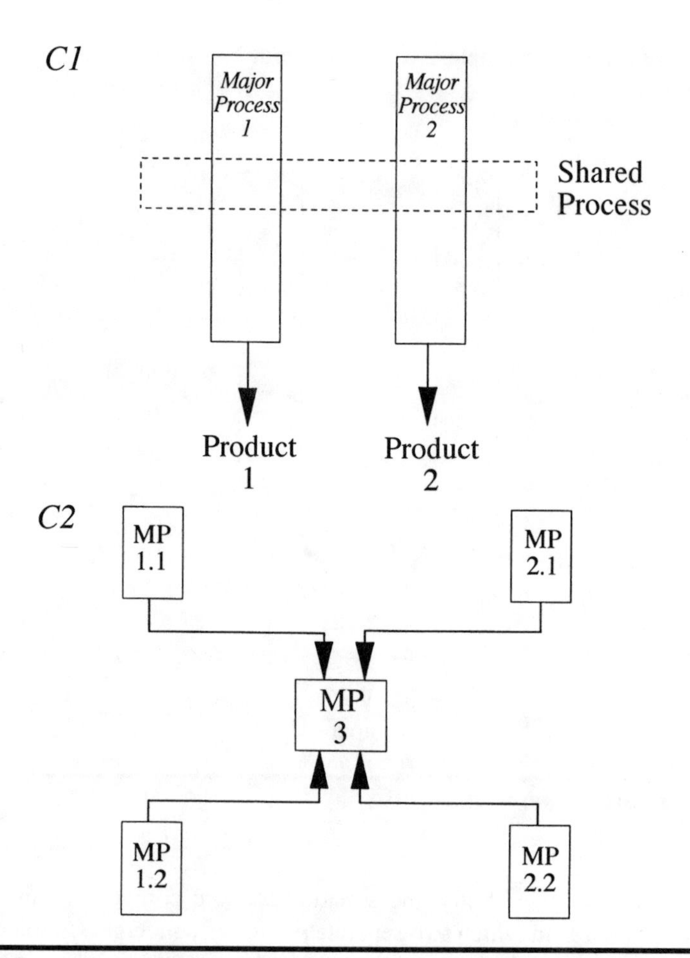


**Figure 7.7** Production work area C.

processes to share some activities. In C1 of Figure 7.7 the shared process is represented by the dashed rectangle, but can be better shown as in C2, with the processes feeding into the common process 3 and then diverging again into their separate lines.

Using these concepts, the work area of any organization can be represented by chains of input–process–output, converging or in parallel, with or without shared processes. Depending on the complexity of the business, the chart produced can be correspondingly more or less complex (the more complex chart may look like a large tree). Where the situation is complex, however, it is best to start with a general but comprehensive chart and, if necessary, add detail later.

Other types of flowcharting and diagramming tools are available and can be obtained from the ISO 9000 Forum (see the profile at the end of Chapter 5).

## SALES AND MARKETING

In Figures 7.2 and 7.3, the starting activity of the operating process is shown as sales and marketing. Again, the organization of this activity can vary widely and be more or less complex. However, at a very general level, the activity can be represented as three stages: (1) inquiry generation and processing (encompassing advertising, direct mail, sales visits, etc.); (2) preparing draft contracts and negotiating with customers, using sales skills to obtain results (although not always successfully); and (3) agreeing upon a final contract with the customer. As indicated by the dotted line in Figure 7.8, only the latter two activities (possibly only the third) are directly relevant to ISO 9000.

Generally, for the purposes of designing a quality system to meet ISO 9000, the representation of sales and marketing shown in Figure 7.8 is sufficient. However, it may be useful to list the specific activities undertaken in each of the three stages under the major headings shown in the boxes (inquiry generation, etc.).

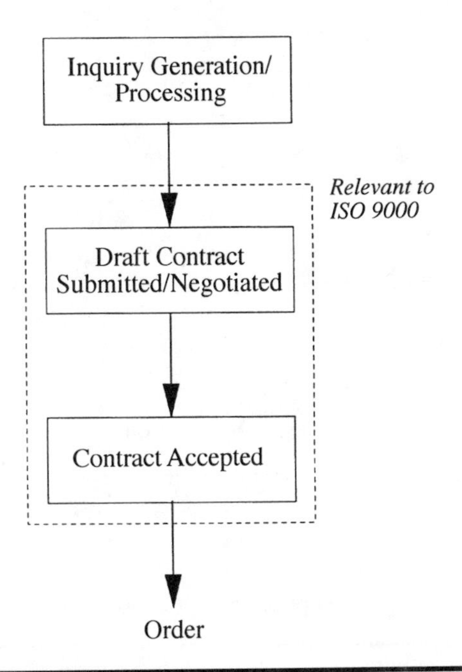


**Figure 7.8** Sales and marketing activities.

## DESIGN

Design only needs to be included in the organization analysis if it is part of the operating process and/or ISO 9000 is being sought. Again, the more involved activities can, at least initially, be represented by a three-box chart as in Figure 7.9. This represents design as carried out within one central department. In some organizations, however, design may be carried out within different parts of the operating process (e.g., in a management consultancy), and in such cases a different representation will be appropriate. The three boxes in Figure 7.9, as shown later, correspond to specific requirements of the standard. As with sales and marketing, it is probably sufficient to leave the analysis at this very general level, with the addition of a listing of the specific activities carried out in the three stages.

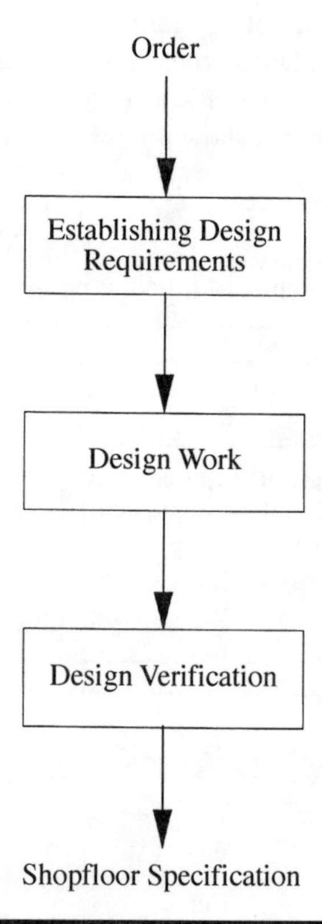


**Figure 7.9** Design activities.

## DISTRIBUTION

The activities covered by distribution in Figures 7.2 and 7.3 consist of three principal areas:

- **Storage:** In a business supplying customers from stock (as in Figure 7.3), storage is a major element in the operating process. It is important commercially: companies must weigh maintaining adequate stock levels to meet demand vs. minimizing stocking costs. Storage also has a quality component: having maximized quality in design and in the production area, the product must not be allowed to deteriorate while it is in stock. The specific action needed to ensure this will depend on the nature of the product: safe keeping of frozen vegetables is quite different from safe keeping of gravel.

  In made-to-order businesses (as in Figure 7.2) the storage requirements are often much less complex; the product is delivered very soon after it is made. For many services, no storage activity is involved.
- **Packaging:** This includes all activities related to protecting finished products while in storage or transit. It normally excludes the type of packaging that is necessary for the product itself, such as the can that is used to hold baked beans. In this case, it is the outer cardboard carton or polyethylene wrapping that is considered the packaging for the beans. Packaging is as relevant to made-to-order as to inventory-based businesses, although some physical products may require no packaging. Again, services seldom require packaging in the usual sense. However, a market research company registered for ISO 9000 regards the physical presentation of its client reports as a packaging activity.
- **Delivery:** This aspect of distribution refers to the transportation of the product using either purchased resources or the supplier's own. Again, services often have no requirements in this area.

Another aspect of distribution that can be thought of as either applying to all activities or as a separate activity in its own right is handling. To ensure that products are not damaged when coming in or out of storage, being packed, or in delivery, they must be handled appropriately. What is appropriate depends entirely upon the nature of the product.

For the purposes of the review (see Chapter 8), it is enough for the analysis of distribution to select which of the preceding three elements are applicable and how they are carried out. Perhaps a short description can be written on what is involved in each case, e.g., *Packaging:* Products M and N are packed in cardboard cartons in either 50s, 100s, or 250s to meet different order sizes.

When developing procedures (Chapter 9), it may be appropriate to prepare a chart of the distribution function analogous to the one suggested for the production work area, built up as a sequence of input–process–output.

## AFTER SALES

Not all organizations have after-sales activities in the sense of supporting products supplied to customers. In the context of ISO 9000, it is only relevant to 9001 registration. After-sales activities may, however, be applied to a service, e.g., in the case of a management consultancy, following up a client's implementation of project recommendations. Some companies also choose to regard positive monitoring of customer satisfaction and complaint handling as an aspect (or the main part) of after-sales service.

As with distribution, for the purposes of the review it is enough to recognize that after-sales services are relevant and to prepare a short description of what is involved. The description should include differences across the product range and the nature and type of service given to customers. A more detailed analysis may be needed for procedures.

## SUPPORT ACTIVITIES

In Figure 7.1, the operating process was shown to rest on a base of support activities. In Figure 7.10, the support activities are divided in two directions. The horizontal layers represent the elements of support activities that are (or are not) relevant to ISO 9000. The vertical lines of the figure divide support activities into three areas: resourcing, records and information, and control and management.

Resourcing includes activities such as purchasing (bringing inputs into the

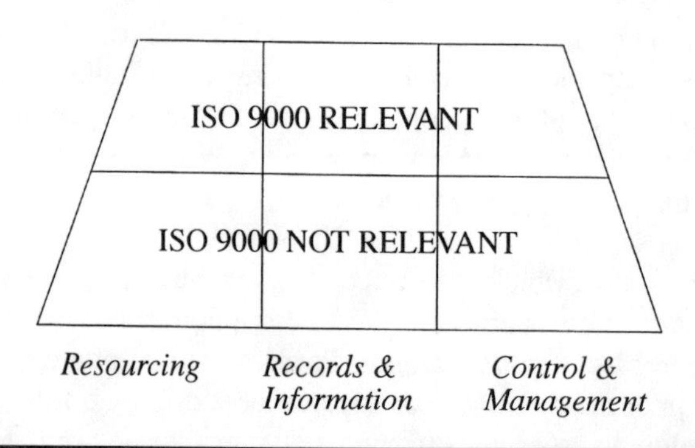


**Figure 7.10** Support activities.

work area), providing equipment needed in the work area (or elsewhere), and recruitment and training of personnel. These aspects of resourcing are relevant to ISO 9000 (to be discussed in the next chapter) and can, therefore, be represented in the upper layer of the left-hand segment. Other types of resourcing, e.g., premises provision and maintenance, are not relevant and fall in the lower layer of the left-hand segment.

Records and information includes the activities connected with accountancy and the provision of financial information, essential in all organizations. However, although these types of records and information are important, they are not relevant to ISO 9000. The standard, however, does have requirements in this area of support activities: those which can be described as *quality records.*

Control and management covers the general management of an organization. In a business this includes the activities of the board of directors when deciding policy issues. This is not directly relevant to ISO 9000. A type of control and management that is a requirement (in fact, several requirements) of the standard is the control of the quality system itself (management responsibility, internal quality audits, corrective action and quality document control). Except in very rare cases, these will not exist in an organization prior to setting up a formal quality system.

For the purposes of the review at least, answering the questions relevant to support activities under item 6 of the Action Plan below provides sufficient analysis.

## ORGANIZATION ANALYSIS ACTION PLAN

The following action plan, which uses the concepts and approaches suggested in this chapter, can be implemented in almost any organization. Reading Chapters 8 and 9, however, will make the point of the analysis work so much clearer.

1. Produce a chart of the operating process modeled, as appropriate, on Figure 7.2, 7.3, or 7.4. Decide whether design and after-sales activities are carried out in the organization. If ISO 9001 is being sought as well, include these in the chart.
2. Produce a chart of the production work area to at least the level of detail of major processes. Decide whether or not products are supplied by customers for incorporation into the final product.
3. Confirm whether or not Figure 7.8 provides a reasonable representation of sales and marketing (if not, prepare an alternative to a low level of detail). Briefly describe the major specific activities carried out in the boxes of Figure 7.8.

4. *For ISO 9001 registration only:* Confirm whether Figure 7.9 provides a reasonable representation of design. If not, prepare a suitable alternative, even when design is spread throughout the company rather than centralized. Briefly describe the major specific activities carried out in the boxes of Figure 7.9.
5. Describe how (or if) distribution activities—storage, packaging, delivery, and handling—are carried out.

   *For ISO 9001 registration only:* Briefly describe the after-sales operation, including any product range variations.
6. Answer the following questions about the support activities of the organization:

   *Purchasing*
   - Is purchasing centralized or decentralized?
   - Is purchasing the responsibility of specialists or is it carried out by staff with a range of other duties?

   *Inspection, Measuring and Test Equipment*
   - What types of such equipment (if any*) are in use in the operating process?
   - To which specific activities are they linked?
   - How are they calibrated, checked for accuracy, and maintained?

   *Training*
   - Is training centralized or decentralized?
   - In broad terms, what type of training is carried out?

   *Product Identification*
   - Can products be individually identified during manufacture and afterward, and if so, how?**

At the start of this chapter, the type of organizational analysis outlined was distinguished from the hierarchical chart. However, once the action plan has been carried out, the charts and descriptions produced should be linked to the personnel and hierarchy of the organization. Specifically, it should be shown on the operating structure and production charts which departments currently carry out the activities (e.g., colored lines can be used to show the departmental responsibilities) and specifically which senior staff are involved. These additions will be useful when deciding who to involve at the procedure development and system building stages.

---

*Some services will have no such equipment in use or could not practically apply such equipment.

**For example, a serial number may be permanently affixed to the product.

# THE JAPANESE DELEGATION AND ISO 9000: INTEGRATING ORGANIZATION ANALYSIS AND TQM

## Introduction

The following information was graciously provided by Dr. Hitoshi Kume to Frank Voehl during a meeting and interview session at the ISO 9000 Forum meeting in Washington, D.C. in October of 1993.

## Overview

Since the creation of the ISO 9000 series and the accompanying assessment and registration of quality systems throughout the world, a substantial number of Japanese companies have requested assessment and registration of their quality systems on the basis of the ISO 9000 series, especially when trading with European buyers. Accordingly, a number of assessment/registration bodies have started operation in Japan, and scores of Japanese companies and factories have had their quality systems assessed and registered by those bodies. This is in marked contrast to the Japanese indifference to ISO 9000 until 1991.

## Deliberation on Accreditation Scheme

In 1991 the Japanese Industrial Standards Committee (JISC) set up the Technical Committee on Quality Systems, chaired by Professor Hitoshi Kume of the University of Tokyo. The purpose of the committee is to conduct surveys and deliberate on a suitable assessment and registration scheme for quality systems in Japan.

## Key Issues for Consideration

The report raised the following issues for consideration:

---

*Source:* Interview with Frank Voehl and excerpts from a speech and unpublished paper by Dr. Hitoshi Kume, Washington, D.C., October 8, 1993.

- The essential objective of the assessment/registration scheme is to create or increase the buyer's confidence in products or services by evidence that the quality system of the manufacturing process has been assessed and registered by an independent third party.
- By using an appropriate scheme, overlapping assessments of a quality system by multiple buyers can be avoided.
- Accreditation of assessment/registration bodies will ensure the reliability of their work.
- Quality system assessment/registration bodies currently operating in Japan are not coordinated in either their assessment procedures or in the validity of their results.

In conclusion, the report stressed the importance of setting up a well-organized quality management and organization analysis and assessment system in Japan and the need to establish a national accreditation body to unify the relevant standards.

## Guiding Principles for the Accreditation Body

The report recommended the following principles for the accreditation body:

1. The accreditation body should be an independent and neutral organization.
2. The body should be newly established as a nongovernmental, non-profit foundation as soon as possible.
3. The body should be established through the initiative of and with the resources of the private sector.
4. The body should also accredit auditor training programs and evaluate quality system auditors for registration as well.
5. The body should formulate criteria for accreditation of quality system assessment bodies and for evaluation of quality system auditors in accordance with ISO/IEC Guide 40 and ISO 10011-2, respectively. The criteria should be made available to the public.
6. The body should be open to quality system assessment bodies from abroad applying for accreditation.

## A Different Quality Management Ethos

Traditionally, Japanese quality management has been rather uneasy with a certification system based on ISO standards. The ISO standards represent quality management from the *purchaser's* standpoint, while the mainstream of Japanese quality management is from the *supplier's* standpoint. Japanese quality management is designed to do more than merely pass the inspection and audit of a purchaser. It attempts to capture market share and foster corporate growth by anticipating a customer's needs and actively developing and providing products that will satisfy them. This quality management ethos has been cultivated as a result of the enlightening and illuminating lectures given by Drs. Sarasohn, Deming, and Juran, and it forms the backbone of modern Japanese quality management.

## Reappraisal of Japanese Quality Management

According to Dr. Kume, Japanese quality management, or company-wide quality management, is a distinctive, supplier-based form of quality management that has helped Japanese firms produce world-class quality. However, it tends to err on the side of spontaneity and emotion. In contrast, the ISO standards are extremely logical and compensate for the weaknesses in Japanese quality management. Reassessing Japanese quality management on the basis of ISO standards and reconstructing it based on the firm foundation that these standards provide could raise it to an even higher level internationally.

At a TC 176 meeting in Brisbane in November 1993, discussion focused on whether to create an international standard for total quality management (TQM). The Japanese were against the proposal. Japanese TQM is based on two main areas of quality management: one deals with the type of human activity that can be controlled by standards, while the other centers on people and must be allowed to develop outside the scope of standards-based control and audit. As a management technique, TQM is more concerned with the latter area. In order for a company to have an efficient TQM system, it must create and develop its own system rather than follow outside standards. Finally, many excellent books on TQM are available and can be used for reference in the implementation of TQM.

Quality management based on the ISO 9000 series is typical of standards-based quality management, while the so-called "Japanese-style" of quality management, although it also uses standards, is typical of people-centered quality management. The two are not mutually exclusive; rather, they complement each other. Neither can achieve good quality alone.

## Is People-Centered Quality Management Uniquely Japanese?

Because people-centered quality management evolved in Japan and is rooted in that country's unique culture, the question arises as to whether it can be applied in other countries. Dr. Kume believes that it can. His involvement in TQM in the United States dates back to 1988, when he was a member of the JUSE counselor team that visited Florida Power & Light. He made the following comments about that experience and the organization analysis that was conducted by the JUSE team:

"In 1989, an American electric utility company, Florida Power & Light, became the first organization outside Japan to win a Deming Prize. As a member of the examination team, I visited it twice in July and August of that year. I learned a lot from those visits. It was an extremely valuable experience for me to be reminded once again of the benefits of people-centered quality management. When examining Florida Power & Light for the Deming Prize, I asked its president, John Hudiburg, what conditions he thought would make TQM possible in an American company. His reply was extremely clear: total commitment of top management, total education, and total implementation of quality improvements. These requirements are exactly the same for a Japanese company. All three are important, but the second and third can be satisfied relatively easily as long as the first is met. Top management commitment is the single most important requirement."

## Quality Improvement through ISO 9000

Will a certification system based on the ISO standards really improve quality worldwide, or will it simply result in mountains of useless paperwork? This is of concern not only to Dr. Kume (who authored the expanded version of this text), but to quality management specialists all over the world. "A system is simply a means to an end," summarizes Dr. Kume, "and however excellent it may be in itself, it will do more harm than good if misapplied. We must keep this fact constantly in mind when applying the ISO standards. Using them merely for the purpose of gaining certification will promote a ritualized form of quality management. We must view the system as providing us with opportunities to review and analyze our organizations with an eye to maintenance and improvement of quality. It is possible that we will make good use of the ISO standards' strengths in order to develop even better and more reliable quality management."

# 8

# READINESS REVIEW

## REVIEW OBJECTIVES

The primary objective of the review is to produce a list of procedures that will be required to meet the standard. Procedures are documented working methods and, for the purposes of this chapter, include work instructions and quality plans (see Chapter 10 for a description of these).

Few, if any, organizations are likely to have formally documented sets of procedures before preparing for ISO 9000. However, most will have effective procedures, even if they are unwritten, covering most of their operation. It is very unlikely that the employees start work each day with no preconceptions of how they will work. For the important areas of the operating process, there will already be established methods, whether or not they are written down, and these are used to develop the formal written procedures. Some of the really critical activities may already have been written down in various forms. In some departments, there may be a small manual; in others, notices are pinned to the wall or memos are circulated. In carrying out the review it is important to establish in what form current procedures exist and are documented. Generally speaking, where a procedure is in place and thought to be working effectively, it is better to incorporate it into the new formal quality system than to change it. Introducing a formal quality system for the first time is a large enough task.

Preparing the list of required procedures effectively determines how the formal requirements of the standard will be met. The second objective of the review is, therefore, to prepare a series of fairly short policy statements describing how ISO 9000 is to be applied in the particular organization. These policy statements will in due course be incorporated into the quality manual, which is a key document in the formal quality system.

The work of the review is carried out by considering in turn each element of the organization identified in the analysis described in the previous chapter. A copy of the relevant standard (i.e., ISO 9001, 9002, 9003, or 9004) is essential.

As illustrated in Figure 8.1, the organization can be divided into two parts: the operating process and support activities.

## ISO 9000 AND THE OPERATING PROCESS

Figure 8.1 is a repeat of Figure 7.2 in the previous chapter and shows the operating process of a made-to-order business. In this case, however, the relevant numbered headings of ISO 9001 are included. This shows which requirements of the standard apply to each part of the operating process. The requirement for *Contract Review (4.3)* of 9001, for example, applies to the sales and marketing activities; *Design Control (4.4)* applies to design. Each element in the operating process has one corresponding standard requirement. The exception is the shop floor, which unfortunately has five relevant requirements. This most complex area is discussed first, and the activities that logically precede the shop floor in the operating process will be dealt with later.

The previous chapter described the two fundamental forms of the operating process, and Figure 7.3 represented the major alternative structure. The requirements of the standard can be easily inserted into Figure 8.3 to provide the counterpart to Figure 8.1.

### ISO 9000 in the Shop Floor

The procedures in place on the shop floor must meet several requirements of the standard: *Process Control (4.9), Inspection and Testing (4.10), Inspection and Test Status (4.12), Control of Non-Conforming Products (4.13),* and *Purchaser Supplied Product (4.7).* These requirements were discussed earlier, but should also be read in their entirety in a copy of the standard. Now is also the time to consider any recommendations set out in guides to the implementation of ISO 9000 in a particular industry, including those from trade associations or assessment bodies.

As previously pointed out, all organizations, without exception, have shop floors consisting of chains of input–process–output. The first four of the requirements of the standard relevant to the shop floor can be applied in any organization, because they concern what happens in a process *(4.9)* or how inputs and outputs are inspected *(4.10)* and controlled once inspected (*4.12* and *4.13*). The

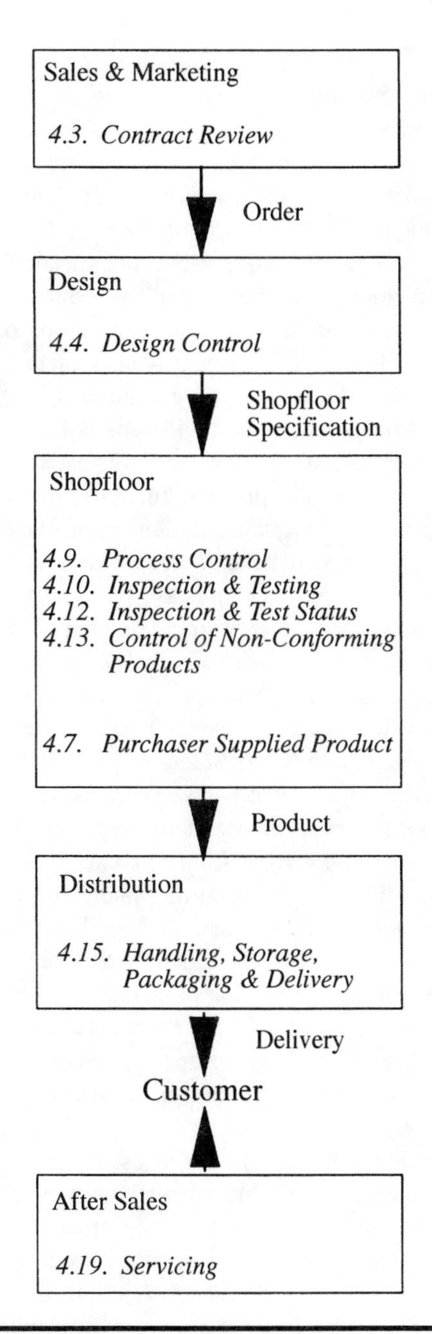


**Figure 8.1** ISO 9001 and the operating process.

remaining requirement of *Purchaser Supplied Product (4.7)* in this context is of a unique status, because some organizations are never involved in processing product supplied by their customers.

Again, the primary objective of the review is to prepare a list of procedures that will meet the requirements of the standard (the contents of the procedures are decided later; see Chapter 9). In the case of the shop floor, a major issue is to resolve whether one procedure (or one group of procedures) will cover all the processes of the shop floor or if a number of procedures/groups of procedures would be more practical. Figure 8.2 reproduces the shop floor represented in the previous chapter (see Figure 7.6): the coat hanger factory. If the two parallel processes 1 and 2 are essentially similar (e.g., both bend wire but one is used for red wire and the other for green), then it will usually be convenient to have one set of procedures covering both processes. Note that there is no objection to having a set of procedures for each process, but at the very least the drafting task will be extended, and once the quality system is in place, a member of staff involved in both processes will have to read two sets of virtually identical procedures. The common set of procedures to cover both processes in Figure 8.2 is labeled SF1, and this will be the provisional number of the procedure that will eventually be prepared. As shown in Figure 8.2, process number 3 is quite different from processes 1 and 2 (perhaps it is where the complete hanger is finally assembled). For this reason a separate set of procedures will be required, and this is provisionally numbered as SF2.

Thus, it has been determined that two sets of procedures will be appropriate to cover the shop floor and meet the standard requirements relevant to this part of the operating process *(4.9, 4.10, 4.12, 4.13),* except for *Purchaser Supplied Product (4.7),* which will be discussed further later. The sets of required procedures can be formally recorded on a chart such as illustrated in Figure 8.3. The two sets of required procedures are recorded as provisional numbers (SF1 and SF2) and their scope described (major processes 1/2 and 3). The ISO 9000 requirements that these procedures will have to meet are also recorded. When the time comes to draft the procedures, the specific requirements will have to be considered in detail. The remaining question is whether or not procedures are actually in place.

It would be surprising if the shop floor processes—the core of the business—were not carried out according to some established rules or procedures, whether or not they were documented or covered all the standard requirements that must be addressed. It is suggested that the list of required procedures include a notation showing whether or not current procedures exist and, if so, in what form. This is shown in Figure 8.3 under Present Status, with a notation indicating that procedures exist but not in documented form.

In this example, with the exception of *Purchaser Supplied Product (4.7),* the

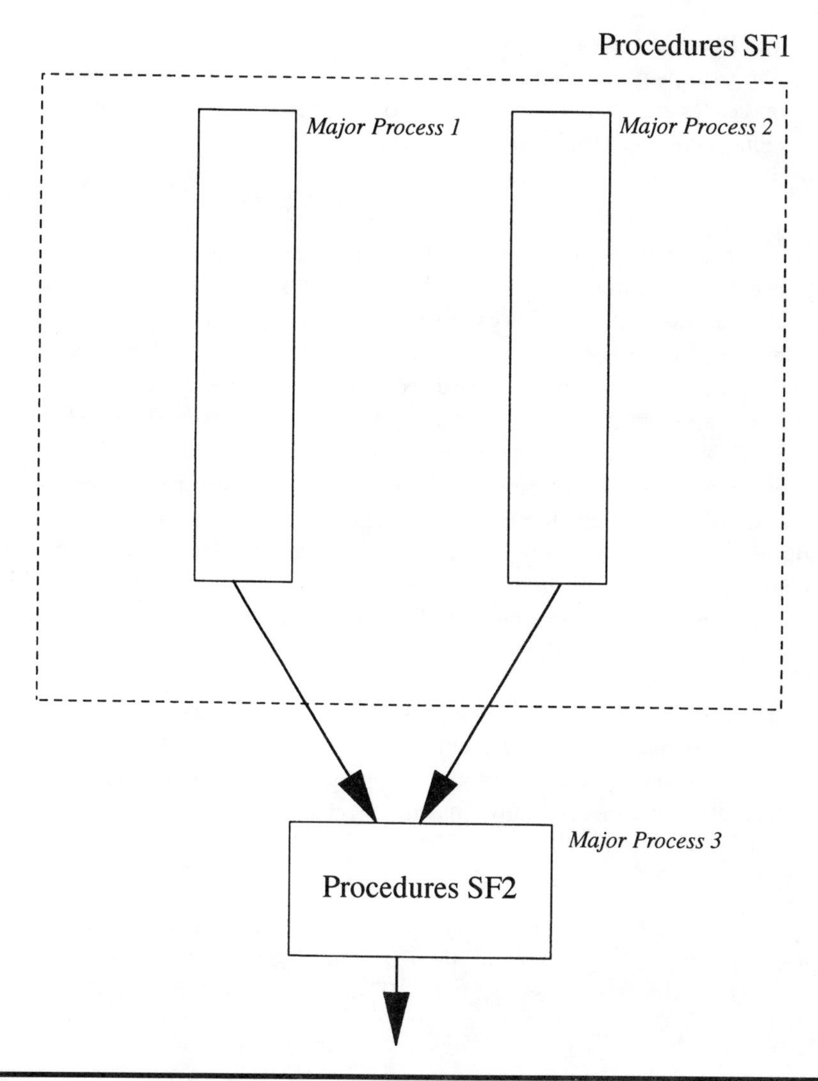


**Figure 8.2** Meeting ISO 9000 in the shop floor activities.

primary objective of the review of the shop floor part of the operating process is complete. All the procedures that will be required are listed. The second objective of the review, which is to prepare a short policy statement showing how requirements of the standard will be met through the company's individual quality system, can now be addressed. In the case of *Process Control (4.9),* for example, an appropriate formal policy statement might take the following form:

**4.9 Process Control**

The Company shall implement formal procedures to ensure that all processes are carried out in a controlled manner with adequate documentation and monitoring to ensure that control is exercised at all times.

*(see procedures SF1 and SF2)*

The formal policy statement is cross-referenced to the specific procedures that ensure the requirement is met in the quality system. As yet, the procedures are simply numbers and still have to be written. In due course the numbering may be altered to fit the nomenclature of the quality manual. Similar formal statements can be made to cover standard requirements *4.10, 4.12,* and *4.13.*

The remaining requirement relevant to the shop floor is *Purchaser Supplied Product (4.7).* At least in smaller businesses, the requirement to verify, adequately store, and maintain purchaser-supplied product can probably be covered by one set of procedures, applicable to all stages of the shop floor and covering all processes. In Figure 8.3 the required procedures are numbered SF3 and are indicated as covering all the shop floor processes, but as yet with no existing procedures in place. A corresponding formal policy statement can be prepared, for example:

**4.7 Purchaser-Supplied Product**

The Company shall implement formal procedures for the verification, adequate storage, and safe keeping of materials supplied by customers for incorporation into the products made for them by the Company.

*(see procedures SF3)*

If in the organization analysis it has been determined that such purchaser-supplied product is not involved, then it would be pointless to design procedures to cover this nonexistent situation. The policy statement would make this explicit:

**4.7 Purchaser-Supplied Product**

The Company does not, in its normal course of business, receive purchaser-supplied product. Accordingly, there are no formal procedures in place to cover this specific requirement.

## ISO 9000 in Other Parts of the Operating Process

Refer to Figure 8.1 for all other parts of the operating process apart from the shop floor. The review for these processes is considered here.

| Number | Scope | ISO 9001 Requirements | Present Status * |
|---|---|---|---|
| SF1<br>SF2 | Major Process 1 + 2<br>Major Process 3 | *}4.9*<br>*}4.10*<br>*}4.12*<br>*}4.13* | }<br>} 1<br>}<br>} |
| SF3 | All Shopfloor | *4.7* | 0 |
| SM1 | All Sales & Marketing | *4.3* | 1 |
| DS1 | All Design Activities | *4.4* | 1/2 |
| DT1 | All Distribution | *4.15* | 1 |
| AS1 | All After Sales | *4.19* | 1 |
| SA1 | All Purchasing | *4.6* | 1/2 |
| SA2 | All Inspection, Measuring & Test Equipment throughout All Processes | *4.11* | 2 |
| SA3<br><br>SA4 | Training of Staff Involved in Major Process 1 & 2<br>Training of Staff Involved in All Other Processes | *}*<br>*}4.18*<br>*}* | }<br>}<br>} 1/2<br>} |
| SA5<br><br>SA6 | Output of Major Process 1<br>Output of Major Process 2 & 3 | *}*<br>*}4.8*<br>*}* | }<br>} 2<br>}<br>} 0 |
| SA7 | All Activities | *4.16* | 0 |
| SA8 | All Activities | *4.20* | 1 |
| SA9 | All Activities | *4.1, 4.2, 4.5, 4.14, 4.17* | 0 |

* **0 = No Existing Procedure**
**1 = Existing But Not Documented Procedure**
**2 = Existing & Documented Procedure**

**Figure 8.3** Sample procedure chart.

The standard requirements to be met in the sales and marketing activities of the business are *Contract Review (4.3)*. In most smaller businesses, it is very likely that the requirements for contract review can be adequately covered by a single set of procedures. This is the case in the example shown in Figure 8.3. The required procedures are numbered SM1, are stated to cover all of sales and marketing, and are designed to meet the ISO 9000 requirement *4.7.* It is assumed in the example that some procedures controlling contracts exist, but are not in a written form; they are perhaps the established methods of the sales manager. An appropriate formal policy statement can also be made, for example:

> **4.3 Contract Review**
> It shall be the Company's practice to establish a clear understanding of the customer's requirements at the outset and continuously review these as the work for the customer is carried out.
>
> All orders shall be matched to a fully documented and corresponding quotation prepared for the customer by the Company, which shall include a specification of the product to be supplied, the delivery date, and the costs to be charged.
>
> *(see procedures SM1)*

It is also worth noting that many of the activities within sales and marketing are not specifically addressed by ISO 9000. In particular, all the marketing methods used to generate sales leads and the discussions with customers that take place *before* a contract is drafted are outside the scope of contract review, which only becomes relevant once a contract has been prepared. The procedures, therefore, can narrowly address what is done once a contract is drafted and leave all other sales and marketing activities outside the scope of the formal quality system. However, a major benefit of ISO 9000 is that it addresses internal efficiency and minimization of errors, and thus it may be decided that problems in contract drafting are best addressed at an earlier stage of the sales and marketing process. This can be accomplished by ensuring that salespeople obtain sufficient details of customer requirements at an initial meeting to enable an adequate contract to be drafted. The inclusion of activities within a quality system that are not formally addressed by the standard, however, has a down side, which must be weighed against the benefits of taking a wider view of the scope of the quality system. Once procedures are in place and included in the quality system, they may be taken into account in the formal assessment, which determines success or failure in initially gaining ISO 9000. In other words, there are some dangers in making the process more detailed than it need be. The wider the scope of the procedures, the greater the chance that someone will fail to follow them. Procedures must not only be drafted, but must be adhered to.

The design activities within the operating process of a typical business seeking ISO 9001 are represented in detail in Figure 8.4. These activities are divided into (1) establishing the design requirement (which logically follows contract approval) (2) the actual design work, and (3) design verification (check-

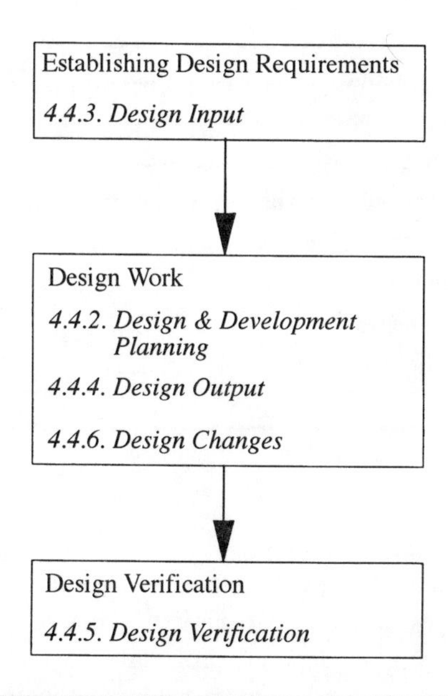


**Figure 8.4** Documenting design activities for ISO 9000.

ing that the design actually meets that which is required). The ISO 9001 requirements in these areas are set out in *Design Control (4.4).* This is a vital element of 9001 because it is its inclusion that differentiates 9001 from 9002. Realistically, therefore, an assessment for 9001 will include detailed consideration of a quality system's coverage and implementation in the design area. The design requirements are actually set out in *4.4* under five subheadings, as shown in Figure 8.4.

In most smaller manufacturing companies that product to customers' orders, design work is likely to be carried out in one department and is usually completed before manufacturing starts (as indicated in Figure 8.1). In such cases, one set of procedures applicable to the one design department is likely to be most appropriate. This is the case in the example illustrated in Figure 8.3, where procedures exist and are to some extent documented in the form of notes within the design department. The procedure group is numbered as DS1. When drafted, it will cover the requirements set out in *Design Control (4.4),* which covers five distinct subheadings, the contents of which must each be considered.

In some businesses, design activities may be split among a number of departments, each perhaps linked to one or more shop floor activities. In this case, it may be appropriate to have a set of procedures for each design unit, particularly if the type of work undertaken by each is very different. However,

| | |
|---|---|
| **Introduction** | QS 0 |
| **Commissioning** | QS 1 |
| **Professional Research** | QS 2 |
| **Structured Interviewing Research** | QS 3 |
| **Data Processing** | QS 4 |
| **Reporting** | QS 5 |
| **Administration** | QS 6 |
| **Quality System Control** | QS 7 |

**Figure 8.5** Sample list of procedure manual headings.

although the particular activities may vary, the general principles of controlling the work will be the same. It may therefore be quite possible to devise a single set of design procedures applicable to various types of work. In general, it is better to have fewer than more separate procedures, even though the purpose of procedures is to control the work. The procedures, therefore, must be specific enough to guide staff.

In service businesses, design may be carried out at various points in the overall process, perhaps with all key staff performing design functions alongside other activities. An individual management consultant, for example, will typically be involved in sales and marketing, developing methods of work to meet a client's requirements (design), collecting data (shop floor), and developing and presenting recommendations (design, shop floor, and possibly distribution). In this situation it may be more practical to include design procedures with procedures covering shop floor activities, rather than to have a separate set of design procedures. The major sections of the procedure manual for a market research company are presented in Figure 8.5. Although this firm is registered for ISO 9001, and therefore includes its design activities, design is not a separate set of procedures; the activity is widely distributed and covered in a number of the shop floor procedures (QS 2 to QS 5). (*Note:* In the sample procedure in Figure 8.5, QS 1 to QS 5 cover the operating process of the company and QS 6 and QS 7 cover the support activities.)

For this particular company, the relevant policy statement is as follows:

**4.4 Design Control**

Much of the work undertaken by the Company contains an element of design. Through specific procedures (including those referenced below) the Company will ensure adequate control of design work, including:

*4.4.2* Planning the design work and assigning responsibility for it to adequately trained and qualified staff and communicating these requirements throughout all parts of the Company engaged in the work.

*4.4.3* Establishing the design requirements of clients.

*4.4.4* Appropriately documenting the design in working papers and other documents used in projects.

*4.4.5* Having checking procedures to ensure that designs meet client requirements.

*(Ref: QS 1.2.1, QS 2.3, QS 3.1, QS 3.2, QS 5.1, QS 5.2)*

In the example, specific reference is made to the subheadings of the requirement of the standard. Given the importance attached to control of design in ISO 9001, this is appropriate. The policy statement of a company in which design is carried out in a specific department would refer to the department (e.g., "The design work of the Company is carried out by the Design Unit...") and give a specific procedure heading reference (e.g., DS1 as in Figure 8.3).

The approach to carrying out a review of the remaining parts of the operating process (distribution and after sales, as in Figure 8.1) is much the same as for sales and marketing and design. Generally, in smaller businesses, both types of activities can be best covered by one set of procedures, and this is the case in the example illustrated by Figure 8.3 (DT1 is distribution, and AS1 is after sales).

In service companies, some of the distribution and after-sales activities which the relevant requirements of the standard address are not carried out. Few if any service organizations store product, for example; packaging may be minimal and delivery carried out by regular mail. Similarly, after-sales activity may not relate directly to the product or service provided. An example of an appropriate policy statement for a service company with limited involvement in distribution or after-sales is as follows:

**4.15 Handling, Storage, Packaging, and Delivery**

For the most part, product handling, storage, and delivery practices of the Company are as normal office practice. Packaging is particularly covered* as per the reference below. Where additional service is required by the client, this shall be carried out as per the contract.

*(Ref: QS 5.1.3)*

*In this case the procedures are applied to the standard for printing and binding clients' reports, rather than to how they are packed for dispatch.

**4.19 Servicing**
The Company's policy shall be to maintain contact with clients in order to determine the effectiveness of work undertaken as well as to obtain new business.

*(Ref: QS 5.4.7)*

## ISO 9004-2 for Service Organizations

Due to the unique nature of service organizations, ISO has created an interim standard called ISO 9004-2, which can be used as a blueprint for most types of service organizations. Unlike ISO 9001 or 9002 certifications, ISO 9004-2 is more top-down and of a general nature. The key aspects of a quality system for service organizations are the interactions between management responsibility, resources, and quality system structure.

As previously mentioned, management responsibility consists of the quality policy and objectives, quality responsibility and authority, and management review. Resources consist of personnel motivation, training and development, communication, and material resources. The quality system structure consists of the service quality loop (see Figure 8.7), quality documentation, records, control and audits, and interface with customers.

Finally, the quality system operational elements are subdivided into the marketing process (which itself has five subelements), the design process (with thirteen subelements), the service delivery process (with seven subelements), and service performance analysis and improvement (with four subelements).

# ISO 9000 IN SUPPORT ACTIVITIES

The parts of a business classified in the previous chapter as support activities are shown in Figure 8.6. These are grouped into three categories: resourcing, records and information, and control and management. The relevant requirements of ISO 9001—over half of all the major headings in the standard—are included in the figure.

Generally speaking, the procedures required to meet these requirements are best applied throughout the company. One set of procedures, for example, will normally cover all the purchasing activities of a company. This is the case in the example shown in Figure 8.3, which lists one set of procedures (SA1) covering all purchasing activities of the business. In the example, relevant purchasing procedures already exist and are at least partly documented. However, even in a smaller company, purchasing may cover two or more very distinct activities. For example, in a service company it might include buying stationery and similar

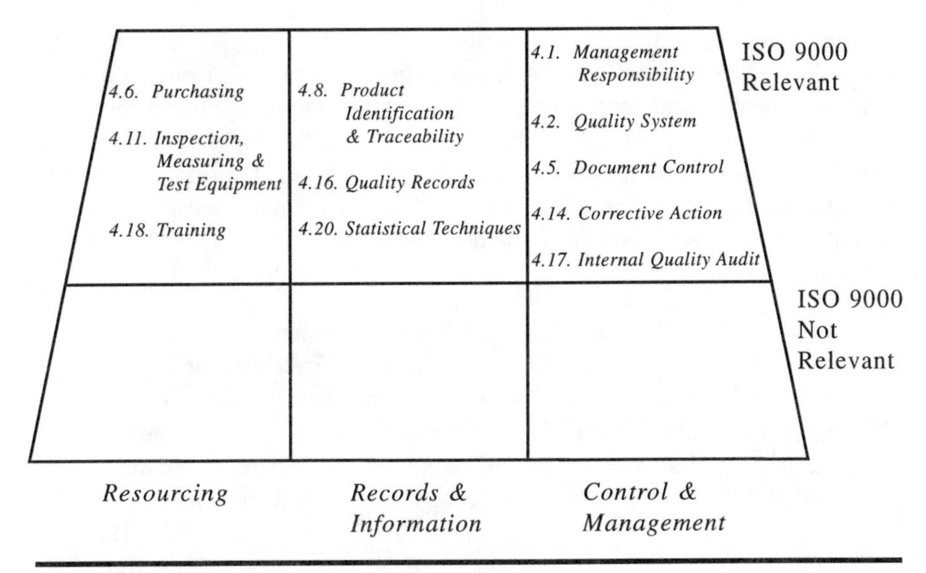


**Figure 8.6** ISO 9001 in support activities.

materials as well as subcontracting work to independent professional freelancers. In these circumstances it may be better to draft two distinct sets of procedures, because different staff are involved in the distinct types of purchasing.

The relevant requirement of the standard *(4.6 Purchasing)* covers the need to assess suppliers *(4.6.2 Assessment of Sub-Contractors)* and ensure that orders are adequately documented. Appropriate procedures would typically include a system of regular performance assessment of approved suppliers (this may include a provision for emergency or probationary suppliers to allow adequate flexibility in sourcing) and a requirement to place all orders with approved suppliers in writing that includes the necessary specified information. The formal policy statement would reflect the approach adopted:

> **4.6 Purchasing**
> Purchases of significance to the Quality System include stationery materials and obtaining services from professional practices and similar sources. The Company shall maintain a system of Approved Supplier Lists which includes a provision for assessment of the quality of product or service provided by these suppliers (meeting *4.6.2* of ISO 9001). Orders placed with these suppliers will be in writing and in conformity with relevant procedures for documentation (meeting *4.6.3 Purchasing Data* of ISO 9001).
>
> *(Ref: SA1)*

The organization analysis (as described in Chapter 7) will have identified the nature and location of the inspection, measuring, and test equipment used in the business. Again, in smaller businesses one set of procedures, applied throughout, is probably the best approach (as illustrated in Figure 8.3, in which procedures, already existing in written form, are labeled as SA2). However, when the procedures are actually drafted it may be necessary to include a separate schedule or subsection for each type of equipment in use. A sample policy statement could be as follows:

> **4.11 Inspection, Measuring, and Test Equipment**
> It shall be the policy of the Company that a register shall be kept of all such equipment, and this shall include the test status of the equipment and the method of calibration used. Where appropriate, this data shall also be shown on the equipment. Wherever possible, calibration shall be traceable to recognized national standards.
> *(Ref: SA2)*

Most manufacturing businesses will have inspection practices and similar procedures of this type in place, but some types of service businesses may not. This should be made clear in the policy statement:

> **4.11 Inspection, Measuring, and Test Equipment**
> The Company has no such equipment in use, and consequently there are no formal procedures covering this requirement of ISO 9001.

A statement such as this should only be made after careful thought at either the organization analysis or review stage. If the independent assessor finds test or measuring equipment to be in use, despite the company's assertion to the contrary, there will be a problem.

Businesses employing staff with a wide variation of skill levels, probably within a number of distinct departments, may find it more useful to have relevant training procedures (addressing *4.18 Training*) for each major grouping of employees. In the example in Figure 8.3, there is a separate set of procedures for people involved in some specific activities and another set for all other staff. In the market research company covered by the list of procedures shown in Figure 8.5, all training is grouped together in QS 6 (Administration), but as the following policy statement indicates, there are separate subsets of procedures for specific groups of staff:

> **4.18 Training**
> It shall be Company policy that all staff shall be adequately trained to carry out the tasks assigned to them and procedures in place for specific groups of staff. The procedures include a provision for

annual appraisal of training needs, plans to implement identified needs, and the keeping of adequate records.

*(Ref: QS 6.–QS 6.4)*

Three requirements of the standard can be regarded as aspects of records and information: *Product Identification and Traceability (4.8), Quality Records (4.16),* and *Statistical Techniques (4.20).* In each case a single set of procedures applied company-wide is generally appropriate. The specific methods used to meet the requirements for product identification will depend on the nature of the product, but in most cases will involve unique numbering of a product or batch, with the number recorded on the product itself and/or in quality records. The example in Figure 8.3 presents two very different approaches: one for the output of a particular process and another for the products of all other activities. In this case it is considered useful to have a set of procedures specific to the particular process (SA5). In the example in Figure 8.3, the outputs of all processes except number 1 have no existing procedure or method for identification, and new procedures will be required in these areas.

The requirements for quality records in ISO 9001 *(4.16)* address how such information is filed and stored. The need for such records is specified under other headings of the standard, e.g., procedures addressing the requirements for purchasing *(4.6)* will be drafted to cover the need for written orders and the data included, maintaining lists of suppliers, etc. A single group of procedures (meeting *4.16)* may, therefore, specify where each type of record is to be kept, in what form, and for how long. It is unlikely that a company will have such procedures in place before setting up a formal quality system (as is the case in the example in 8.3, in which the required procedures are identified as SA7). An example of a relevant policy statement in this area is as follows:

**4.16 Quality Records**

Records relating to both the Quality System and individually identified projects shall be maintained to provide evidence of the operation of the Quality System.

Procedures shall specify where, how, and for what length of time each type of record shall be kept.

*(Ref: SA7)*

The inclusion of statistical techniques in the standard (*4.20*) is somewhat arbitrary. Where a specific technique is regularly in use in order to control a specific operation, it can be described in a specific set of procedures (as in the example shown in Figure 8.3, identified as SA8). However, the appropriateness of such methods may not be so clear in some businesses. In such companies it may be sufficient to make a general statement without including any specific procedures in the quality system, for example:

**4.1 Management Responsibility**

*4.1.1 Quality Policy*

The Company has a formal documented quality policy.

*4.1.2 Organization, Responsibility, and Authority*

The Company has a formal management structure.

All staff have responsibilities concerning quality, and these are specified in relevant procedures and covered in staff training.

A member of staff shall be appointed as management representative and have specific responsibilities for the implementation and maintenance of the Quality System.

*4.1.3 Management Review*

The Company shall hold formal review meetings to consider the working of the Quality System and ensure that the Company Quality Policy is followed.

*(Ref: SA9.1)*

**4.2 The Quality System**

The Company has developed and implemented a quality system to meet the requirements of ISO 9001.

The system is documented at two levels. The first is a quality manual which sets out the Company's policy in relation to the requirements of the standard and relates this policy to specific procedure references. The second level is a procedure manual which describes how quality is to be achieved in each area of the Company's activities.

*(Ref: SA9.2)*

**4.5 Document Control**

Quality System documents are controlled in such a way that all copies are kept up to date. Procedures cover the authority to draft and amend documents and the documentation of any changes made.

*(Ref: SA9.3)*

**4.14 Corrective Action**

It shall be the Company's policy to investigate all occurrences of non-conformity to the Quality System, with a view to preventing recurrence and making necessary changes to the Quality System so as to minimize the occurrence of such problems. This will be achieved through formal procedures for Corrective Action.

*(Ref: SA9.4)*

**4.17 Internal Quality Audits**

A program of Internal Quality Audits shall be carried out covering all aspects of the Quality System. These audits shall establish whether the Quality System is being correctly implemented by the Company and its staff.

A formal procedure shall ensure that Internal Quality Audits are carried out by trained and appropriate staff and according to a planned schedule.

*(Ref: SA9.5)*

**Figure 8.7** Sample policy statements for control and management requirements of ISO 9001.

**4.20 Statistical Technique**
The Company shall use selected statistical techniques as and where appropriate in quality improvement exercises.

The final area of support activities relevant to ISO 9000 is referred to in Figure 8.6 as control and management. Whether or not a company has defined procedures applicable to various areas of activity, it will almost certainly *not* have any procedures relevant to this area, because they are only meaningful in the context of a formal and fully documented quality system. Additionally, policy and procedures in these areas are likely to be broadly similar across companies, regardless of the type of business. A procedure for corrective action, for example (meeting requirement *4.14*), can be as equally applicable to a brick manufacturer as to a law firm, although the wording of the procedure, as well as some of the finer details, may vary in order to account for the differences in the organization of the two businesses. In Figure 8.3 the procedures to cover all these requirements are referenced simply as SA9. They are applied across the entire company; it would be rare even in smaller businesses if any other approach were used.

An example of policy statements relevant to meeting the standard requirements for control and management is shown in Figure 8.7. Sample procedures are provided and will be discussed in the next chapter.

# ISO 9000 READINESS FOR A TQM-BASED ORGANIZATION: CREATING ALIGNMENT

## Making Total Quality Work: Aligning Organizational Processes, Performance Measures, and Stakeholders

The following material is an abstract of an article by Judy D. Olian and Sara L. Rynes published in *Human Resources Management.* Throughout this article, four 1991 survey sources are used: the KPMG survey of 62 companies, 2 Conference

*Source:* Judy D. Olian and Sara L. Rynes, "Making Total Quality Work: Aligning Organizational Processes, Performance Measures, and Stakeholders," *Human Resources Management,* Vol. 30, Issue 3, Fall 1991, pp. 303–333.

Board surveys of 149 firms and 158 Fortune 1000 companies, and the AQF/Ernst & Young study of 500 international organizations. The cornerstone of this 30-page article revolves around the authors' statement: "The goals of total quality can be achieved only if organizations entirely reform their cultures. Total quality (TQ) is increasingly used by companies as an organization-wide system to achieve fully satisfied customers through the delivery of the highest quality in products and services. In fact, TQ is the most important single strategic tool available to leaders to effect the transformation of their organizations. Traditional management, operations, finance and accounting systems are reviewed against changes that are needed in organizational processes, measurement systems, and the values and behaviors of key stakeholders to transform the status quo and shift to a total quality culture that permeates every facet of the organization."

Total quality must reflect a system-wide commitment to the goal of serving the strategic needs of the organization's customer base, through internal and external measurement systems, information and authority sharing, and committed leadership. In this sense, the objectives are very similar to ISO 9000 readiness for registration. Therefore, the concepts presented by the authors are also valid for those TQM-based organizations that are seeking ISO 9000 certification. The article contains the following pertinent data: (1) organizational synergies critical to achieving a pervasive culture, whether it be for TQM, ISO 9000, or other types of quality assurance; (2) the essentials of TQ; (3) organizational processes that support TQ; (4) establishing quality goals, including a look at Six Sigma and benchmarking; (5) training for TQ; (6) recognition and rewards; (7) measuring customer reactions and satisfaction; (8) developing four areas of measurement: operation, financial, breakthrough, and employee contributions; and (9) stakeholder support. Of significant added value are over 60 references on the subjects discussed, which is reason enough to obtain a copy of this extremely worthwhile article, in spite of its formidable length. This article is highly recommended reading for TQM-based organizations seeking ISO 9000 registration.

9

# DEVELOPING PROCEDURES

## INTRODUCTION

The dictionary defines *procedure* as a manner of proceeding, a way of performing or effecting something, a series of steps taken to accomplish an end, or a set of established forms or methods for conducting the affairs of a business.

A quality system runs on its procedures on a daily basis, and developing them accounts for a large part of an ISO 9000 project. However, in procedure development it is not only *possible* to spread the workload, it is *essential.* The more key employees that are involved, the fewer the implementation problems.

This chapter explains in some detail what procedures are, appropriate formats for their documentation, and how to organize effective drafting of procedures. The principles are illustrated by two major examples.

## WHAT IS A PROCEDURE?

Procedures show how an organization's quality policy will be implemented, day to day, in specific areas and activities. A procedure manual is, therefore, a practical, how-to-do-it guide for all employees. Figure 5.3 represented a quality system to meet ISO 9000 as a pyramid, and Figure 9.1 reproduces this concept.

The top of the pyramid is a formal quality policy that commits the organization to implementing an effective system. However, no staff member can actually

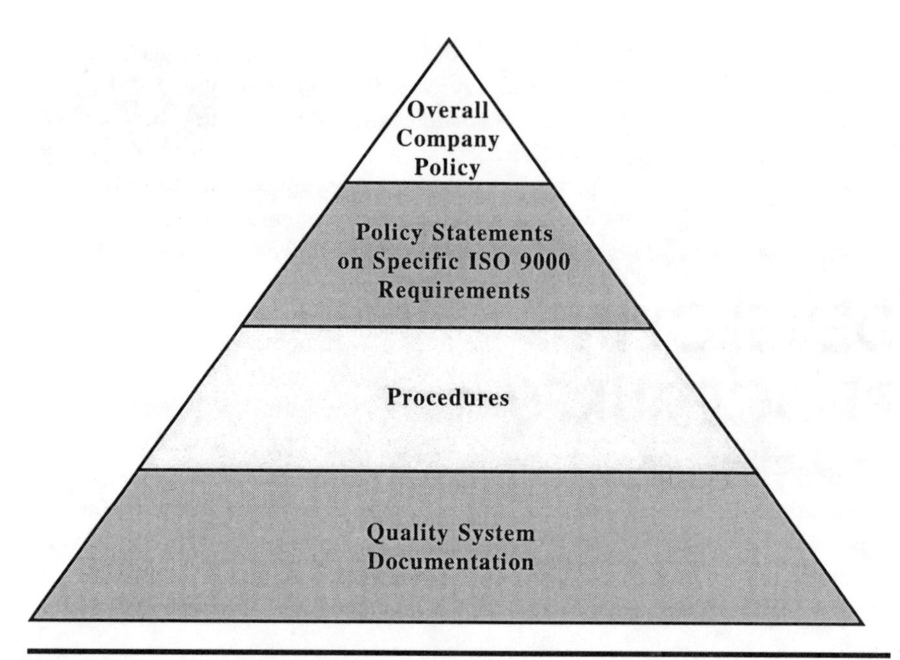


**Figure 9.1** The quality document pyramid.

*do* anything specific on the basis of the policy statement; it is not a practical guide. The next level of the documented system includes, among other things, a number of more specific policy statements describing how each requirement of the standard is going to be applied in a particular organization. In the previous chapter, preparing such statements was recommended as part of the review work, and examples were provided. In a few cases such policy statements provide adequate guidance for staff to implement the requirements of the standard, but generally this is not so. The policy statements demonstrate commitment and intention, but are short on practical guidance. Consider the following example of a statement taken from Figure 8.7:

**4.1 Management Responsibility**

*4.1.1 Quality Policy*

The Company has a formal documented quality policy.

*4.1.2 Organization, Responsibility, and Authority*

The Company has a formal management structure.

All staff have responsibilities concerning quality, and these are specified in relevant procedures and covered in staff training.

A member of staff shall be appointed as management representative and have specific responsibilities for the implementation and maintenance of the Quality System.

*4.1.3 Management Review*
The Company shall hold formal review meetings to consider the working of the Quality System and ensure that the Company Quality Policy is followed.

Some parts of this statement stand alone in that nothing further must be said in order to implement the policy. The formal documented quality policy, for example, has been written, and nothing else needs to be done to implement *Quality Policy (4.1.1)*. The same can be said for the formal management structure. For other important parts of the statement this is not the case. Consider the part of the statement concerning management review: more detail is needed to implement this. How often will such meetings be held? Who will attend them? What will be discussed? Only with such information or instructions can the policy be implemented. An appropriate procedure describes how the commitment to management reviews will be implemented. An example is provided below.

**PROCEDURE SA9.1**

**Title** Management Review

**Purpose** To define procedures to ensure that the Quality System and its working is regularly reviewed

**Scope** All parts of the Quality System

**References** Quality Manual
Procedure Manual

**Definitions** *Quality Audit:* An activity carried out by persons independent of the area under review, to establish whether the Quality System is complied with in the area.

**Documentation** Management Review Meeting Agenda (SA9.1.3/1)

**Procedures**

**SA9.1.1** *Frequency of Management Review Meetings*
Management Review Meetings will be held at least every quarter.

**SA9.1.2** *Management Review Meeting Attendees*

The Meetings shall be chaired by the Company Chairman, who may nominate another person to chair a particular meeting.

The Management Representative shall attend all meetings and act as meeting secretary.

Other persons entitled to attend the meetings shall be all Directors of the Company and any other persons invited by the Chairman to attend a particular meeting.

A quorum for a meeting shall be the Chairman (or his/her nominee), the Management Representative, and one other person entitled to attend a meeting.

**SA9.1.3** *Agenda for Management Review Meetings*

An agenda for each meeting shall be as per Form SA9.1.3/1.

The subjects to be covered in "Any Other Business" shall be determined by the Chairman (or his/her nominee) in consultation with the Management Representative before the meeting and included in the written agenda.

The written agenda, using Form SA9.1.3/1, shall be circulated by the Management Representative, one full day before the date of the meeting, to all persons entitled to attend the meeting.

**SA9.1.4** *Minutes of Management Review Meetings*

The Management Representative shall prepare minutes of each meeting within five days of the meeting and circulate these minutes to all persons entitled to attend the meeting. The minutes shall be signed by the Chairman as a true record at the next meeting held.

**SA9.1.3/1** *Management Review Meeting Agenda*

1. Date _________
   Time _________
   Place _________
2. Minutes of last meeting
3. Points arising from 2
4. Report from the Management Representative covering:

- Results of internal or external Quality Audits
- Corrective Actions
- Changes to Quality System documentation carried out since the last meeting

5. Points arising from 4
6. Report from the Chairman of customer comments and complaints received since the last meeting
7. Points arising from 6
8. Any other business
   (a) ________
   (b) ________
   (c) ________
9. Action points arising from the meeting
10. Date of next meeting

All organizations seeking ISO 9000 are required to hold management reviews, and the preceding sample procedure can be used a model. However, the specific contents can be varied considerably to meet the needs of a particular business. The procedure, for example, could be less formal. A specific layout format is used for this procedure, but again this could be quite different. Procedure formats are discussed below.

In terms of the quality system, the point of the procedures is that they enable the requirements of ISO 9000 to be implemented. Therefore, each procedure can in principle be related back to the standard. The link is through the policy statements; the management review procedure in the above sample is tied into the policy statement at the beginning of this chapter and, therefore, to *Management Review (4.1.3)* of ISO 9001. The only exception to this principle—that the purpose of a procedure can be related to one or more specific requirements of the standard—is where it has been decided to include in a quality system procedures over and above the requirements of the standard, e.g., financial activities.

Procedures within a quality system are always documented. However, they are not just verbage; they must be *effective.* To be effective, procedures must meet four tests: they should be *understandable, actionable, auditable, and mandatory.*

Employees involved in the area covered by a particular procedure should be able to do what is required, on the basis of what is stated in the procedure and on that basis alone. This requires that a procedure be clearly expressed and understandable by everyone involved in implementation. Therefore, procedures should be written in the simplest language possible, with the writer bearing in mind the comprehension abilities of the least literate member of staff involved.

It is also important that a procedure can be implemented in practice. It is unlikely that anyone preparing procedures would purposely design a procedure that cannot be followed, but it is often found in the early stages of implementation that something prescribed in the procedures is not possible. For example, a procedure requiring that a certain member of staff carry out a particular check is impractical if that person is rarely on the premises. Consultation with a wide range of personnel who will be involved will reduce the chance of preparing well-written but impractical procedures.

A procedure must also be auditable. A quality system must be more than well intentioned; it must include mechanisms to demonstrate that the system has been followed. It should be possible, therefore, to establish in retrospect whether or not each procedure has been followed, and this usually requires that some form of objective evidence be built into the procedure itself. The preceding sample procedure, for example, is auditable by consulting the minutes of the meeting.

Clearly, a procedure must be mandatory. If it is a matter of discretion whether or not employees do a particular thing, it cannot be regarded as a procedure. If a procedure is needed at all, everyone involved must be expected to follow it. Implementation is largely about ensuring that the procedures are followed, through setting in place mechanisms to monitor compliance (auditing), as well as methods to sort out problems (corrective action). In the end, a quality system requires some underlying authority structure, and an organization without one cannot have an effective quality system. However, although procedures are mandatory, they are not immutable. An important part of the system is a mechanism to change ineffective or poor procedures in a controlled way (see Chapter 10).

In addition to understanding what procedures are, it is useful to know what procedures are not. First, a procedure manual is not a handbook describing how all the activities of an organization are carried out. Some activities may be described in detail, but only as a means of stating how the quality system is to be implemented. Other activities that may be critical to the overall process may not be mentioned at all, simply because there is no specific quality-related action to undertake.

A related point is that a procedure manual is not intended to be a training manual. It is assumed that any employee engaged in the activity covered by a procedure is already adequately trained to do his or her job. (Training procedures will also be covered by the quality system.) The procedure manual is, therefore, not used to learn how to work the process, but to ensure that quality levels are maintained. A procedure for a machine, for example, may provide no details about how to start up and operate it, but will detail how critical settings are to be determined *(process control),* the testing methods to be used, and the records to be kept about the output *(inspection and testing)*. With such procedures in place, a trained machine operator will be able to ensure that the quality standards sought are attained, but an untrained person would not even be able to switch on the machine. A common problem with procedure manuals is that they are too long. Recognizing that a procedure manual is not a training guide will help to keep the procedure manual to a reasonable length.

## PROCEDURE FORMATS

The particular format that was used in the earlier sample procedure is the same format that will be used in other examples elsewhere in this book. The format includes a number of features that all documented procedures should include, and these will be discussed shortly. However, this is not to say that this format must be used; other styles can encompass the required features just as well. It is for each organization to develop its own format. The important point, though, is that whatever format is adopted should be common to *all* procedures.

Through training or in other ways, workers become familiar with the procedures that directly affect their day-to-day work. Often, however, they may be required to carry out tasks in other areas of the business and consult written procedures with which they are less familiar. Auditors, including external assessors, certainly will. Comprehension is quicker and better if the format is familiar, because the reader knows where to look to obtain specific types of information. A direct analogy is newspapers: there is perhaps nothing intrinsically better about the layout of a particular newspaper, but the reader will find it easier to check TV listings in whichever paper he or she normally reads. Moreover, with a common format it will be easier to recognize that sets of procedures are official quality system documents and that they are up-to-date. The latter point is an aspect of document control, an important topic which is discussed in Chapter 10.

In the drafting process, several authors may carry out the work. Problems will clearly occur if each uses a different format. It is best if a model is agreed upon at the start of the process. People who are perhaps not used to writing substantial documents will find the task much easier if there are examples to follow.

A standard format also makes the final documents look better. This may seem trivial, but an attractive document is more likely to be read and the procedures followed. Also, at the assessment, the first task is the desk investigation: checking that the documented system meets the requirements of the standard. The assessors will not add points for neatness, but they will feel more positive about a quality system that is professionally presented.

The sample procedures contain a number of features worth highlighting:

- **Numbering:** A numbering system allows for accurate cross-referencing and the integration of separate procedures into a complete system, i.e., the procedure manual. The system used in the sample procedures relates to the numbering first introduced in the review stage (see Figure 8.3). Many different methods of numbering are possible, and none is intrinsically superior. Numbering is mentioned again in the next chapter.
- **Title:** The need for this is self-evident.
- **Purpose:** Every procedure must have a purpose, and it is a good discipline to make this explicit. It also aids implementation; staff know why the procedure is being followed. The purpose statement should be succinct. If it seems difficult to write, there is probably something wrong with the procedure—possibly too much is being attempted to be covered in one procedure. The purpose statement is a bridge to the policy statements discussed in the previous chapter and, therefore, to the requirements of the standard.
- **Scope:** The scope of a procedure states where in the organization it is to be applied. This might be described in terms of department (e.g., sales), activity (e.g., purchasing), process (e.g., wire cutting and bending) or, in the case of system management procedures, the quality system itself (as in the earlier sample procedure). Making the scope explicit helps practical implementation; staff know where a procedure applies.
- **References:** To carry out a procedure, it may be necessary to consult other instructions or guidelines. These may be either internal or external to the quality system. Internal references are usually to other specific procedures (which can be identified by name or number), although in the sample procedure the reference is to the whole of the documented quality system. External references are to a document that was not created within the quality system itself. A good example is a machine supplier's handbook, which details how a machine is to be set.
- **Definitions:** Although all procedures should be written in clear and simple language, it is sometimes essential to use a term that might not be understood by everyone (including auditors) involved in using a procedure. Most commonly, this will be a technical term applied to some part of a process or it may be a quality system term. The solution to such a problem is to include formal definitions. However, this leads to the very practical problem of where to draw the line. Which terms should be defined? There is no simple answer to this, although a general rule is that a term need not be defined if it can be confidently expected that someone trained in the activity covered would recognize and understand the term. (For example, "questionnaire editing" may not be generally understood, but is likely to be a familiar term in a market research company.) Also, a set of procedures should need relatively few accompanying definitions; if there is a large number, the procedures should be rewritten using simpler terms. Abbrevations can also

be explained, including those that are familiar in house but are incomprehensible to outsiders such as an assessor.

- **Documentation:** As previously pointed out, a procedure must be auditable, and therefore requires objective evidence to determine that it has been followed. Generally, this requires documentation, which can be of various types (including electronic data), but in most systems means forms or ledgers. It is this aspect of a quality system that sometimes has given ISO 9000 the reputation of being nothing but a lot of useless forms. On the contrary, the quality system should only be adopted if it leads to net benefits to the organization. All procedures in a system should, of course, be necessary to the system. A procedure can only be effective if it is auditable and therefore the documentation required is beneficial. If forms do become too numerous, it may be possible to eliminate some of them.

  It should clearly identify any external documents (such as drawings, equipment operating manuals, industry standards, or detailed work instructions) that are needed in conjunction with the procedure. It should also be supported by process flow diagrams whenever possible.

  While objective evidence is required for every procedure, it does not follow that each needs its own and separate form. One form or ledger may provide the quality data for several procedures. Although a particular procedure may not call for a record to be made, other procedures to which it is linked, logically or through workflow, will most likely have a documentation requirement.

  Just as users of procedures should be able to clearly understand them, it should be made obvious what documentation is required to carry out a procedure. This is best achieved through a numbering system (in the sample procedure, the form is numbered to match the relevant part of the procedures) and by explicitly identifying the documentation adjacent to the relevant text. As in the example, the forms relating to a set of procedures can also usefully be listed at the beginning or end of the procedure.
- **Procedures:** These are best presented as short paragraphs, perhaps with numbering as in the sample procedure and with subtitles. The reader can then quickly find what is required.
- **Responsibility:** It should be clear in procedures which staff are responsible for doing particular tasks. In the sample text this responsibility is mentioned at appropriate points within the procedures themselves. Another approach is to state explicitly the responsibilities under a separate subheading.

The example discussed is just one approach to the layout and formatting of procedures. It is a workable model, but it is not necessarily the best possible. Others may be much better. What is important, though, is consistency—decide on a suitable layout and format and use it for all procedures.

## FROM THE REVIEW TO PROCEDURES

The review (see Chapter 8) will have identified a list of procedure headings (tentatively numbered SF1, SF2, etc. in Figure 8.3). This list will also show the scope of the procedures (the parts of the operation they apply to), the requirements of ISO 9000 to be met through the procedures, and whether the procedures already exist, in written or unwritten form. The procedures under each heading can now be developed, and this is demonstrated by a detailed example.

In a small organization the person responsible for the development of procedures—often the project manager—may have a good working knowledge of all the activities of the business. In these circumstances, this person may be tempted to go off into a corner and start writing procedures. This must be resisted. It is essential that the development of procedures involve as many employees as possible. Only through this type of involvement will staff feel that the procedures are their own rather than imposed from above. This is vital, because procedures must be implemented as well as written. Those that are not felt to be "owned" will not be followed. Neither is this a case of management public relations. Procedures developed without staff involvement will fail, not just because they are resented (which they will be), but because they will be flawed and impractical. However knowledgeable the writer of the procedures, he or she will not know the processes in sufficient detail to develop valid descriptions. The level of understanding required can only be gained from those involved day to day in working the process.

There are various possible ways of organizing staff involvement. At the simplest level, all staff from the relevant department or process area can meet together and, starting with a blank sheet of paper, decide what procedures are needed. In practice, however, this group must be effectively led. The person given the leadership task by the project leader will need to focus the group, i.e., enable them to understand what the goal is and provide the tools necessary to produce satisfactorily documented procedures. The leader may even start with his or her own rough set of procedures as an opener to discussion, but this has the danger that novices will just accept the suggestions without becoming really involved. Where the group involved is too large to meet comfortably together at once, or cannot all be spared at the same time from day-to-day work, a representative subgroup can be brought together or the larger group can be split into two or more parallel groups. If a subgroup is used to represent the whole, it should be reasonably representative and certainly not just the department manager and shift foreman.

The most effective tool to use with a group is the flowchart. As discussed earlier (see Chapter 7 on organization analysis), all activities of any business can be represented as a sequence of input–process–output. At the organization analysis stage, it is a good idea to chart the entire organization, but only at a fairly general level, with the specific details left unrepresented. The processes involved in cutting and bending the wire to produce a coat hanger, for example, might be left as one box representing all the processes involved. At the procedure writing stage, however, a detailed flowchart should be produced for all the activities making up the process to be covered by the procedures. In the example in Figure 8.3 of the previous chapter, the procedures numbered SF1 require a detailed flowchart to be produced for processes 1 and 2 (see Figure 8.2). However, in this case, both processes are substantially the same, and a single set of procedures would probably cover each adequately. Therefore, one flowchart can probably adequately represent both processes. (It is probably best to produce a flowchart for process 1 and then double check that it also represents process 2.)

The advantage of using a flowchart as a tool in procedure development is that any process is usually easier to understand in chart form than in word form: one can see the flow of input, process, and output. This is true even if the work is being carried out by someone accustomed to using words as a descriptive tool, but it is even more the case for a group who may rarely write anything longer than messages or read material more demanding than short articles. A graphic representation will be grasped very quickly, and members of the procedure development group will soon feel confident enough to create their own charts or amend a first draft. In practice, the group leader can either develop a first draft by questioning the group or can prepare a very rough and even deliberately vague chart and then have the group amend it once they have become familiar with the flowchart language.

Once a flowchart is prepared it will, of necessity, incorporate all existing procedures because they are part of the process being drafted. Preparing a formal written set of procedures will be a relatively easy task, because what needs to be stated is already there in graphic form (even partly in written form, as the chart will include verbal descriptions). How all this is done is illustrated below through the use of an example.

Because the chart is produced by the group involved in the process, it should represent a universally approved understanding of what actually happens in practice, rather than what someone believes should happen, i.e., actual rather than ideal procedures. The process of drawing the chart will probably uncover some inefficient methods of operation and may lead to suggestions for improvement. However, on the whole it is generally better to base initial procedures on what actually happens rather than on what should happen. It is a big enough task to train staff to follow formal documented procedures without changing the working practices at the same time. Procedures can always be changed later, once the quality system is working. In fact, the formalization of working methods represented by written procedures provides a means of identifying the need for change; a quality system is always dynamic in this sense. However, some inefficiencies will be so glaring that change will be irresistible at the time of procedure development. Also, the procedures must be adequate to meet the requirements of the standard; if the existing practices omit activities that are judged to be needed in order to meet the standard, some changes (usually additional procedures) will be essential. If, for example, the final product is never inspected, new procedures will have to be introduced to meet the ISO 9000 requirements for final inspection.

To ensure that the requirements of ISO 9000 are met through the procedures, the persons responsible for their development must know both which requirements are to be met and the contents of these requirements. The review will have identified for each set of procedures the requirements of the standard that must be covered (e.g., in Figure 8.3 procedures SF1 must meet *4.9, 4.10, 4.12,* and *4.13* of ISO 9001). Clearly, the contents of these requirements must be understood by the person responsible for developing the procedures and leading the staff group involved. However, the group itself does not need to know the requirements in any detail. The best approach may be for the leader, having read and considered the requirements, to make up a very brief summary in headline form, as shown below:

- Control what is happening (*4.9 Process Control*)
- Inspect:
  - What goes in
  - What is done
  - What comes out
- Keep records (*4.10 Inspection and Testing*)
- Determine if the product has passed inspection (*4.12 Inspection and Test Status*)
- What happens to it if it does not pass (*4.13 Control of Non-Conforming Product*)

At an appropriate time the group can then be asked to consider whether the activities represented in the flowchart adequately cover the requirements summarized in the headline list. Once the procedures are written, the author can reconsider, by referring to a copy of the full standard, whether or not the necessary requirements of the standard are being met.

The group involved in preparing the flowchart will not normally be involved in the actual writing of the finished procedures; even if the individuals are skilled wordsmiths, a committee is a poor author. Instead, the task will probably be undertaken by the group leader or a member of the group selected as likely to be a capable author. As mentioned earlier, there should by this stage be an agreed upon format and layout and possibly a sample set of procedures to use as a model. Once a first draft is prepared, the group should be reconvened, the leader should show the link between the flowchart and the procedures, and he or she present the written document. The group can then be asked to comment on both the coverage achieved by the procedures and their clarity and to decide if these written procedures will be usable by the group most involved in implementation.

## DEVELOPING PROCEDURES: A PRACTICAL EXAMPLE

The example used to show how procedures are developed is based on the wire coat hanger manufacturer introduced in earlier chapters. All the shop floor activities of the business are represented in Figure 9.2. Fundamentally, the process is split into two parts: cutting and bending the wire and final assembly. The following discusses the procedure for cutting and bending, which in the review was numbered as SF1 (covering two parallel lines). The review identified that procedures existed for this process, but in an unwritten form. The requirements of ISO 9001 to be met through procedures for *all* shop floor processes—i.e., both procedures for cutting and bending (SF1) and final assembly (SF2)—were also identified in the review (*4.9, 4.10, 4.12,* and *4.13*).

The first task in developing the procedures for cutting and bending is to prepare a flowchart. This is done with the active contribution of staff working in this production area. The procedure author leads the group and prepares a rough flowchart during the meeting (either from a completely blank sheet or from his or her initial rough draft). The flowchart emerging in the meeting will be rich in detail through the contributions of all participants, but will also be a mess—marked up with deletions, changes, and notes added as a result of the group's participation.

Following the meeting, the procedure author neatens and redraws the flowchart in legible form. Figure 9.2 shows this first neat draft. If the author has any doubts, the chart should be presented to the group for checking.

The flowchart as it stands could be the basis for one set of procedures. However, the author should consider if it might be better to cover the entire cutting and bending process in a number of separate procedures. The chart in Figure 9.2 is fairly complex, and it may be better to consider splitting it into a number of separate charts with corresponding sets of procedures developed. Possible changes of this type to consider in the example include:

- The setting of the cutting machine and the associated inspection could be dealt with separately with its own set of procedures.
- The inspection of the initial output of the bending machine could similarly be covered separately.
- There is a natural division of the process between cutting and bending, and it might be better to cover the two stages separately.

Also, the process as described in the chart assumes that something important happens beforehand. The material used to make the hangers is checked by stores.

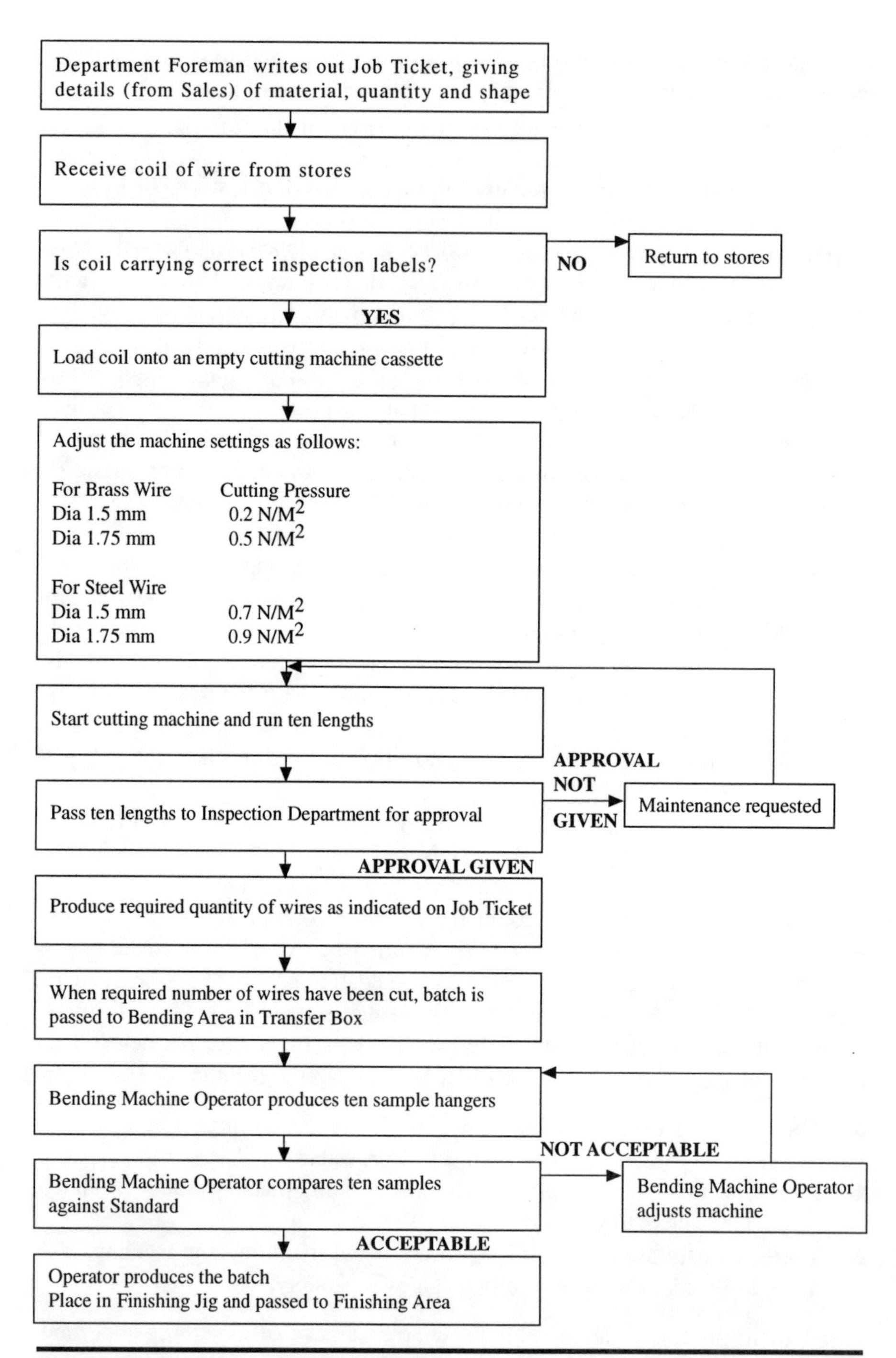


**Figure 9.2** Flowchart example: initial.

This points to the need for a separate procedure in this area (later to be numbered SF1.1).

Undoubtedly other changes to and subdivisions of the flowchart could be considered; there are no hard and fast rules. The best approach is whatever leads to the clearest and most easy to implement procedures. All that can be said is that procedures are generally easier to use if they are shorter rather than longer.

In the case of the example, it was judged appropriate to regard the setting and checking of the cutting machine as a separate activity with its own procedure (this separate procedure could be developed with the information already available). The flowchart is then modified as Figure 9.3. The chart now includes references to separate procedures for coil inspection, cutting machine setting, and the next process down the line—assembly and finishing.

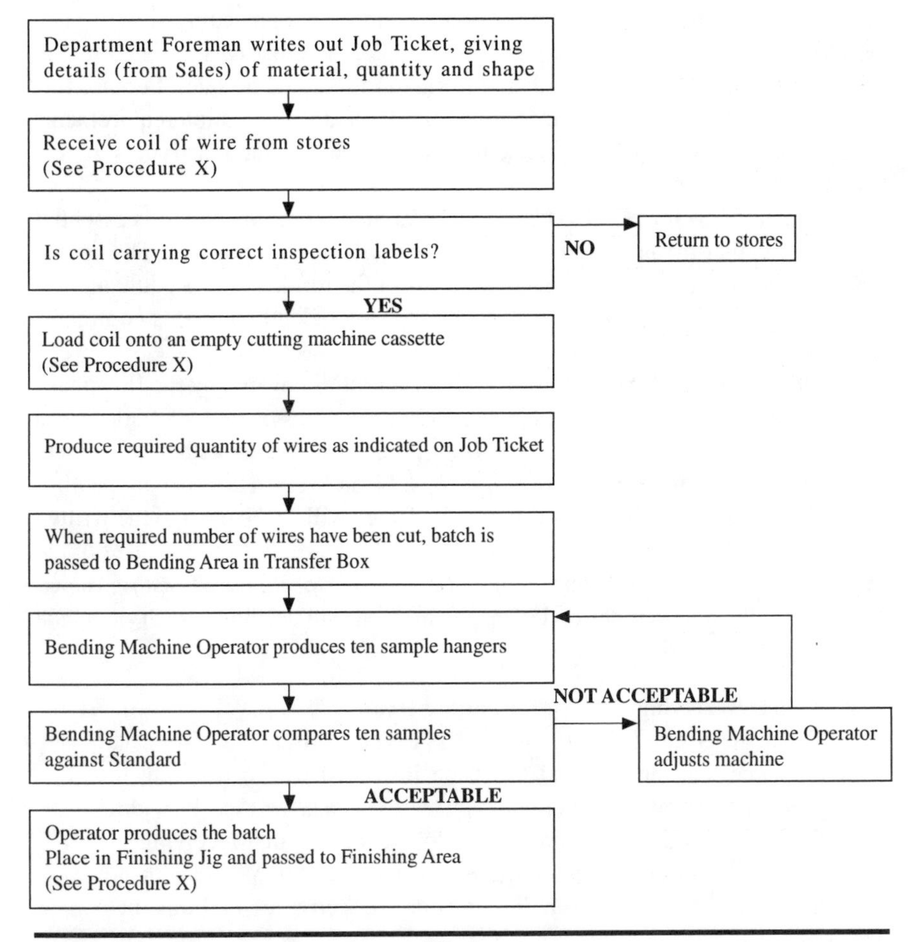


**Figure 9.3** Flowchart example: modified.

As discussed earlier in this chapter, all procedures should be auditable; after the event, it should be possible to establish that the procedures have been followed. As it stands, the process produces little in the way of documentary evidence. Any occurrence of uninspected coils will be shown on the relevant inspection label (or by its absence), but this documentation really belongs to a separate procedure. Nothing is produced to show if the correct number of lengths have been produced or if the shape test carried out in the bending area has actually been completed. The most obvious remedy is to design separate forms to provide these records. However, across the whole company, this will lead to the kind of proliferation of paperwork that can give ISO 9000 a bad name. Although documentary evidence is a necessity, the number of forms in use should be kept to a bare minimum.

A good practice when developing procedures is to consider if any existing documentation (including documentation arising from a preceding activity) can be adapted to provide the record. In the example, the process is initiated by the foreman writing out a job ticket from information supplied by sales. Perhaps this existing document could be adapted to cover all the documentation requirements of the cutting and bending procedures, and even the later activities in the finishing and assembly area.

Whether a new form has to be produced or an old one adapted, it is essential to check whether the proposed documentation will work in practice. The people best qualified to do this are the eventual users of the form. The procedure author, therefore, prepares a rough draft of the revised job ticket and invites comments from the cutting and bending areas.

Another important consideration is if the activities covered by the flowchart, and eventually by the procedures, meet the requirements of ISO 9000 identified in the review. In this case all the shop floor processes, taken together, must meet four requirements of the standard: *4.9, 4.10, 4.12,* and *4.13.* The procedure author now needs to compare the charted activities, which will be the basis of the written procedure, with what is actually required in the standard. For the purposes of the example, the focus below is on whether or not *4.10 Inspection and Testing* is met. This particular requirement of ISO 9000 has four subheadings, each of which may be relevant to the activities:

**4.10.1 Receiving, Inspection, and Testing**

The material entering into the process is wire coils, and the flowchart indicates that the material has been inspected before reaching the process and that there is documentary evidence for this. Providing that the relevant procedure is developed for the area receiving the wire coils (supplies), this requirement will be met. Whether or not this is the case, however, lies outside the activities of immediate concern.

**4.10.2 In-Process Inspection and Testing**
In-process inspection and testing is carried out during the process, e.g., the bending stage. Also, the cutting operator certifies that the pieces are of the right size (how the test is carried out is covered by a separate procedure). If the procedures, therefore, cover this type of inspection (as they will), the requirement is met.

**4.10.3 Final Inspection and Testing**
The final product is not an output of this process and, therefore, this particular requirement does not arise. It will, however, be relevant to the finishing and assembly process, which is referenced in the flowchart.

**4.10.4 Inspection and Test Records**
As discussed, thought has been given to providing documentary evidence that all the procedures have been carried out, and this includes inspection and testing activities.

In this way, the procedure author is confident that, where appropriate, requirement *4.10* of the standard has been met. Using a similar approach, conformity to the other three requirements can also be checked. If this checking process indicates that the activities do not cover the requirements of the standard (e.g., if no shape test was in use), additional activities within the process would have to be considered and incorporated into the procedures. When this situation arises, consultation with the staff involved is particularly vital. In most cases the procedure author will not be qualified to decide how the additional activities (e.g., shape testing) can be practically carried out.

With these checks completed, the procedure author can now turn the flowchart into a set of written instructions. Before doing so, however, it is very useful to add an appropriate numbering notation to the chart. This will be the numbering used in the drafted procedures. This is illustrated in Figure 9.4. Numbers are given to steps in the flowchart (e.g., SF1.2.1), and these numbers are then used in the drafted procedures. Other procedures are also given numbers (e.g., SF1.1)

The procedures produced are shown below and follow the format used earlier. A form—the job ticket—has been designed to provide auditable records that the procedure has been followed (assuming that a job ticket already existed prior to developing the procedures). References are given in the sample document to other procedures that can be assumed to be as yet unwritten, but which can be numbered. The numbering system is based on that used in the review (see Figure 8.3 in the preceding chapter). The final reference is to an "external" source: a machinery supplier's handbook.

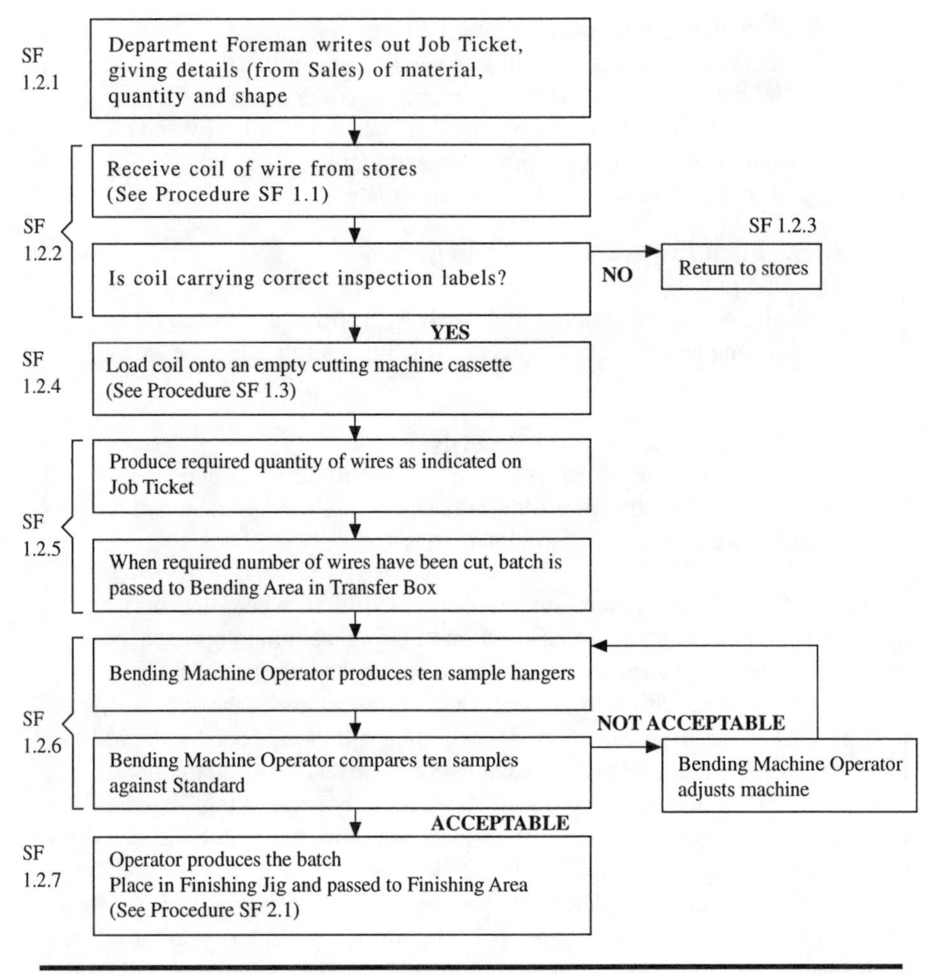


**Figure 9.4** Flowchart example: numbered.

**PROCEDURE SF1.2**

**Title** Cutting and Bending Processes

**Purpose** The procedure describes the process to be used in the cutting and bending processes of the production of wire coat hangers, from the receipt of materials to passing the cut and bent wire to the finishing and assembly process.

**Scope** The wire cutting and bending processes.

**References** Material Stores (SF1.1)
Cutting machine setup procedures (SF1.3)
Finishing and assembly procedures (SF2.1)
Bending machine supplier's handbook

**Definitions** None

**Documentation** Job Ticket (SF1.2.1/1)

**Procedures**

**SF1.2.1** *Preparing the Job Ticket*

The foreman of the cutting and bending process area shall prepare a Job Ticket (SF1.2.1/1) and record details of the material to be used, the quantity to be produced, and the shape required.

**SF1.2.2** *Receipt of Materials*

The required materials shall be obtained from Suppliers.

The cutting machine operator shall determine whether the materials supplied have the correct inspection documentation attached (see SF1.1x).

If this inspection documentation shows that the material has been appropriately inspected, the next procedure will be as per SF1.2.4.

If the inspection documentation is missing or is not signed as "passed," the next procedure will be as per SF1.2.3.

**SF1.2.3** *Uninspected Material*

Uninspected material (as per SF1.2.2) shall be returned to Suppliers with a note attached stating the reason for the return.

**SF1.2.4** *Loading and Setting of the Cutting Machine*

The cutting machine is then set and loaded with the material. See Machine Setting Procedure SF1.3 (including Cutting Machine Setting Inspection—SF1.3x).

The cutting machine operator shall complete the relevant parts of the Job Ticket (SF1.2.1/1) to record the machine loading and that the setup is correct.

**SF1.2.5** *Cutting of the Batch*

The cutting machine is then run to produce the quantities shown on the Job Ticket (SF1.2.1/1).

If, while the batch is being run, the material runs out, all procedures from SF1.2.2 will be followed.

When completed, the cut lengths making up the entire batch shall be placed in a Transfer Box.

The complete Transfer Box will then be passed to the bending machine area with the Job Ticket (SF1.2.1/1) attached and the batch quantity recorded.

**SF1.2.6** *Setting of the Bending Machine*

The bending machine operator shall set the bending machine as per the Supplier's Handbook to produce the shape specified on the Job Ticket (SF1.2.1/1) for the batch.

The bending machine operator shall then produce a sample of ten bent hangers.

The bending machine operator shall compare these samples against the Standard Shape appropriate to that specified on the Job Ticket (SF1.2.1/1).

All Standard Shapes shall be available at all times in the vicinity of the bending machine.

If the sample shapes match the appropriate Standard Shapes, the operator shall make entries on the Job Ticket (SF1.2.1/1) to show that the machine has been set and the setting tested and shall then proceed as per SF1.2.7.

If the sample shapes do not match the appropriate Standard Shape, the operator will repeat procedure SF1.2.6 until a match is obtained.

**SF1.2.7** *Bending of the Batch*

The full batch shall be run through the bending machine and the Job Ticket (SF1.2.1/1) completed.

The bent pieces shall be placed on a Finishing Jig with the Job Ticket (SF1.2.1/1) attached and then passed to the finishing and assembly area (see SF2.1).

**SF1.2.1/1** *Job Ticket*

**SF1.2.1**

Batch No. ______ Number Required _______

Material Finish: Brass ( ) Steel ( )

Diameter ______ mm

Shape_____________________

Signed ____________________ Date _______

| | | |
|---|---|---|
| **SF1.2.4** | Machine Loading ____________ | |
| | Signed ____________________ | Date ________ |
| **SF1.2.5** | Number of Cut Pieces________ | |
| | Signed ____________________ | Date ________ |
| **SF1.2.6** | Bending Shape Check________ | |
| | Signed ____________________ | Date ________ |
| **SF1.2.7** | Number of Bent Pieces _______ | |
| | Signed ____________________ | Date ________ |

## DEVELOPING PROCEDURES FOR THE ENTIRE BUSINESS

The practical example concerned procedures for a shop floor process within a manufacturing company. A service company could just as well have been used in the example; the basic approach would be no different. The method suggested can also be used throughout a business to produce almost all the procedure requirements identified in the review. The approach of using groups of staff closely involved in the area to be covered by the procedure is just as practical in other parts of the operating process as on the shop floor. Sales and marketing, design, distribution, and after-sales service all involve groups of people who have the essential knowledge required to produce workable procedures and whose positive participation will be crucial to successful implementation. In all these areas of the operating process, flowcharting is both practical and strongly recommended. The only situation in which it may prove difficult to produce a working chart is when the process being studied appears too complex to be illustrated on one sheet. When this problem arises, the entire process should be broken down into a number of smaller, linked processes, even if the divisions are artificial (e.g., one production line can be split into subprocesses, even though they all happen together). In this way, a full picture of the whole is constructed from the smaller parts, each of which can also be the basis of discrete procedures. To repeat a point made earlier: shorter procedures are generally more effective at both the drafting and implementation stages.

The same principles of procedure development can also be used for some of the support activities of a business. Purchasing, for example, will involve existing personnel with established if unwritten procedures, and this activity can be very well described through a flowchart. However, when developing procedures for some areas of the support activities, the approach may not be relevant. This is particularly the case for the procedures described in the review as control and management. The procedures required here arise mainly because a quality system is being developed. Therefore, there are no existing procedures of any sort, no existing process to chart, and no staff involved in the activity (because it has not been carried out). The flowchart approach either does not work at all or provides insufficient detail for procedure drafting. Rather than using flowcharts, it is usually more appropriate in these areas to base the procedures directly on the policy statement generated in the review. Procedure writing in this case then becomes a matter of fleshing out the policy in such a way that staff can practically implement it and provide evidence that the procedure has been followed. Sample procedure SA9.1 showed how this might be done to meet the requirement for management review, for example In various parts of this book, sample procedures are provided to cover all the requirements for control and management. (In addition to procedure SA9.1, which provides an example of management review procedures, see also Chapter 10 for document control procedures and Chapter 11 for internal quality audit and corrective action procedures.) These examples provide a basis for drafting procedures to meet the needs of most small to midsize companies.

## THE GERMAN DELEGATION: A LOOK AT DEVELOPING ENVIRONMENTAL MANAGEMENT PROCEDURES AND PRACTICES

Germany has taken a leadership position in the integration of environmental management practices into ISO 9000. This profile is based upon material presented at the October 1993 ISO 9000 Forum meeting in Washington, D.C. by Klaus Patrick, managing director of DQS (the German association for quality system certification), and a follow-up discussion with Frank Voehl.

*Source:* ISO 9000 Symposium Proceedings ENVIROMEN/8.93.

## Overview

In the last three years there have been several initiatives from a variety of sources on environmental management. These initiatives were partly related to the environmental summit in Rio de Janeiro in 1992, as well as to various EEC activities, Dutch and Japanese charters, Canadian management programs, and the German compendium of environmental protection laws.

In April of 1991, the International Chamber of Commerce published the *Business Charter for Sustainable Development.* The proposals and requirements referred to environmental policy, comprehensive management, improvement processes, training of personnel, research, transfer of technologies, environmental assessments, responsible care, resources and processes, subsuppliers, emergency control, and dialogue of the interested parties.

All of these sources agree that environmental management of companies should be handled systematically and should be supported by international standardization. This quality system should combine all the different rules and environmental practices that may be prescribed either by governments or by other interested parties. Such standardization can be used as a guideline for environmental activities within a company.

An international group of leading personalities from industry and trade (the Business Council for Sustainable Development, BCSD) established a Strategic Advisory Group on Environment (SAGE) that identified the following themes: environmental performance, environmental product labeling, life cycle analysis, environmental systems, and environmental audits. The SAGE group recommended that an international standardization be initiated for all these subjects. Late in 1992 it was decided by the member bodies of ISO to establish a new technical committee, the ISO/TC 207, for environmental management.

ISO/TC 176 adopted the following three new work items:

- Application and expansion of ISO 9004 for environmental management
- Application of ISO 9001/9002/9003 for environmental management
- Application of ISO 10011 Part 1, Part 2, and Part 3 for the audit of environmental management systems

## TC 176 Discussions

The quality management system of an organization ensures that the requirements for quality (which includes environmental requirements) of the products offered to the market are fulfilled. The environmental management system of a company ensures that the environmental requirements for the intended and unintended products are fulfilled. Unintended products are emissions, waste, consumption of energy, consumption of land, by-products, and other effects of a company. The environmental management system may be integrated within the quality management system or may be established parallel to it. Accordingly, the quality management system covers some of the main parts of the environmental management system and vice versa. Standards for environmental management systems, therefore, need to be fully compatible, element by element, with the standards for quality management systems. In the same way, the content of audits of quality management systems overlap with the content of audits for the environmental management systems.

The development and success of the ISO 9000 series should be used as a model. It should also be noted that there are already results of standardization on national levels. There is a British standard (BS 7750, "Specification for Environmental Management Systems") which in some respects relates to the ISO 9000 series and provides comparison charts with the requirements of ISO 9001 and the proposed regulations. There is a strong demand, especially from the side of quality management standardization, for an international environmental management system standard that presents the environmental management system elements in a form compatible with the ISO 9001 quality management system elements, as does the British standard, and includes more reference to design control and the understanding that processes and all their results should be designed with a systematic approach to environmental aspects in mind.

The new South African Standard SABS 0251:1993, "Environmental Management Systems," is a good example of how to structure such a standard. Another example is the French Standard X30-200 (April 1993), "Environmental Management System."

The following list of examples shows how, according to Dr. Patrick, environmental protection management aspects can be attached to the quality management system elements and how ISO 9001 requirements can be interpreted and complemented for environmental purposes:

- **Quality Policy:** Environmental policy (in conjunction with the quality policy) of the company concerning intended and unintended products and concrete environmental objectives, e.g., reduction of the use of resources in production, supply of environmentally acceptable material, and reduction of emissions).
- **Organization:** Responsibilities of all members of the organization in all environmentally relevant fields. Nomination of a management representative concerning environmental issues.
- **Management Review:** Management review of the environmental management system.
- **Quality System:** Environmental management system (in conjunction with the quality management system) fulfillment of the governmental and internal environmental policy for the intended and unintended products.

- **Contract Review:** Relevant contract partners: purchaser, authorities, societal groups. Contracts: laws, regulations, supplier–purchaser contracts, internal requirements.
- **Design Control:** Design control concerning environmentally relevant aspects of material, semi-products, final products to be offered, processes, packaging, waste, design of measurement, acceptance and test methods.
- **Document Control:** Environmentally relevant documents, environmental management plans, environmental management handbook.
- **Purchasing:** Environmentally relevant criteria for supplies.
- **Purchaser-Supplied Products:** Environmentally relevant governmental and company-specific requirements for the purchaser-supplied products.
- **Product Identification and Traceability:** Traceability of pollutants.
- **Process Control:** Production processes that pollute the environment tangibly or intangibly: waste, wastewater, emissions, by-products, consumption of energy, risks.
- **Inspection and Testing:** Inspections concerning environmentally relevant requirements and danger potentials.
- **Inspection, Measuring, and Test Equipment:** Equipment for environmentally relevant inspections, environmental monitoring.
- **Inspection and Test Status:** Laboratory test result documents for toxic waste.
- **Control of Non-Conforming Product:** Non-conformities as non-fulfillments of environmentally relevant requirements, alternatives for disposal, emergency plans.
- **Corrective Action:** Measures to avoid and reduce the recurrence of environmental problems.
- **Handling, Storage, Packaging, and Delivery:** Handling of waste and toxic materials, preventive actions (operational procedures, training, protection equipment).
- **Quality Records:** Records concerning the fulfillment of governmental or internal company environmental requirements, environmental records for concentrations of toxic material, waste, audit records.
- **Internal Audits:** Internal audits of the company-specific environmental management system.
- **Training:** Definition of environmentally relevant need for training, procedures for training to cover the need.
- **Servicing:** Servicing concerning environmentally relevant aspects of products, cooperation with authorities, environmental information for the public.
- **Statistical Methods:** Statistical methods for the analysis of environmental data and for the determination of the trends and correlations concerning environmental effects and risks.

10

# BUILDING/INTEGRATING THE SYSTEM

## INTRODUCTION

Work carried out as part of the review (Chapter 8) and procedure development (Chapter 9) will produce most of the substantive material required for a quality system to meet ISO 9000. This chapter shows how to draw the material together and integrate it into a coherent whole.

The topics covered include a description of and practical recommendations for each part of the complete system. Also discussed is document control and its practical implications.

## THE PARTS OF THE SYSTEM

The formal documented system can be regarded as consisting of three distinct parts: the quality manual, the procedure manual, and documentation.

- **Quality manual:** The quality manual is a statement of policy. It includes the overall company quality policy (see Chapter 5), together with statements on how the requirements of ISO 9000 will be implemented in the particular circumstances of the company. The quality manual has a number of roles, including providing important signposting to the outside assessors, whose first task in an assessment is to establish whether or not the documented system covers the requirements of ISO 9000. A well-formatted quality manual provides an effective bridge between the standard and the actual activities (as per the procedures) of a company. A quality manual can also be a useful marketing tool; copies can be made available to customers seeking confirmation of the supplier's quality assurance.

If the recommended approach to the review is followed as outlined in Chapter 8, the substance of a quality manual will already be available, i.e., the statements of policy relevant to each requirement of ISO 9000. All that is additionally required is to draw this together and add a suitable introduction and similar formal material.

- **Procedure manual:** Obviously, the procedure manual brings together all the procedures that have been developed to meet the requirements identified at the review stage. The procedure manual requires nothing more than a coherent numbering system (which may also have been determined at the review stage), a short introduction, and a listing of the procedures contained in the manual.

  The ISO 9000 standard refers to documents termed *Work Instructions* and *Quality Plans.* Neither is relevant to all organizations seeking ISO 9000. For convenience, these will be considered specialized types of procedures and will be discussed later, when more details on building the procedure manual are provided.
- **Documentation:** Documentation includes the blank forms required by the procedures, as well as the completed forms and other records kept to provide evidence that the quality system has been followed. The master copies of the blank forms are part of the procedures to which they relate and are therefore within the procedure manual. Clearly, however, these forms are not available for use, and the system requires that copies be made available wherever they are needed. A system is also required for the safe-keeping of completed records. Where they are to be kept, how long they are to be kept, and who is responsible for them are all relevant issues which need to be covered in an appropriate procedure.

Later in this chapter more detail is given on each of the above elements of the complete system. Underlying each part of the system, however, is the concept and the important practical implications of document control.

## DOCUMENT CONTROL

Most companies seeking ISO 9000 succeed at their first assessment. Of those who do not pass at the first attempt, the most common cause of failure is inadequate document control. However, with reasonable planning, document control should not be a problem.

There are a number of facets to document control, and each will be covered in turn. The core of the concept is that a quality system consists of the various documents previously outlined, and at any one time all personnel in the organization should be working from one and the same set of documents. This is particularly vital in the case of the procedure manual. As already stated, procedures must be mandatory and uniform, and they clearly cannot be so if different parts of the organization are using different versions of particular procedures. Without adequate controls to ensure uniformity, divergence is almost inevitable, particularly once a quality system starts to change. Document control also implies authority: the documents making up the system are authorized by responsible staff following an agreed procedure. Document control is achieved by following a number of principles and developing a procedure based on these principles:

- **Finite and definite number of copies:** Within a quality system there should be a stated number of controlled copies of both the quality manual and the procedure manual, and the whereabouts of each copy should be known (e.g., copy number 4 is kept in the sales office). There should be a person responsible for the safe-keeping of each copy. This person is the copy owner, often the manager of the department where the copy is kept. To ensure that the number, location, and ownership of each copy is controlled, a circulation list is kept, and this forms part of the document control procedure. Only the copies identified on this list should be regarded as controlled copies. A specimen circulation list is provided in Figure 10.1.
- **Only controlled copies in use:** Within the organization only controlled copies of the quality and procedure manuals (which are finite in number) should be used to implement the quality system. No other uncontrolled copies should be in use within the company, although uncontrolled copies of the quality manual (not the procedure manual) may be circulated *outside* the company (see below). Controlled copies of the documents should, therefore,

| Procedure Manual Copy | Keeper | Location | Remarks |
|---|---|---|---|
| 1 | Management Representative | Administration | Master Copy |
| 2 | Management Representative | Administration | Auditors' Copy |
| 3 | Factory Manager | Factory Office | |
| 4 | Sales Manager | Sales Office | |
| 5 | Buyer | Purchasing Office | |
| 6 | Distribution Manager | Warehouse | |

**Figure 10.1** Sample circulation list.

be distinctive and not easily copied by unauthorized staff. There are various ways of achieving this, including printing the copies on special paper and having the person in charge of issuing the copies sign each page. (Bear in mind that signing will also be required as parts of the documents are revised, which can become extremely tiresome if the system includes more than a very few copies.)

- **Accessible controlled copies:** The corollary of the principle that only controlled copies of the documents should be in use is that they must be accessible to the workers required to use them; an employee can hardly be taken to task for not following a procedure if the written version is not available to him or her. Although it is possible to make controlled copies available to every member of the organization, this is not recommended. The more numerous the copies, the greater the problems in controlling them and, when the time comes, revising them.
- **An appropriate number of copies:** A decision has to be made on how many copies of the controlled documents should be printed (and listed on the circulation list). In practice, a reasonable balance should be struck between having enough to be accessible, but not so many that control breaks down. No general guidance can be given because organizations vary so much in structure, size, and physical layout—all factors that influence the decision. By way of illustration, in one organization there are seven controlled copies of both the quality and the procedure manuals; in practice, this has been found adequate for around 75 employees spread over five distinct departments. There is a copy available in each department, one used by the auditors, and the master copy kept by the person acting as management representative.

  As a general rule, it may be better to start with as few copies as possible and increase the number only when it is clear that the restricted number limits practical accessibility. It is not necessary that each manager above a certain level have a personal copy. A few departmental managers may be designated as manual owners, but even they should keep the documents where they are accessible to all their staff, not locked up in an office.
- **All copies in use are up to date:** As discussed below, it is essential that a facility for *controlled* change of the system be built in. However, once the system starts to change, mechanisms must be in place to ensure that each controlled manual is up to date and complete. This requirement is the main reason that uncontrolled copies cannot be allowed. Because they are not controlled, they are not changed at the appropriate time and become out of date. The mechanisms for ensuring that copies are up to date include (1) having master copies of the documents in the direct charge of the management representative, to provide a yardstick against which any other controlled copy can be judged; (2) a system of periodic inspection of all copies to check they are up to date; and (3) page "plating." Plating of each page of

**SF2.1 Page 1/5**
**Reason for Issue: Revision**
**Revision: 2**
**Date: January 1, 1994**
**Authority: John Evans**

**Commentary**

| | |
|---|---|
| *SF2.1* | The procedure number |
| *Page 1/5* | The procedure consists of five pages, of which this page is the first. |
| *Reason for Issue: Revision* | This version has been issued because of a change in procedures. |
| *Revision: 2* | This is the second revision (the first and original issue might be numbered 1 or left unnumbered). |
| *Date: January 1, 1994* | This is the date the version was issued. There needs to be a consistent policy on whether this is also the date the revised procedure was implemented. If this is not the case, there should be a method of determining the implementation date. |
| *Authority: John Evans* | The change has been made on the authority of John Evans. From other sources it should be possible to establish that Mr. Evans is indeed authorized to make the change, e.g., he is the management representative. |

**Figure 10.2** Example of page plating.

the manual provides an easy means of checking if all pages making up the procedure or section of the manual are present and identifying the version (and, therefore, whether or not it is the latest version) and who has authorized the document. An example of such a plate is provided in Figure 10.2. For various reasons, plates have not been used in the sample procedures included in this book.

- **Controlled change:** It is essential that a quality system be adaptable. The first attempt to build a system will inevitably have problems that will need to be addressed soon after implementation if the system is to work. Moreover, even an initially "perfect" system will have to be revised to meet changes within the organization and the environment in which it operates. Change to the documented system is, therefore, inevitable and desirable, but it must be carried out in a controlled way to ensure that the changes have been thought through adequately and that they are implemented uniformly across the company.
- **The origin of change:** If change is to be controlled, it should originate and be agreed upon in a formal way. In practice, this is best achieved by allowing

change only through a corrective action procedure. The next chapter discusses this type of procedure in detail and provides an example. For the purpose of this section, it is enough to know that the procedure provides a mechanism for both investigating problems and opportunities for improvement in a quality system and, where appropriate, for agreeing upon and authorizing necessary changes to solve the problems found. Figure 10.3 illustrates the mechanisms by which change to a quality system is made through corrective actions. The top layer of the chart represents how the problems or opportunities arise (including via good ideas). The Corrective Actions box indicates the stage at which the problem is investigated and a recommendation made for change, if appropriate. Management review provides a means of deciding whether or not a recommendation for change should be implemented; when this is approved, the change mechanism ensures that all relevant copies of the documented system are updated appropriately.

- **Responsibility for making changes:** Once changes are approved and authorized through the corrective action procedure, someone should be assigned responsibility for implementing the changes. This is usually the management representative (see the next chapter for a discussion of this role). He or she is likely, at least in smaller companies, to actually perform all the functions associated with document changes.
- **Preparing the revised documents:** The first task is to retype the section of the document being changed. The minimum document level at which revisions are made should be determined. This can be down to the individual page, but it is more common, in the case of the procedure manual, to change an entire procedure whenever a change to any part of the procedure is required. If, for example, a change is to be made regarding who shall prepare the Job Ticket in SF1.2.1 of the sample procedure provided in Chapter 9, then all of SF1.2 (which is only three or four pages) will be reprinted and replaced in all controlled copies of the procedure manual. The quality manual can also be divided according to levels of change. However, since this document is fairly short and changes are generally much less frequent than in the procedure manual, it may be better to change the entire document if any part of it is changed. After being retyped, the revised pages required to change each controlled copy of the document are printed, including an additional copy (see later).
- **Highlighting changes:** In retyping the part of the document to be changed, it is good practice to indicate in some way the part that has been revised. This can be done by underlining the text (provided that underlining is not used for other purposes), drawing a vertical line beside the text, or, as in the sample procedure that follows, highlighting the text as shown. In this way, the changes are immediately apparent to the users of the document. In the future,

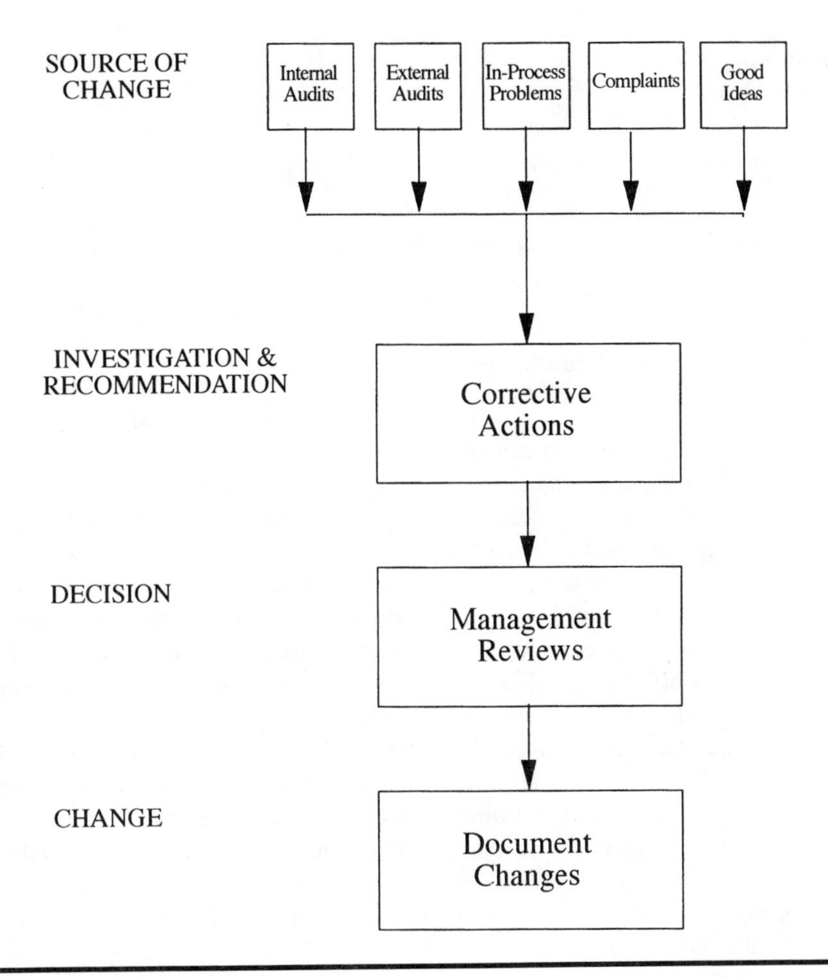


**Figure 10.3** The change process.

if the document is revised a subsequent time, the latest change is highlighted and the highlighting of the previous change is removed. The page plate (discussed earlier) can be used to show when the change was made.

- **Document list:** The procedure manual should include a list of all documents making up the complete manual *down to the level at which changes are made.* The list would, therefore, show procedure SF2.1 and its title as one entry (followed by SF2.2, etc.). Next to the entry for each document listed, the latest revision number is shown, together with the date of the latest change. An example of such a list is provided in Figure 10.4 (no number in the revision column indicates that the document is the original issue). Such a document list serves a number of purposes: it is in effect the table of

| Procedure Manual<br>Procedure No. | Title | Revision | Date of Revision |
|---|---|---|---|
| I1.1 | Introduction | 1 | March 1, 1993 |
| SF1.1 | Material Store | | January 1, 1994 |
| SF1.2 | Cutting and Bending | | January 1, 1994 |
| SF1.3 | Cutting Machine Setup | | January 1, 1994 |
| SF2.1 | Finishing and Assembly | | January 1, 1994 |

**Figure 10.4** Sample document list.

contents of the procedure manual, it enables a check to be made that the manual is complete, and it summarizes all changes made to the system. A document list is also needed for the quality manual, unless it is decided to completely change it whenever any change is needed.

- **Records of the changes:** Records should be kept of all changes. This can be conveniently organized by filing the copies of the former pages superseded by the change (which can be those replaced in the master copy of the document) in a suitable place, together with a copy of the new revised pages. It is a good idea to annotate the superseded document with the corrective action number (see Chapter 11) that led to the change and through which it was authorized. It may also be useful to keep a log of all changes in the change file, numbered in sequential order and showing for each change the document reference (e.g., the procedure number and the corresponding corrective action number). Keeping records in this way is normally the responsibility of the management representative or staff working under his/her direct control.
- **Making the changes:** A mechanism is required to ensure that *all* controlled copies are changed within a short time. In a small company the work may be done by the management representative or by a member of staff reporting directly to that individual. However, once the number of controlled copies exceeds ten, for example, or the copies are widely distributed, such personal control becomes impractical and time consuming. An alternative is to circulate the new pages to the keepers of the manuals, with instructions to insert the new pages in order, when practical to do so, and to *return the replaced pages to the management representative.* The latter is important, both to provide evidence that the change has actually been carried out and to ensure that outdated documents are removed from circulation. Regardless of who makes the changes, the replaced pages should be destroyed, except for the copy required for the records previously mentioned. Whether the changes are carried out by the management representative or through circu-

lation, it is wise to have some sort of checklist on which to check off each controlled copy as it is changed; a copy of the circulation list can be adapted for this purpose. Because of the importance of ensuring that all copies of the controlled documentation are changed and kept up to date, it is recommended that some form of routine checking of all copies be built into the procedures. Alternatively, periodic checking can be carried out as part of internal auditing work (see Chapter 11).

- **Date of change:** All staff should know when a change comes into effect, and all should implement a new procedure at the same time. This is best achieved by making the date on the page plates of the procedure correspond to the implementation date. The setting of this date should allow for typing, printing, and changing each copy of the controlled documentation.

A sample procedure covering all the areas referred to in the preceding discussion of document control is provided below. Such a procedure is not only practical, but is also a formal requirement of the standard *(4.5 Document Control* in ISO 9001). However, this is only one example of an appropriate procedure (suitable for a smaller company) and may need modifying, if not significant reworking, to meet the needs of a larger organization.

**PROCEDURE SA9.2**

| | |
|---|---|
| **Title** | Document Control |
| **Purpose** | To define procedures relevant to controlling Quality System documentation and making authorized changes to this documentation. |
| **Scope** | All contents of the Quality and Procedure Manuals and any revision of these documents. |
| **References** | Quality Manual<br>Procedure Manual (I1.1 SA9.4) |
| **Definitions** | *Manual Owner:* A member of staff—defined by job title—responsible for the safe-keeping of Controlled Documents. |
| **Documentation** | None |
| **Procedures** | |
| **SA9.2.1** | *Responsibility*<br>The Management Representative is responsible for implementation of Procedures SA9.2.<br>Manual Owners are responsible for the safe-keep- |

ing of Controlled Documents in their charge. This includes ensuring that no changes are made to Controlled Documents except as per SA9.2.4.

**SA9.2.2** *Circulation and Document Lists*

A Circulation List and Document List are part of the Procedure Manual (see I1.1). A Circulation List is included in the Quality Manual.

A Circulation List identifies each copy of the Manual and shows the owner of the copy and where it is kept.

The Document List lists all Procedures making up the Procedure Manual, and for each shows the current revision number and the date that revision was made. Whenever any changes to procedures are made (as per SA9.2.5), the Document List shall be amended accordingly.

**SA9.2.3** *Controlled and Uncontrolled Copies of the Quality Manual and Procedure Manual*

Controlled copies of the manuals are printed on special paper which shall be easily identifiable.

The use of uncontrolled manuals within the Company is not permitted.

Uncontrolled copies of the Quality Manual may be circulated outside the Company. These shall be identified as uncontrolled, and the Company cannot give any undertaking that such uncontrolled copies are up to date.

No copy of the Procedure Manual, whether controlled or uncontrolled, shall be passed outside the Company.

**SA9.2.4** *Authorized Changes to Controlled Documentation*

Changes to the Quality Manual and Procedure Manual may only be made as authorized according to the Corrective Action Procedure (see SA9.4).

Any change to a Procedure shall require change of the entire Procedure (to the second level of numbering—e.g., SA9.2).

Any change to the Quality Manual shall require the change of the entire Quality Manual.

**SA9.2.5** *Document Change Procedure*

The Management Representative shall have a revised copy of the relevant document prepared to the usual format.

The specific changes in the document shall be identified by highlighting the text as shown here. The highlighting of text for any previous revisions shall be removed.

The required number of copies of the document shall be printed on the paper used for controlled documents (the required number shall be the number of copies of the document as per its Circulation List plus one).

The Management Representative or a member of staff to whom the Management Representative shall delegate the task shall insert the new version of the document in all controlled copies of the Procedure Manual (or replace the Quality Manual with the new version) and at the same time remove the documents which the new document supersedes.

One copy of the new document and one copy of the superseded document shall be filed suitably with the relevant Corrective Action reference annotated to the superseded document to show the authority for the change.

All other copies of the superseded documents shall be destroyed.

Following any changes to the Procedure Manual, the Document List (see I1.1) shall be amended appropriately and entries shall be made in Corrective Action records as required by the Corrective Action Procedure (see SA9.4).

**SA9.2.6** *Inspection of Controlled Documents*

Twice a year, the Management Representative shall inspect each controlled copy of the Quality Manual and Procedure Manual.

The inspection shall be recorded by annotating the reverse side of the front sheet of the Manual.

Any deficiency found in a Manual shall be immediately corrected and the cause of the deficiency investigated by the Corrective Action Procedure (see SA9.4).

Each element of the documented system is discussed below, and some practical suggestions are offered for building them into a system.

## THE QUALITY MANUAL

The core of the quality manual is a series of statements that describe how each requirement of the standard is to be applied in the particular company and provide cross-references to the procedure manual. Suggestions for how to draft these statements were made in Chapter 8, which also gave an example of a suitable formal statement covering *Management Responsibility* (*4.1* of ISO 9001), including a procedure reference (SA9.1). If all the required statements were prepared at the review, they can now be arranged in the number sequence of the relevant standard, whether it be ISO 9001, 9002, 9003, or 9004. Assembled in this way, the statements may comprise about ten pages. These would represent the last but largest section of the quality manual. This section would perhaps be preceded by a statement such as:

> The structure of this section follows the clause numbering of ISO 9001 (or 9002, etc.).

Apart from this section, the quality manual is essentially formulaic. In some form or another, the contents should consist of the following items:

- **Title sheet** (i.e., Quality Manual of ABC Company, Inc.): This sheet should also contain the controlled copy number (1, 2, etc.). If it is an uncontrolled copy, this should be indicated clearly, and the copy should perhaps be printed on plain rather than on the special paper reserved for controlled documents (see below for the role of uncontrolled copies).
- **Contents:** If the quality manual is to be split into a number of sections, each of which can be changed independently, the document control list can serve as the table of contents. If, on the other hand, the manual is treated as a unitary document (for change purposes), a list with page references can be provided instead.
- **Foreword:** This brief section might state that the quality manual forms part of the quality system of ABC Company and that other parts of the system include the procedure manual. The purpose of the quality manual within the quality system can then be stated:

  > This manual defines the quality policy and objectives of ABC Company and describes how the system is implemented to ensure that the highest quality of service is provided to clients. Where appropriate, relevant cross-references to the procedure manual are provided.

- **Circulation:** A circulation list should be part of the manual. This lists all controlled copies and the keepers responsible for them (see the example given previously). It should be stated how controlled copies are to be identified (e.g., printed on special paper). It should also be mentioned that uncontrolled copies of the quality manual are not to be used within the company, but that they may be made available *outside* the organization. If customers request copies of the quality manual as evidence of the supplier's quality assurance, or the company decides to use the document as a positive marketing tool and mails it to key customers, then because only uncontrolled copies of the manual go outside the company, no commitment can be made that any such copy is up to date (it clearly will not have been changed as part of the document control procedure).
- **Introduction:** This part of the manual is usually a very brief description of the company, including the nature of its business and its location. Half a page is probably sufficient to provide some background to a reader with no other knowledge of the organization. A hierarchical type diagram of the organization can also be included in this section of the manual, although a good alternative is to attach this to the policy statement once the standard's requirement for management responsibility is met.
- **Overall company quality policy:** The wording of an overall company quality policy and an example of one were given in Chapter 5. This should certainly have been drafted by the time the quality manual is put together and should be included within the document.
- **Scope of the quality system:** The quality manual should state which parts of the organization are covered by the quality system. In most smaller companies, this statement might simply be in the following form:

  > All activities in all departments and at all sites of ABC Company are covered by the Quality System.

  If it is intended to apply ISO 9000 to only a specific part of the organization, careful thought will have to be given to defining which parts are covered and which are not.

Suitably numbered, these various sections make up a quality manual. Each page in the controlled copies could include the "plating" discussed earlier and should be printed in the appropriate way. The complete document will usually be less than 20 pages and a fixed binding is quite suitable. Alternatively, the controlled copies of the manual can be inserted in a loose-leaf binder as a separate section, but together with the procedure manual. Copies sent outside in order to market the company should be presented as attractively as possible. If a significant number are involved, professional printing should be considered.

The quality manual is a vital part of the entire system and is usually the starting point for the outside assessors' investigation. However, the manual has only minimal day-to-day practical application within the organization. It should certainly be available to employees as evidence of the organization's commitments, and the management representative and the internal audit team may need to refer to the document, but it cannot be anticipated that the rest of the staff will be using the document with any frequency. Whether in daily use or not, however, every quality system must have a quality manual in some form.

One suggestion for improving the usefulness of the quality manual is to include the organization's mission, vision, guiding principles, and annual objectives. In fact, many organizations are pursuing total quality management based policy deployment. This manual can be used as a link and a bridge between ISO 9000 and total quality management.

## THE PROCEDURE MANUAL

Unlike the quality manual, the procedure manual is in daily use and provides practical guidance for the implementation of the quality system. The contents of the manual consist mainly of the procedures themselves. Once these are developed (as per the last chapter), all that is needed is to put them in sequence. If a numbering system was developed before or during the development of the procedures, then the sequence is already determined. Otherwise, a suitable numbering system needs to be adopted and the procedures referenced and arranged in logical order.

Forms are an integral part of their relevant procedures and are usually attached at the end of each separate procedure (as in the example in Chapter 9). Some additional comments on the control and circulation of forms are appropriate at this point.

Apart from the procedures and the related forms, the only other element of the procedure manual is a brief introduction. This can be limited to a statement on the purposes of the manual, a warning that only controlled copies of the procedure manual may be used within the company, and an instruction that compliance with the procedures is mandatory. The circulation and document lists for the procedure manual can follow the introduction, with the latter also acting as a table of contents. Because the introduction is technically part of a controlled document, it needs to be brought within the scope of the procedure for document control. This is best done by treating it as a procedure with its own number in the system (e.g., I1.1), although the layout will not match that of the other procedures. The circulation lists and the document lists can then be treated and numbered as forms relating to this section (e.g., I1.2.1/1 Circulation List, etc.). It should be remembered that whenever changes are made to the procedure manual, the document list must be updated.

## Format and Binding

Loose-leaf is the only practical binding for a procedure manual. Each procedure can then be replaced individually as the need arises. It may be worth investing in a form of binding not commonly used within the company (e.g., four-hole) to discourage unauthorized tampering with the manuals. It may also be worthwhile to have special binders printed for the controlled copies. For a very reasonable cost, the finished documents will look much more professional and be easily identifiable as controlled documents.

## Hierarchy of Manuals

In a smaller company the procedures are likely to be few enough that they can be bound together as one document, but in large companies the scale and diversity of the operation may mean that the procedures run to several volumes. In this situation, and even when they can fit in one binder, it may be considered appropriate to provide specific departments with only those procedures that affect their own operation. Careful thought will be needed to establish just which procedures may apply; some (e.g., document control) apply to every part of the operation. Also, this specialized distribution of the manual must be carefully specified on the circulation list.

It is particularly important that only controlled copies of the procedure manual be used within the company. This can present some problems at the training stage, which is discussed in Chapter 11. As with the quality manual, uncontrolled copies of the procedure manual can be made available outside the company, but after developing the procedures to meet the needs of the company, it would seem unwise to make copies easily available to all, including direct competitors. Generally it is better to regard the document as commercially sensitive and restrict circulation to controlled copies within the company. However, it may be necessary to deviate from this policy by making specific procedures available to outsiders on a need-to-know basis (e.g., to subcontractors). In practice it may not be worth the trouble of being overly concerned about confidentiality. Copies of at least part of the manual eventually are likely to go outside. As long as the manuals are registered as copyrighted (©), they will be sufficiently protected.

The final aspect of the procedure manual is the role of *Work Instructions* and *Quality Plans,* covered here for convenience rather than by strict logic. Both work instructions and quality plans are specifically mentioned in the standard (e.g., see *4.2 Quality System* and *4.9 Process Control* of ISO 9001). However, the reference is in a form that indicates that neither type of document is required in all situations and in all organizations. In fact, the use of both is relatively exceptional—in most small companies at least.

Work instructions are applicable in organizations making standard products where it is thought useful to supplement the procedures with a "recipe" for each individual product. Such instructions would contain specific details to make the particular model. In the case of the coat hanger factory, instructions could be developed for each model of hanger and specify the materials to be used, the cutting machine setting, the required shape, how the finished products are to be bundled and packed, and the like. With both a model reference and the instructions available, each part of the factory would know how to make the specific hanger required. In this case, instructions of this type are not essential, as the information could be provided in other ways. However, they may prove to be convenient in the longer run. If they are to be used, they should, of course, be controlled documents and formally linked to the procedure manual; they might all be grouped together to form a distinct procedure within the manual and, where appropriate, cross-referenced in other procedures (and therefore numbered in a way compatible with the overall numbering system). In general, it is not a good idea to build work instructions into the system initially, unless they are already in use in some form and are required by the assessors. Later, once the system has been successfully implemented, work instructions can be added, if it is agreed that they offer real practical benefits.

While work instructions apply to standard products, quality plans are appropriate for large, one-time projects (although they can also be used to control a new product when it is first introduced). The most typical fields of application are building, civil engineering, and large plant construction. Another feature of these plans is that their use is normally agreed upon by the supplier and customer, and they are specifically included in the contract documentation. Quality plans also generally require the active involvement of the customer at various critical stages of manufacture; for example, there may be a provision for the customer to carry out quality inspections. Where they are used, specific quality plans would form part of the documentation of the quality system rather than be within the procedure manual. However, a specific procedure (or part of a wider procedure) would control when such plans should be used, their format, and the responsibilities for implementation. Again, it is recommended that quality plans not form part of an *initial* quality system unless they are already in use within the company, in which case the need for their inclusion will be apparent. Finally, quality plans are considered so specialized as to make further discussion of them inappropriate in a general book.

## QUALITY DOCUMENTATION

Quality documentation includes both blank forms and completed ones (and other similar records). As stated previously, all blank forms should be bound in with the relevant procedures and are best numbered such that they can be linked with a specific procedure (e.g., the form numbered SF1.2.1/1 in the sample procedure represented in Chapter 9 is first referred to in procedure SF1.2.1). Like the procedures themselves, forms will be changed to meet identified problems and to adapt to changing circumstances; it should be apparent whether a particular form is the current version or an earlier (and outdated) version. This can be controlled by the type of plating discussed earlier, but often this will be impractical. One problem is that if a form needs to be of full-page size, there is no room for the plating box. An alternative is to follow the form reference number with a revision notation. Thus, the first and original version of the job ticket in the example mentioned earlier would be numbered SF1.2.1/1, the first revision would be SF1.2.1/1 R1, and so forth.

A copy of each form is bound in the appropriate place within each controlled copy of the procedure manual, printed on any special paper that is in use, and is, of course, part of the controlled documentation. Forms, however, are designed to be used. Clearly, those bound in the procedure manual cannot be used. In the case of the coat hanger factory, a job ticket form is completed for each and every batch going through the factory. The forms in use can be regarded as uncontrolled copies of the controlled documents. However, it is essential that whenever a form is changed (as per the document control procedure), the forms in use are changed to match.

In smaller companies, at least, it is probably better to integrate the replacement of old versions of a form by new ones with the procedure of document control. As part of changes to a procedure (including where the only change is to a form associated with a particular procedure), the management representative (or someone under his/her direct control) can print an appropriate number of the new version of the form, take it to the location where it is kept ready for use, and at the same time destroy all old versions. Variations on this type of approach include making the print room operator, for this purpose, an agent of the management representative. Such processes for ensuring that up-to-date versions of forms are always in use can be detailed in the relevant procedure (document control).

It is often effective to print blank forms on distinctively colored paper reserved for that use only. It is then easy to find the quality documentation among all the other papers on the premises.

The completed forms and similar records comprise *Quality Records* as per the requirements of *4.16* of ISO 9001. In the wording of the standard, specific procedures are required for:

> Identification, collection, indexing, filing, storage, maintenance and disposition of quality records.

Identification can cover both the reference of the form (e.g., SF1.2.1/1) and the product identification to which the particular copy of the form relates. Collection, indexing, filing, and storage all relate to how and where the records are to be kept together. Elsewhere, the standard mentions the need to have the records easily retrievable, as obviously there is no point to them if specific records cannot be found. Maintenance covers the need to keep the records in a usable form for a defined period. How long is acceptable will vary according to the nature of the product and the practice of the business. For purposes of quality auditing, two years will generally be a sufficient time, but if the product has a long life, other factors may dictate that records be kept for a longer period. However, for the purposes of the quality system, all that is strictly necessary is to keep the records long enough to allow internal or external auditing to be carried out, which at a minimum would take 18 months.

The ISO 9000 certification (registration) process is usually a very good time to begin a detailed forms analysis. This function can be handed over to a quality improvement team for streamlining once the certification is completed.

In general, there are two major approaches to handling the record keeping: either all the records belonging to a particular product or project can be collated and kept in a central location, or each department or process can keep the records as they arise out of their own work. The former approach may be suitable for a service activity, where records relate to discrete and sizable jobs (e.g., market research commissions), and the latter may be more suitable for standard product runs. However, the appropriate choice should be made on an individual basis.

Formal procedures are required for quality records specifying responsibility, where records are to be kept, how, for how long, etc. Such procedures can either be integrated into the procedures that generate each record or can be specialized to cover all activities (including those designated support activities, e.g., training and inspection, measuring, and testing equipment). A patchwork approach can even be used, with the procedures both integrated and drawn together as a summary procedure. Whatever approach is adopted, the variation in this area among different companies and types of activities will be very wide. For this reason it is not practical to provide useful sample procedures.

Because quality records are the principal means by which auditing, including that by outside assessors, is carried out, they are clearly a very important aspect of a successful quality system. No company can expect to achieve ISO 9000 without keeping adequate quality records.

# THE CZECH DELEGATION: FOCUS ON BUILDING A QUALITY SYSTEM FOR A MARKET ECONOMY

The following material is based upon excerpts from an article by Zdenek Rosa, who is the head of the CSNI Department of the Czech member body of ISO, COSMT (phone: 422 2 547 751 ext. 258). Because earlier attempts at establishing quality systems had failed in the state-controlled environment, the renewed effort toward ISO 9000 as a bridge to a market-based economy in a country of small businesses is a bold move forward.

## Overview

Developments in the Czech Republic related to ISO 9000 are taking place within the context of a succession of rapid political and economic changes. Czechoslovakia, with the breakup of the Eastern bloc, regained its independence. Since then, the Czech and Slovak Federal Republic has split into two independent states, the Czech Republic and Slovakia. At the economic level, the Czech Republic is undergoing the transition from a centralized, command economy to a market-oriented one. Mr. Rosa reports that more than 100 Czech businesses or organizations are currently seeking ISO 9000 registration. He also describes the intention to create an infrastructure in the country for assessment and registration activities in order to avoid a costly dependence on foreign-based organizations.

The ISO 9000 series was adopted in January 1992, by what was then Czechoslovakia, without modification as CSN ISO 9000.

The adoption of the series as a national standard was made possible after changes in the state management system and a new legal framework for standardization necessitated revising the terminology for quality so that it complies with ISO 8402, *Quality—Vocabulary*.

---

*Source: ISO 9000 News,* Vol. 2, No. 6, Nov./Dec. 1993, pp. 16–17.

The standards were published in two-column format with the corresponding Czech and English texts side by side.

There is at present a great impetus in the Czech Republic to implement quality systems based on the ISO 9000 series. This arises from the development of the market-based economic system and the growing demand by customers who, when drawing up a contract, require the supplier to have a quality system certified as conforming with the appropriate ISO 9000 standard.

Certification (registration) of quality systems has mainly been carried out up to now by foreign organizations such as RW TUV, Lloyd's Register Quality Assurance, Bureau Veritas Quality International, and Det Norske Veritas, although they have recently been joined in this activity by Czech bodies.

The first company to be assessed and registered was the machine tool plant TOS Kurim, which was issued a certificate of conformity to ISO 9003 by RW TUV in 1991. There are now approximately ten Czech organizations registered to ISO 9001 or ISO 9002.

Many other companies are currently preparing for ISO 9000 certification. They are active in the following sectors: mechanical and electrical engineering, chemistry, and construction. The registrations will principally be carried out by the foreign auditors mentioned above.

Substantial know-how is being transferred to Czech companies, particularly concerning procedures for setting up quality systems. A year of preparation for certification performed with the help of a Czech organization is less expensive than when such preparation is carried out with the assistance of a foreign body.

## Accreditation

A national accreditation system has undergone intensive development in the Czech Republic.

In all, 37 testing laboratories and 6 calibration laboratories have been accredited under the Czech accreditation scheme, and more than 100 companies or organizations are at different stages of preparation for assessment and registration to ISO 9000 by the four certification bodies listed earlier.

## Restructuring

In the Czech Republic, many of the difficulties in implementing quality systems are the result of problems encountered in the restructuring of companies and organizations in order to establish a decentralized market economy.

The Czech Republic fully participates in ISO/TC 176.

ISO 9000 has great potential for further development, and the gradual implementation of quality systems by the service industries in particular is expected to reach higher levels.

# 11

# IMPLEMENTATION: INSTALLING THE SYSTEM

## INTRODUCTION

A quality system is more than just documents. Well-planned quality and procedure manuals are vital, but a quality system also depends on the people implementing it. The employees, including those with some specialized quality management tasks, determine whether or not the system succeeds.

This chapter outlines how to successfully install the quality system. Topics covered include quality system management, auditing and auditors, staff training, startup, and what to do when the system breaks down. Sample procedures for internal quality audits and corrective action are also included. A 22-step checklist for ISO 9000 registration is provided in the profile at the end of Chapter 12.

## QUALITY SYSTEM MANAGEMENT

The ultimate responsibility for the management of the quality system lies with the senior managers of the organization (in smaller companies, the directors). However, in order for the system to work effectively, a number of tasks must be managed on a daily basis. These include:

- Responsibility for document control, including issuing of forms to be used for quality system documentation
- Leading the audit team
- Administering the corrective action procedure
- Ensuring that senior management reviews the system and approves any necessary changes, and also keeps minutes to provide records of the meetings
- Implement agreed-upon changes
- Training staff in the use of the quality system
  - Dealing with the outside assessors
  - Seeing that quality records are filed appropriately

These tasks should be the responsibility of one member of staff (who in turn may delegate activities), and in the terminology of the standard this is the *management representative.* This title is used in the sample procedures in this book, but it is acceptable to substitute another if it better fits the existing language within a company. The role of management representative often conveniently dovetails with another management job, such as company secretary, financial director, office manager, or quality assurance manager; providing it is anticipated that this will be the case for some time, the existing job title can be used instead of "management representative" in the procedure manual. However, if such is the case, it should be stated in the quality manual under the policy statement relating to *Management Responsibility—Organization (4.1.2)*:

> The Office Manager shall act as the Management Representative and be responsible for implementing and maintaining the Quality System.

Whatever the approach, it is vital that everyone within the organization know who has the role of management representative.

Because he or she has a crucial role in the successful implementation of a quality system, the choice of the management representative is very important, although in most smaller companies there will be few candidates from whom to choose. In Chapters 5 and 6, the choice of the project leader was discussed; often whoever has that role, by default, becomes the management representative. This often works out well: at least initially, the project leader is probably the best qualified for the job. However, in the longer term someone else can certainly take over the role. In other cases, the management representative reports to the Director of Quality.

The qualities required for a successful management representative are those that make any line manager successful, such as the ability to plan and to lead staff. In many ways, successful implementation of a quality system depends on getting the details right, and the management representative needs to be concerned about the operation of the system at a detailed level: that each procedure is followed, that the right forms are used for recording quality data, that records are filed in the correct place, and similar concerns. The management representative also needs enough authority to ensure that all staff fully participate in the quality system. "All staff" includes a company's senior managers, who, in their functional activities, will themselves have to follow procedures as well as exhort their staff to do so. The management representative must, therefore, have the confidence to hold his or her ground with senior managers, as well as other staff, and should be not much lower in standing than the main decision makers within a company. More and more organizations are providing specialized project management training for their management representatives, which includes a systems approach to planning, scheduling, and controlling projects.

In many smaller companies, a director will have to take on the role of management representative and juggle his or her time between this and primary line management responsibilities. Enough time must be available to carry out the role effectively, although like most successful management, delegation of tasks will be a major factor in success. As discussed earlier, for example, although one of the jobs of the management representative is the updating of the controlled documentation, this individual does not personally have to change all the pages in the procedure manuals.

According to Henry Lucas, the key to successful implementation lies in the understanding of basic implementation techniques. Specifically, the general understanding of how to implement tends to lag behind the understanding of the technology. In the case of ISO 9000, the technology is the standard and its interpretation. Thus, it is crucial that the management representative become the company expert, or "guru."*

Although important to successful implementation, the management representative cannot be the only senior member of staff involved; a quality system must not be a private domain. Other senior managers, as well as all members of the organization, have to be involved, both in their individual daily work and together, through management review meetings. In Chapter 9 a sample procedure for management review meetings was provided; this can be adapted to meet the circumstances and style of most companies. Formal meetings of this type need to be held at least several times a year (quarterly in the sample procedure), and in the early stages of implementing the quality system, the meetings should be even more frequent, probably monthly. In most smaller companies the main members of the meetings are usually the directors of the company (with one acting as chairman) and the management representative (if he or she is not also a director). If regular formal board meetings are held, it may also be convenient to hold management review meetings.

---

*H. Lucas, *Implementation: The Key to Successful Information Systems,* Columbia University Press, New York, 1981.

A formal agenda should be part of the procedure for management review meetings, and subjects for discussion will include the results of audits, corrective actions taken (including the resulting decisions, which will be discussed shortly), changes made to the system documentation, and any customer comments (or complaints) received. Most of the information provided to the meeting will come from the management representative. It may be convenient to have this material submitted in advance as a short written report, leaving plenty of time in the meeting for discussion. Minutes also form part of the formal procedure for a management review meeting, and the management representative will probably be the best person to act as meeting secretary. At the assessment, evidence will be sought that management review of the quality system is carried out, and the minutes of meetings will provide appropriate records.

## AUDITING AND AUDITORS

Even if internal auditing were not a formal requirement of ISO 9000), this very important activity would still have to be undertaken. It is not possible for a quality system to work unless its implementation is checked and monitored. Only through actively seeking out deficiencies can problems be identified and solutions found.

At the simplest level, auditing is establishing whether or not the requirements of the formal quality system are being followed *in every particular aspect.* For example, in the sample procedure for the coat hanger factory (see Chapter 9), the cutting machine operator is required to make certain records on the batch job ticket. In auditing this part of the quality system, it should be established that these records were prepared in the right form; this might be checked from a sample number of job tickets or, more rigorously, by tracing a sample batch of hangers through the production process and establishing whether or not the appropriate records have been provided.

Auditing focuses on objective evidence of compliance with the quality system. A procedure has either been followed or it has not. (If it is impossible to determine this, there is something wrong with the procedure.) No judgment is made in auditing on *why* a procedure has not been followed. Possibly the required information was not entered on the job ticket because the machine operator simply forgot or was too busy with other things. Perhaps the procedure just could not be followed, even with the best of intentions. Any of these or other reasons may explain why the procedure was not followed, but at the *auditing stage* no judgment is made about the cause of the deficiency, nor is any blame apportioned. The auditing task is, therefore, simply to identify noncompliance, not to provide solutions; these come later.

Auditing requires auditors. In a smaller company auditing is usually carried out by staff with other mainstream jobs. Once the system is established, audit work may take up about one or two days per month of each auditor's time; therefore, in this sense, it is not an overly heavy burden. It is advisable to have at least two auditors available at any one time; they may work efficiently as a pair, and auditing can still continue if one is not available. The management representative leads the audit team and in this sense is part of it, but does not have to take part in actual audits (and it is probably better if he or she does not).

The choice of part-time auditors and the use of outsiders is important. Again, in smaller companies there are often few candidates, but whoever is selected for the work will need at least three qualities (see the case study on Bailey Controls in Chapter 14 for further detail):

- **Independence:** This has two aspects. First, auditing of any area of the business must be carried out by someone who is not involved in the day-to-day activities. This is a practical matter: someone involved in an activity is more likely to focus on what *should* happen than on what *actually* happens (for much the same reason, an author does not proofread his or her own work well). Auditors, therefore, are better selected from among staff not involved in the core activities of the business and may be better drawn from the administrative (e.g., financial) staff.

  The second aspect of auditor independence concerns the ability to arrive at judgments and stick with them despite pressure from other, possibly more senior, staff. Although auditing should be factual—the procedure has or has not been followed—and nonjudgmental, a line manager may well feel threatened by any deficiencies discovered in the operation of the quality system in his or her domain, particularly if it appears that the problem is that employees are not putting enough effort into following the system. In such circumstances, a manager may seek to solve the problem through browbeating the auditor and trying to convince him or her that the procedures have been followed or at least followed as well as they can be. The auditor must resist this and, despite any hostility, report that the requirements of the system are not being followed in this instance. Such independence is a personal quality, although the auditor must also feel confident that in carrying out the job, he or she is following the policy (and has the support) of the senior managers of the company.
- **Tact:** Tact is clearly linked to the second aspect of independence. In order to minimize the possible stresses inherent in being audited, auditors must deal tactfully with the staff of a department. Auditors are not there to seek out and punish the wicked. If a deficiency is found, both auditor and auditee

should agree that this objective fact exists, e.g., some job tickets do not record the machine setting. The auditor must not imply that because of this deficiency he or she feels that the departmental workers or manager are not doing their jobs properly. In addition, the auditor has to take up time of the staff whose work is the subject of the audit. Tact will be required to persuade staff to give the necessary time to the audit (although often this is minimal, because much of the work consists of looking at records, which should be in an accessible form). Sometimes the auditor will have to deal with staff who use shortage of time as an excuse for avoiding an audit altogether. If (after training) the auditor does not have the interpersonal skills necessary to deal with this or similar situations, the individual is not suitable for the work.

- **Attention to detail:** An auditor does not need technical expertise in the area subject to audit. At least in principle, auditing in the coat hanger factory requires no knowledge of wire bending. The auditor must, however, pay attention to detail. It is not enough that the machine operator appears to write something down now and again; the records of the machine setting and other quality checks must be in the prescribed form on the right document. The auditor must be capable of identifying in detail both what is required and what has actually been done. In this case, nit-picking is very much a virtue.

Once selected, internal auditors must be trained (ISO 10000 is the standard relevant to audit work). One of the obvious benefits of using outside auditors, at least in the initial stages of ISO 9000 implementation, is the avoidance of training and payroll costs. Eventually, every organization that is ISO 9000 certified should have in-house audit capability, where feasible. Various commercial organizations run courses aimed specifically at internal auditing. These no doubt offer valuable training, but for the smaller company it is possible for training to be organized internally by the ISO 9000 project leader or, if different, the management representative. At the least, this person can act as the leader of a seminar in which both he or she and the auditors discuss their auditing responsibilities and how they will actually carry out the work in practice. The first few audits, although for real, can be regarded as part of the auditor training process.

Auditor training needs to be started well before the startup day for implementing the quality system because auditing should be started soon after the new system is put into action. Only through audit work can any judgment be made as to whether or not the system is working reasonably well.

Auditing as a process should have its own procedure—a component of the system control part of the quality system. A sample procedure for auditing is provided later in this chapter, following a discussion of some of the underlying principles.

## Audit Records

As in other parts of the quality system, it is not enough that a procedure applies. There must be some objective evidence that it has been followed as well. In the sample procedure, the records include a schedule of audits, a register, and individual reports on each audit carried out. Adequate records could be kept in other ways, although the information included should be much the same.

## Frequency of Audit

The required frequency of internal audits depends on the size and complexity of the operation. At a minimum, every part of the quality system should be audited at least once a year, and the frequency of audit should be whatever is necessary to achieve this. For the smaller company, on average, the minimum frequency is one audit in every quarter of the year. Bearing in mind that the frequency of audit actually achieved should itself be audited (because it is a formal part of the quality system) and may be checked by the outside assessors, it is advisable to set the requirement in the formal audit procedure at the minimum level ("...audits shall be carried out at least once in every quarter"). In practice, it is better to do more than the minimum, and, in some cases, monthly audits are often useful and good practice, although they may not be cost effective. Sometimes the temptation to over-control should be resisted. A monthly audit may be too much of a good thing. As already mentioned, audits should begin as soon after startup as practical. It is advisable to hold more, rather than fewer, audits in the period between startup and assessment. In this way problems can be identified and steps taken to remedy them at the earliest opportunity.

## Scope of Each Audit

Before an audit starts, its scope must be defined. An audit taking one day, for example, including writing up the records, cannot possibly cover more than a part of the quality system. Which part it is planned to cover should be decided at the outset of each audit assignment. This coverage can be broadly defined either in terms of the quality system itself, i.e., a specific number of procedures, or in organizational terms, e.g., the cutting and bending department and all quality procedures that apply there. Determining the scope of a particular audit is the responsibility of the management representative. Some form of audit register should be kept to record the scope of each audit (which can be numbered sequentially) along with other pertinent details.

## Planning a Schedule

A schedule should be prepared for each year, showing the planned audits for the year and the scope of each audit. Taken overall, the schedule will demonstrate that the whole of the quality system will be audited at least once in the year. The schedule can be in various forms, but might be as simple as a one-sheet yearly planner or Gantt chart with the dates and coverage of each audit shown appropriately. The date on the schedule might be approximate: the month rather than a specific day. The schedule is usually drawn up by the management representative and distributed so that concerned staff, including the auditors, know when audits are to be carried out in the year. Although on an ongoing basis such schedules should be prepared at the beginning of the year, it may be better to delay preparing the first schedule for a month or two after the startup date. The reason for this is that through lack of experience, the management representative may find it difficult to anticipate what can be achieved in one audit and thus how many will be necessary over the year to cover the entire system.

A final consideration about the audit schedule is that although it demonstrates that the activity is planned, it should never be inflexible. Sometimes problems arise which suggest that a particular area should be audited as a matter of urgency even though it is not due according to the schedule.

## Pre-Audit Planning

The activities of each audit should be planned beforehand. The scope of the audit should be discussed at a meeting of the management representative and auditors. Any reports of previous audits of a similar scope should be read to see what was found before; if there was a problem in a particular area, it may be appropriate to pay special attention to it and see if the problem has recurred. The pre-audit meeting is also an opportunity for the whole team (management representative as well as auditors) to review general progress in auditing and discuss any problems. The need for additional auditor training may also need to be considered. If auditing is being carried out on a monthly basis, such general matters may not be thought worth covering at every meeting—once a quarter should be enough. Such special meetings may include a training element, and at least a brief record should be prepared showing what has been covered. This can then be offered as evidence that the requirements of the standard for trained auditing staff are being checked and met.

In addition to the pre-audit meeting, other preparation includes compiling a checklist and arranging dates and times with the auditees. A checklist is purely for the benefit of the auditors and is prepared by them. It can take several forms, but a common approach is to note each specific part of the system to be covered (e.g., in the example provided in Chapter 9, a suitable notation might be SF1.2.5

Cutting) together with the records that will be examined in relation to this part of the system (e.g., the job ticket). Although an important part of the audit is to look at the evidence of objective records, it may also be considered appropriate to ask relevant staff to describe what they are supposed to do in relation to the quality system. The outside assessors may do this, so it is worth rehearsing the employees. The checklist can, therefore, include questions to be asked as part of the audit.

The final part of pre-audit planning is making arrangements with the departments concerned. This is not just a matter of courtesy; there is no point in showing up at a department to carry out an audit if all the staff have gone off on other business. The formality of such arrangements will vary depending on the size, geography, and style of the organization. In a smaller company it may be enough to make a phone call the evening before the audit, but in other cases even two weeks' notice may not be enough. No excuses about the pressure of work should be allowed to delay auditing work indefinitely. The successful implementation and eventual certification to ISO 9000 depends on auditing.

## The Audit Work

For the purposes of this book, it is difficult to be more specific about what actually happens in an audit. The crux of the matter is that the auditor establishes what should happen according to the quality system (in most cases, what is prescribed in the procedure manual) and then seeks to find what happens in practice. The latter may involve observation (e.g., watching the cutting machine operator to see if the procedures are followed), asking questions (e.g., asking the operator what he or she does), and, most important of all, looking for documentary evidence that the system is being followed (e.g., examining job tickets). In the case of documentary evidence, it is clearly impractical to look at all records relevant to the procedure (e.g., every job ticket); a sample should be drawn. There are various practical ways of doing this, and in most cases a suitable approach should be apparent. However, the aim should be an approximation to a *random* sample, i.e., a sample in which each item has an equal chance of selection. What must be avoided is a biased sample, e.g., one that excludes all those jobs that went wrong, or for that matter one that only includes bad jobs. (These situations should be analyzed and evaluated by competent employees using various types of quality tools and techniques). One type of bias is self-selection: a sample picked by the department manager in an attempt to prove that he or she is following the system to the letter, where the records that are incomplete are hidden.

Where the auditor finds evidence of a deficiency, e.g., lack of a record where one is called for, he or she should discuss the occurrence with the auditee. The point of this, however, is not to find out why the deficiency has occurred (although if a reason is suggested it can be noted) and still less to argue whether the system can or cannot be applied in the particular case. All that should be sought from the discussion is agreement that the deficiency exists for whatever reason. Because the auditor is dealing with objective evidence, it should not be difficult to reach this agreement; the job ticket either has or has not been completed. Above all, lengthy debate about the practicality of following the procedure should be avoided. An investigation of causes of deficiency is a separate process that should come after an audit.

A quality system will not be perfect at the start, and deficiencies identified through internal audits must be expected. They are not an indication that the entire system does not work; they are a means of identifying and implementing real improvements. The internal auditor's work mirrors that of the independent assessors, who *expect* to see evidence of internal audits identifying deficiencies, which are then solved through corrective actions. Too many audit records showing that no problems have been found are probably evidence that the audit work has not been done thoroughly enough.

## Audit Reports

While carrying out the work, the auditors should make notes of all their findings and, on completion, prepare a written report. This does not need to be a lengthy document. A couple of pages is usually sufficient. The information provided in the report should include:

- The date of the audit.
- Who carried it out.
- The scope of the audit (as discussed, this is decided beforehand).
- A statement of any deficiencies identified during the audit. Because, as will be discussed, any and every deficiency should lead to a corrective action, all that should be recorded on the audit report itself is a cross-reference to the relevant corrective action form (e.g., "See Corrective Action Form Number 23"). Such a statement of deficiencies can be labeled "audit results"; if no deficiencies are found in the audit, the correct entry under results would be "none."
- Any further comments or observations that may be useful in either reviewing the working of the quality system or in carrying out future audits in the same area, such as:

    Complaints that preparing the records takes far more time than anticipated.

While the records were completed, it is suspected they were filled in after the event. In the next audit, try to test if the records were made during the event.

The report should be signed by the auditor and then handed to the management representative to attend to (i.e., through corrective actions) and file in an appropriate place. Relevant entries should also be entered in the Register of Audits to show that the audit has been carried out and that a report has been prepared.

## Follow-Up Audits

The purpose of auditing is not just to identify problems but, through the corrective action procedure, to lead to eventual improvements in the quality system and its implementation. The auditor's role, as such, is not to propose solutions to problems, but the auditor does have the additional task of establishing whether or not satisfactory solutions have been found to deficiencies identified in an initial audit. This is achieved through the process of follow-up audits.

Follow-up audits are carried out if an initial audit uncovers deficiencies. These always lead into the corrective action procedure, resulting in a recommendation for some action to overcome the problem identified. These actions fall into two broad groups: a change in procedure, which is appropriate where the problem is essentially system based (e.g., data cannot be recorded on a form because there is no space allowed to enter it), or a change in how a procedure is implemented. The second may simply amount to an exhortation for staff to try harder. The purpose of the follow-up audit is to establish whether or not the deficiency identified in the original audit has been solved. The scope of a follow-up audit is, therefore, narrow; the only parts of the quality system audited are those where deficiencies were originally identified. If in an initial audit of the cutting and bending area a problem was found in the recording of batch numbers on the job ticket, the re-audit would only focus on whether or not the data were now being adequately recorded.

Follow-up audits assume that a full corrective action has been followed, with the problem investigated, a solution proposed, a decision made on whether or not to implement the solution, and, where appropriate, a controlled change made in the system. Obviously, all this will take time, and therefore the re-audit should not be carried out until a suitable time has elapsed since the original audit. How much depends on the nature of the organization and the working of its quality system. However, assuming that the solution to the deficiency is a change to the system, the time from initial to follow-up audit needs to be at least as long as it takes to effect such a change. This includes the corrective action to recommend a change, management agreement to make it, and the change procedure itself. In the sample procedure for audits provided, a period of 45 days is allowed for follow-up audits. In some organizations this period may be unrealistically short.

A report should also be prepared to show the outcome of a follow-up audit (with entries made in the register of audits to complete the records). The follow-up report can be even more succinct than that for the original audit; all that is necessary is to record whether the problem has been dealt with or still exists. This can be expressed as "complete" (problem solved) or "incomplete" (problem not solved).

When it is found on re-audit that the problem has not been solved and the deficiency still exists, two alternative approaches may be considered and built into the procedures. One is to regard the matter as at an end as far as the auditing process is concerned. However, the matter cannot be left there. Presumably the quality system is not working in this area, and some action is essential. This may be brought about through a decision taken at the next management review meeting at which all audit reports, including "incomplete" follow-up audits, are discussed. Alternatively, a corrective action can be raised as a result of the follow-up audit and a further follow-up audit conducted. This cycle can be repeated until the problem is finally solved. (Often, by this time, everyone will be so anxious to resolve the matter that a solution will certainly be found.)

The following sample procedure, with fine-tuning, can be incorporated into the quality system of most companies. It will be seen that the auditors' report is prepared after a review meeting with the management representative, during which any corrective action forms required are issued. The main purpose of this is to tie into the sample corrective action procedure provided later. Auditors, however, generally find it useful to discuss the outcome of an audit before preparing the formal report.

**PROCEDURE SA9.3**

| | |
|---|---|
| **Title** | Internal Quality Audits |
| **Purpose** | To define procedures relevant to internal auditing of the Quality System. |
| **Scope** | All of the Quality System. |
| **References** | Quality Manual<br>Procedure Manual (SA9.4) |
| **Definitions** | *Internal Quality Audit:* Establishing compliance with the Quality System through the activities of members |

of the Company's staff independent of the area under review.

**Documentation** Audit Plan (SA9.3.V1)
Register of Audits (SA9.3.3/10
Audit Report Form (SA9.3.4/1)
Follow-Up Audit Report (SA9.3.5/1)

**Procedures**

**SA9.3.1** *Internal Quality Audit Team*

The Management Representative shall appoint staff to act as Internal Quality Auditors (IQA).

The IQA shall include a minimum of two.

The Management Representative may act as an IQA.

The Management Representative shall ensure that the IQA are adequately trained and shall prepare and file records of this training.

**SA9.3.2** *Frequency and Coverage of Audits*

At least one audit shall be carried out in each quarter of the year.

Over a year, all parts of the Quality System shall be audited at least once.

In January of each year the Management Representative shall prepare an Audit Plan (SA 9.3.2/1) for the whole year.

**SA9.3.3** *IQA Meetings*

Before each audit, the Management Representative shall convene a meeting of IQA to:

- Assign audits to the audit team or individual auditors by reference to specific elements of the Quality System. The audits shall be numbered sequentially with the relevant details recorded in the Register of Audits (SA9.3.3/1).
- Review progress of audits during the current year to date.
- Assess IQA performance and review training needs.

**SA9.3.4** On receipt of an audit assignment, the IQA shall review the records of any relevant previous audits carried out within the preceding two years and consider any implications of these for the planned audit.

An appropriate audit checklist shall be prepared by the IQA in advance of the audit.

The IQA shall arrange convenient times for the audit with staff involved in the working areas to be covered in the audit.

The IQA shall then carry out the audit and discuss the results with the Management Representative and the staff covered by the audit.

Where appropriate, the Management Representative shall issue Corrective Action Forms (see SA9.4). The IQA shall then prepare a report of the audit using the form SA9.3.4/1 and give this to the Management Representative along with any appropriately completed Corrective Action Forms raised as a result of the audit.

The Management Representative shall make relevant entries in the Register of Audits (SA9.3.3/1), file the audit report, and, where appropriate, follow the Corrective Action Procedures (see SA9.4).

**SA9.3.5** *Follow-Up Audits*

If a Corrective Action is raised as a result of an audit, the Management Representative shall assign the IQA to carry out a follow-up audit within 45 days of the date of the original audit.

The purpose of such follow-up audits shall be to establish the results achieved for each Corrective Action raised by the original audit.

On completion of a follow-up audit, the IQA shall prepare a Follow-Up Audit Report (SA9.3.5/1) and pass this to the Management Representative, who shall make appropriate entries in the Register of Audits (SA9.3.3/1).

**SA 9.3.2/1** **AUDIT PLAN**

| AUDIT NO | PLANNED DATE | SCOPE |
| --- | --- | --- |
| | | |
| | | |
| | | |
| | | |
| | | |
| | | |
| | | |
| | | |
| | | |
| | | |
| | | |
| | | |
| | | |
| | | |
| | | |
| | | |
| | | |
| | | |
| | | |
| | | |
| | | |
| | | |
| | | |
| | | |
| | | |
| | | |
| | | |
| | | |

**Figure 11.1A** Sample procedure.

**SA 9.3.3/1** **REGISTER OF AUDITS**

| Audit No | Date Started | Scope of Audit | Auditor | Date Report Received | Date Follow-up Audit |
|---|---|---|---|---|---|
| | | | | | |
| | | | | | |
| | | | | | |
| | | | | | |
| | | | | | |
| | | | | | |
| | | | | | |
| | | | | | |
| | | | | | |
| | | | | | |
| | | | | | |
| | | | | | |
| | | | | | |
| | | | | | |
| | | | | | |
| | | | | | |
| | | | | | |
| | | | | | |
| | | | | | |
| | | | | | |
| | | | | | |
| | | | | | |
| | | | | | |
| | | | | | |

**Figure 11.1B** Sample procedure (continued).

**SA 9.3.4/1** **AUDIT REPORT**

Audit No.: ________ Date of Audit: ________ Date of Report: ________

**SCOPE:**

**Findings - As per Corrective Action Form Numbers:**

________________________________

**NOTES:**

Signed: ________________________________ (Auditor)

**Figure 11.1C** Sample procedure (continued).

## SA 9.3.5/1 FOLLOW-UP AUDIT REPORT

Audit No _______ Date of Follow-Up Audit _______ Date of Report _______

| Corrective Action Form No | Complete | Not Complete |
|---|---|---|
| | | |
| | | |
| | | |
| | | |
| | | |
| | | |
| | | |
| | | |
| | | |
| | | |
| | | |

**Notes:**

Signed ________________ (Auditor)

**Figure 11.1D** Sample procedure (continued).

## TRAINING

Implementing a quality system involves everyone. All key employees must be trained before the startup day. The most important training for each person involves following the procedures that affect his or her day-to-day work. As part of the procedure development process, key employees may well have already read the procedures in draft form. Therefore, training staff in their own procedures should be relatively simple. However, all staff need a fuller understanding of the quality system beyond knowing how to follow the procedures of their own jobs.

The required depth of understanding of the quality system will not be uniform throughout a company. The senior management should understand most of the system in detail (how else can they participate in management reviews?). All employees have to understand how to work the procedures that cover their specific jobs, but they also need a broader understanding of what lies behind and beyond the part of the system that affects them directly. This is partly a matter of motivation, for it is easier to follow rules when their purpose is understood than when they appear to be mere whims of management. However, many employees will become involved in procedures beyond those that cover their normal jobs. Examples include auditing ("Why are these people checking up on me?") and corrective actions ("What have I done wrong this time?"). Additionally, the staff in certain areas are affected by the procedures of processes both up and down the line.

Quality system training should at least cover the following:

- Why a formal quality system is being introduced and why ISO 9000 is thought to be worth all the effort.
- The involvement of all employees in the quality system and why participation is central to the business from now on. Excuses such as "I don't have time to follow the procedures" are unacceptable.
- The overall quality policy of the company. By this time, this should be in written form, and copies should be displayed around the company, including in the reception area for the benefit of visitors. The policy should also be explained to all employees, who should be encouraged to think about what the policy means to them in practice. Incidentally, during an assessment, individuals may well be asked to state the company quality policy. They do not have to be able to recite it word for word, but should be able to explain in their own words what it means.
- The documents making up the system, with emphasis on the procedure manual and its accessibility to workers (where the manuals are kept).
- What procedures mean in general (everyone using the same blueprint).

- The layout of the entire procedure manual: the role of each group of procedures and how they are interrelated.
- Use of forms or other records built into the quality system. The forms used by particular work groups, day by day, need to be discussed in some detail.
- The role of internal auditors.
- Corrective actions, including the accessibility of this procedure to all staff.
- What assessment for ISO 9000 will involve.

Whereas these topics should be covered in meetings with all employees, they may have to be expressed in different ways to suit individual audiences. In a very small company, general topics might be covered at one or two meetings with all employees, followed by smaller work group meetings to focus in detail on relevant procedures and quality records.

Clearly, training meetings to cover the necessary ground will need careful planning and scheduling. This includes assigning tasks to selected training leaders, who almost certainly will need some training themselves in the quality system.

As part of the training period, it is important that employees read for themselves the procedures that affect their day-to-day work. This can present practical problems because, as discussed in the previous chapter, the number of controlled copies of the procedure manual should be strictly limited. There should certainly not be one per person. Furthermore, as mentioned before, uncontrolled copies of a manual should not be in use within an organization. One solution is to spread training over one or two weeks prior to the startup day, so that there is time for each department's controlled copy of the manual to be read by all employees in turn. It can also be reasonably argued that all the documentation is still in the draft stage prior to implementation, and therefore, it is acceptable for additional copies of the manual or parts of it to be made *for training purposes only.* (Because the system has not yet been implemented, these uncontrolled copies are not technically in use.) These copies should be withdrawn, destroyed, or filed securely by the startup day.

In a smaller company, often one person is the project leader, chief author of the procedures, organizer of the training, and management representative. Even though employees should have been involved throughout, this person will come to be regarded as the ultimate authority on the quality system and its implementation. A practical consequence is that during training and afterward, this individual will be asked to explain, elaborate on, or resolve inconsistencies in the written procedures. As far as possible, employees should be told to follow the procedures as they are set down in the manuals, and no deviation should be allowed, even by the author of the documents, unless the reasons are well documented. The reason for this is that once procedures have been elaborated in this way, they exist in multiple version—the written version and the interpreted version available to the group who consulted the authority—and there is no longer a common set of procedures throughout the company, unless, of course, the interpretation becomes part of the written procedure. In reality, despite all efforts, some procedures will be ambiguous, unclear, or difficult to apply in circumstances that the authors did not foresee. One solution is to amend them through the change procedure, after the problem has been identified and investigated by a corrective action. The latter may follow from an audit or arise from the initiative of the individual who identified the problem.

## STARTUP

The only major issue to be decided about startup is whether it takes the form of a "big bang" or "roll-out." With the big bang approach, the quality system starts throughout the company at the same time, e.g., nine o'clock on Monday, September 1. Everyone in all departments is thereby expected to comply with the quality system. The advantage of this approach is that it is clear-cut; there should be no uncertainty. Furthermore, compared with roll-out, big bang usually provides a shorter route to assessment and ISO 9000, the culmination of the project. The major disadvantages of the big bang approach are the disruption and the demands on the management representative. The disruption may be such that for the first week or so, all the attention of the company may be focused on the formal side of following the new system to the neglect of day-to-day business. There is no point to gaining ISO 9000 if its implementation so distracts from revenue-earning activities that the future of the business is threatened. However, this would be an extreme situation and would probably reflect that the system had not been thought out well in the first place.

In the period after a big bang startup, the management representative will be very much involved in seeing that the system is working, and the initial demands on his or her time will be considerable. If, as is common in smaller businesses, the management representative combines this role with other critical activities, the pressure can become too much.

If the big bang approach is followed, Quality Day should be made a big event. Advance publicity as well as training should leave staff with no doubt about the date or its importance. On the day, the chief executive or chairman may make a short speech reinforcing the benefits to be obtained from the new system and the requirement for company-wide involvement. Depending on the culture of the company, badges, posters, balloons or other visual aids might all be useful to dramatize the event. The company's quality policy should by now be displayed around the premises. For many organizations following the total quality management philosophy, this may not be consistent with the quality culture (e.g., Deming recommends eliminating slogans, banners, etc.).

The roll-out approach to startup is to introduce the quality system in only one or two departments and then extend it to others until the whole company is up to speed. This approach may overcome the problems of disruption, excessive demands on the management representative, and the hype that can be experienced with the big bang. Furthermore, the quality system can be tried out in less problematic areas. This experience can be built up before the whole company is involved. The disadvantages are that the period until assessment may be lengthened, confusion may be created about the company's commitment to the quality system, and there may be problems of interface: although the quality system may initially be attempted in one department only, departments are usually so closely interlinked that following a set of procedures in one department may, for, example, require actions in up-the-line departments. In the coat hanger factory example, the finishing department cannot make entries on the job ticket if it is not available because the cutting and bending department has not yet implemented the quality system.

In some types of business a problem found on startup, regardless of whether the approach is big bang or roll out, is that jobs are in process at the time the quality system is implemented. A choice must be made between applying the new system only to jobs initiated after startup or to jobs as they enter each department. The former approach is better when the complete process cycle is reasonably short. The latter may be better when it is long; otherwise, processes well down the line may not be in a position to follow the system for quite some time, and the time to assessment can be lengthened as a consequence. Either way, the rule must be clear and known throughout the company.

Auditing should begin very soon after startup. Only through the audit process can a judgment be made about the effectiveness of the system. It is not enough that the system seems to be going well in general. Following a quality system involves attending to all the details. Evaluation of initial effectiveness requires the disciplined approach of the audit.

## WHEN THINGS GO WRONG

No quality system is perfect, especially at the beginning. It is to be expected that problems will be found in using the system immediately after implementation. Even if the system is near perfect to begin with, in the long run adaptation to a changing environment will become necessary. In a coat hanger factory, new materials may be introduced that the original process procedures simply do not cover. Furthermore, even if it could be perfect, the system has to be implemented by fallible human beings, and in practice this is usually the source of some problems. These may be particularly acute at the start when, despite training, familiarity with the system is less than complete. Even once the initial learning curve is over, problems and mistakes due to human error will always occur. The quality system must have a built-in mechanism to deal with all of these problems. This is a formal requirement of the standard (*4.14 Corrective Action* of ISO 9001). Corrective actions provide the means to solve quality system problems.

The mechanism of corrective action involves four stages:

1. Identification of the problem.
2. Investigation and recommendation of a solution.
3. Decision on whether or not to implement this recommendation.
4. As appropriate, either the system is changed or improved implementation follows.

Each stage is discussed in turn. A sample procedure for corrective action is also provided.

## Problem Identification

The sources of quality system problem identification were mentioned in Chapter 10 (see Figure 10.3). The internal audit process will inevitably identify deficiencies and problems in the operation of the quality system, and at the start most corrective actions will be initiated through the work of the internal audit team. Later, when the system is examined by independent assessors, they too will identify deficiencies (or nonconformities) and expect these to be addressed through the corrective action procedure. However, in an effective quality system, problem identification is not solely the province of the quality professionals. Anyone within a company who understands the purpose of the quality system—and this should be everyone—is in a position to identify problems in its working or identify quality problems in the processes. Because the quality system is intended to address all sources of these problems, to identify a process problem (defective coat hangers) is to identify a quality system problem. The best people to spot problems in a process are those who work with it day after day.

Another aspect of corrective action procedure is that it can offer a means of depersonalizing issues. The problem may be that Joe is not giving Fred adequate job instructions, and all too often this can become a major conflict. With a corrective action procedure in place, Fred now simply reports that the prescribed job instructions are not being passed to him, and this is then investigated as a quality system problem (rather than Joe vs. Fred). Once the quality system is in place, therefore, it is a healthy sign for a range of employees to initiate the corrective action procedure.

Another means of problem identification is customer (or possibly supplier) complaints. These might arise spontaneously or through a process of actively establishing customer satisfaction. Either way, it is important that complaints are dealt with at two levels. First, if the customer is unhappy, the specific problem must be solved, wherever possible. The customer may well insist on this. If the complaint is that the coat hangers are misshapen, the first priority is to try to satisfy the customer by replacing the defective products. However, the fact that the mistake has happened at all points to a deficiency in the quality system, and it is essential to investigate the root causes in order to prevent their recurrence. Therefore, through corrective actions, problem solving is no longer just fire-fighting. Instead, permanent solutions to quality problems are found.

Incidentally, a quality system should have a formal method (i.e., procedures) for monitoring customer satisfaction with the service provided by the company. This can take various forms, depending on the nature of the business. Some assessors also feel that there should be a customer complaint procedure, covering the logging and investigation of such complaints, with feedback to the customer stating how the problem has been dealt with.

The last source of problem identification is the "improvement idea." The system is working well enough, but someone believes that a change would bring improvement. Such suggestions are a mark of an organization committed to quality. The fact that an improvement is suggested implies that the existing quality system is in some way less than optimum. Improvement ideas are, therefore, another method of identifying deficiencies in the broadest sense of the term.

Of course, with well-motivated staff, problem identification can get a little out of hand. As part of the corrective action procedure, therefore, it is best to build in some form of test to decide whether or not there is a prima facie case worth going to the trouble of investigating. This can be achieved by requiring problems and deficiencies to be stated on a special form issued by the management representative, who effectively makes the judgment that the issue is appropriately dealt with through a corrective action.

It is important that the initiator of the corrective action (the person identifying the problem) simply state the problem *and not suggest the solution.* It may be obvious that the reason the hangers were misshapen was because of a fault with the bending machine, but the initial entry on a corrective action record should state the problem, and that alone, so that the causes can be fully investigated. Perhaps the machine caused the problem, but why were the faulty products not taken out of the line? The management representative must, therefore, ensure that the initiator confines his or her comments to a statement of the problem, instead of jumping to the solution.

## Investigation of Possible Solutions

Once the problem has been identified and recorded, the next step is to investigate the cause of the problem and recommend a solution. The management representative must therefore select someone to carry out this work. It is generally better for the corrective action initiator *not* to be the investigator of the problem. However, an exception is the corrective action that arises as an improvement idea. In this case the separation of initiation and investigation is artificial: the problem only arises because the initiator has a proposed solution. Even so, the management representative may still require an independent investigation before a management decision is made. There is certainly no need for the investigator to be independent of the area where the problem has occurred. On the contrary, often the only staff qualified to identify the causes of the problem and suggest remedies are those closely involved in the process. As will be discussed, the causes of a deficiency may well be in how a procedure is implemented, rather than a fault in the procedure itself. This situation may be obvious to the management representative at the outset, and he or she may decide that the best investigator is the person who is having difficulty following the procedure. This can be a very practical approach, but with a possible negative side effect: corrective actions are not, and must not be seen as, disciplinary actions against staff who do not comply with the system. If employees willfully choose not to follow the system, then sooner or later disciplinary measures may be needed, but they are not part of the quality system.

The investigator must recognize that deficiencies do not necessarily imply system faults. The procedure may be perfectly reasonable and workable, but because of inadequate training, or for other reasons, the staff concerned are not following the procedure. Initially, many problems of this type will be found. The first task of an investigation, therefore, is to establish whether the deficiency is system-related or people-related (occasionally, the problem may be both). When it arises from the system, the recommendation will be in terms of changing the system, whereas when people are the problem, the solution is likely to be in terms of retraining. In practice, the investigation may itself solve a people problem: Mary was not following the procedure because she did not know she had to; she now knows and from now on she will do it. In such a case, while the formality of a management decision will still be needed after the investigation (because this is a step in a formal procedure), it may amount to no more than noting that the solution to the problem is well in hand.

## Decision to Implement

Once the investigation is complete, an appropriate management decision is needed to implement a solution. Again, this may involve an amendment to the system through the change procedure (see Chapter 10) or staff training in how to implement the procedure. Either decision might be made at a full management review meeting or by someone acting for management (usually the management representative). Whether a decision is to be referred or acted on by the management representative alone might depend on how fundamental the change is and the degree of confidence in the management representative. In the upcoming sample procedure, the management representative can decide to implement the recommendation of the investigator on his or her own initiative or to refer the matter. In some organizations it may be perceived that this gives the management representative too much power. However, in most organizations it becomes impractical to defer all decisions until they have been considered at the relatively infrequent meetings, particularly when the issue is one of implementation rather than change. Whoever is authorized to make a decision does not have to be bound by the solution recommended by the investigator. Another or a better solution may suggest itself.

Whether the outcome of the corrective action is a change in procedure or in how it is implemented, the management and staff of the department concerned must be consulted. Implementation through retraining or encouragement can only be achieved within the work area concerned; if a change in a departmental procedure is planned, it would be unwise not to involve the staff. Without this involvement, there is a good chance that the procedure would still not be appropriate or not implemented because it would not felt to be owned by the workers who perform it.

## Changing the System

If the outcome of the corrective action is a decision to change the system, this must be done through the formal change procedure, with a definite schedule established, probably within the period allowed for the follow-up audit. Indeed, as discussed in the previous chapter, change procedures and corrective actions are linked together; change can only be initiated through following the corrective action procedure. The quality triad introduced in Chapter 2 is reproduced in Figure 11.2. Problems are identified and investigated through corrective action; management review decides on action and, if necessary, implements changes; and internal audits establish whether or not the problem has been solved. If a problem is still apparent, the cycle goes through corrective actions again until it is finally solved. The three elements in the triad not only ensure that the quality system is effective but, used correctly, lead to a continual process of improvement.

This chapter concludes with a sample corrective action procedure that is probably adaptable to most smaller organizations. As with all formal proce-

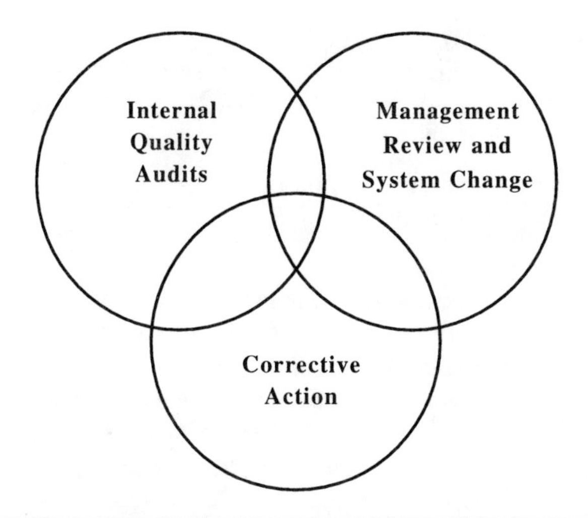


**Figure 11.2** The quality triad.

dures, a mechanism for records of compliance is built in. In the sample, this mechanism takes the form of a corrective action register and sequentially numbered corrective action forms. The latter records a statement of the deficiency, the results of the investigation and recommendations made, the management decision and, if relevant, the date changes are made to the quality system (through the change procedures). Details of the staff involved are also recorded on the form. The same information could, of course, be kept in a different format or another way.

**PROCEDURE SA9.4**

| | |
|---|---|
| **Title** | Corrective Action |
| **Purpose** | To define procedures relevant to determining the causes of any deficiencies in the Quality System and their implementation, and to consider what should be done to remedy such deficiencies. |
| **Scope** | All of the Quality System. |
| **References** | Quality Manual<br>Procedure Manual (SA9.1, SA9.2) |

**Definitions** *Customer Complaint:* Negative or unfavorable comments of a specific and substantial content on the performance of the Company's services made in any form by a customer.

**Documentation** Corrective Action Form (SA9.4.1/1)
Corrective Action Register (SA9.4.V1)

**Procedures**

**SA9.4.1** *Initiation of a Corrective Action*

Any member of staff identifying a deficiency in the Quality System or its implementation or receiving a customer complaint shall initiate a Corrective Action by requesting a Corrective Action Form (SA9.4.1/1) from the Management Representative.

**SA9.4.2** *Issue of a Corrective Action Form*

On receiving a request as above, the Management Representative, if he or she considers the action to be appropriate, shall issue to the initiator a Corrective Action Form (SA9.4.1/1), which shall have a number written on it to correspond to the next sequential form number in the Corrective Action Register (SA9.4.2/1).

The Management Representative shall on issuing a Corrective Action Form (SA9.4.1/1) make appropriate entries in the Corrective Action Register (SA9.4.V1).

**SA9.4.3** *Statement of Deficiency*

The initiator shall complete the relevant part of the Corrective Action Form (SA9.4.1/1) and state the nature of the deficiency.

The initiator shall return the Form to the Management Representative who shall make appropriate entries in the Corrective Action Register (SA9.4.2/1).

**SA9.4.4** *Investigation of the Deficiency*

The Management Representative shall appoint a member of staff he or she considers suitable to investigate the causes of the deficiency and make a recommendation on whether a change to the Quality System is required and, if so, the nature of the change. The investigator may also or may instead make a recommendation on the implementation of the Quality System including any requirement for staff training.

The Management Representative shall pass to the investigator the relevant Corrective Action Form (SA9.4.1/1) and make appropriate entries in the Corrective Action Register (SA9.4.V1).

The investigator shall record the results of the investigation on the Corrective Action Form (SA9.4.1/1) and pass the Form with the relevant parts completed to the Management Representative.

**SA9.4.5** *Referral or Action by the Management Representative*

The Management Representative, as he or she considers appropriate, shall either take action in relation to the Corrective Action or refer the matter to the next Management Review Meeting (see SA9.1).

In either case, the decision shall be recorded on the Corrective Action Form (SA9.4.1/1) and in the Corrective Action Register (SA9.4.V1).

**SA9.4.6** *Management Decision*

The Management Representative or a Management Review Meeting shall then review the Corrective Action and decide:

- To make changes to the Quality System, either as proposed by the investigator or otherwise, and set a timetable for making the change. Such a change shall be made through the Document Control procedure (SA9.2).

*Or*

- To make no change to the Quality System but, if appropriate, take action on the implementation of the Quality System with due regard for any training requirements. The Management Representative shall record this decision on the relevant Corrective Action Form (SA9.4.1/1) and in the Corrective Action Register (SA9.4.V1).

**SA 9.4.1/1** **CORRECTIVE ACTION FORM** **Form No: ____**

1. Statement of Deficiency

______________________________

______________________________

______________________________

Signed: __________ (Person Reporting Deficiency) Date: ______

2. Investigation Report

______________________________

______________________________

______________________________

Signed: __________ (Investigator) Date: _______

3. Referral/Management Representative Action

Referral [ ] MR Action [ ]

4. Procedural Change Decision

Implement Investigator's Recommendations ( ) No Change ( )

Other Changes - As Below

______________________________

______________________________

5. Date of Change Implementation (If Relevant) ____________

**Figure 11.3A** Sample procedure.

SA 9.4.2/1

## CORRECTIVE ACTION REGISTER

| FORM NO | DATE ISSUED | ISSUED TO | BRIEF DESCRIPTION OF DEFICIENCY | DATE RETURNED | INVESTIGATOR | DATE TO INVEST-IGATE | DATE RETURNED | REFERRAL/ MR ACTION | PROCEDURE CHANGE DECISION | DATE OF IMPLEMENTATION (If Relevant) |
|---|---|---|---|---|---|---|---|---|---|---|
| | | | | | | | | | | |
| | | | | | | | | | | |
| | | | | | | | | | | |
| | | | | | | | | | | |
| | | | | | | | | | | |
| | | | | | | | | | | |
| | | | | | | | | | | |
| | | | | | | | | | | |
| | | | | | | | | | | |
| | | | | | | | | | | |
| | | | | | | | | | | |
| | | | | | | | | | | |
| | | | | | | | | | | |
| | | | | | | | | | | |
| | | | | | | | | | | |
| | | | | | | | | | | |
| | | | | | | | | | | |
| | | | | | | | | | | |
| | | | | | | | | | | |

**Figure 11.3B** Sample procedure (continued).

# BUILDING THE ISO 9000 MEASUREMENT SYSTEM

*"If you can't measure it, you can't manage it."*
Peter Drucker

## Introduction

While many organizations are embarking on some form of an ISO 9000 quality system, few have implemented an accompanying measurement system which can be used to figure out how good a job is being done. Because so few have done this well enough to be considered examples for industries to follow, it is difficult to do any real benchmarking in this area.

From the studies conducted on the practices of excellent companies, however, some operating models have resulted. One of the most useful is the Corporate Measurement System (CMS), based on the work of Jack Rockart of MIT and others. This model suggests the use of a vital few critical success factors, which are linked to the business objectives and processes, around which to build the ISO 9000 corporate indicator system.

What formerly took three years or more to accomplish can now be done in three to six months using available software packages such as COMSHARE or PILOT. In addition to implementation speed and economy, the CMS approach is extremely flexible in terms of environment, future needs, and changes. Finally, it is user-friendly, with high-level macros and commands that greatly facilitate its use.

## Overview

Organizations embarking on ISO 9000 need a measurement system that is simple and flexible in design, easy to use and modify, and is integrated into key functions and processes. The information provided needs to be timely and accurate and must be perceived by employees as truly useful and not just another

---

*Source:* This material is adapted from *Building the Corporate Measurement System* by Frank Voehl (Strategy Associates, 1992, Coral Springs, Florida). Used with permission of the author.

way that management can monitor them. Instead, what is needed is a measurement system that people can use to better manage their efforts and to link all areas of the company, from the field or office, to the corporate vision.

The following are the attributes that are needed in ISO 9000 measurement:

- Simple system that is easy to understand
- Employee commitment and motivation
- Specific objectives, procedures, and guidelines for use
- Consistent, continuous monitoring
- Assignment of specific responsibility and accountability
- Top management interest and support
- Timeliness
- Good lines of communication
- Good monitoring staff who provide competent analysis
- Periodic reports
- Useful and relevant information
- Accurate, reliable information linked to the ISO 9000 strategy and business objectives

## Measurement System Principles and Objectives

There are two guiding principles to be followed when developing ISO 9000 measurement systems: (1) people on the front lines of the organization respond best to information relevant to their piece of the world and (2) when people have relevant information about things they deem important and can influence, they become very committed to using the information.

The following is a summary of ISO 9000 measurement system objectives:

- Translate the vision to measurable outcomes all employees understand.
- Focus and align the direction of employees based on measurable results.
- Track ISO 9000 breakthrough and continuous improvement results.
- Foster accountability and commitment.
- Integrate strategic plans, business plans, quality, and benchmarking.
- Provide standards for benchmarking.
- Problem-solve business operations.
- Provide a basis for ISO 9000 reward and recognition.
- Create individual and shared views of performance.

## Measurement System Overview

Two types of measures must be considered when implementing an ISO 9000 measurement system: outcome (or macro) measures and process (or micro) measures.

Outcome measures are often called macro due to their broad nature, which generally reflects an after-the-fact type of indicator. Examples are return on investment, or equity, overall customer satisfaction, etc.

Micro, or process, measures represent work-in-process types of situations and are often used for "upstream control" or prevention of problem situations. Most effective measurement systems have a combination of macro and micro indicators.

Micro measures act as tripwires to enable examining processes to determine whether speed of actions can be increased and time, cycle, and steps can be decreased. Macro measures help focus on measuring the results of leadership on the ISO 9000 outcomes and help to communicate the vision to find out whether the message is being received. Conversation among people in the field needs to be encouraged to help determine if the processes attributable to a particular corporate function enhance or inhibit the ability to create external customer satisfaction. In other words, do the functions and processes enhance or inhibit the journey along the path of ISO 9000?

## Categories of Measures

There are seven general or broad categories into which most types of ISO 9000 measures can be classified or grouped: accuracy, responsiveness, timeliness, customer satisfaction, cost, safety, and corporate responsibility.

The first three—accuracy, responsiveness, and timeliness—refer to the manner and speed with which the organization conducts its business transactions. The fourth category—customer satisfaction—can also include employee satisfaction when employees are viewed as internal customers. The fifth and sixth categories—cost and safety—can be broken down into a wide variety of subcategories. The final category—corporate responsibility—is often replaced in smaller organizations with a more relevant category that relates to the competition.

Templates, or flowcharts, are used to first link all existing measures to the corporate vision and objectives. Once existing indices are linked, gaps and missing indices are identified and added to the system where appropriate. Decisions are also made to modify or eliminate existing indices as new ones are added. Overall, there are generally between 25 to 50 detailed indicators that are distributed among the seven broad categories.

## Role of the ISO 9000 Consultant

The following services can be provided by the consultant in support of the ISO 9000 measurement system:

- Coach and guide the executive management team in the planning, development, and administration of the ISO 9000 measurement system.
- Assist corporate management in developing a linked chain of business objectives for the overall organization.
- Facilitate the development of critical success factors for key business areas, including elements of measure, related indices, and benchmarks.
- Develop a detailed master plan for implementation, including resources and infrastructure required.
- Pull together current measurement indices, help analyze their validity and usefulness for ISO 9000, and recommend areas for streamlining and improvement.
- Consolidate all measurement efforts into an ISO 9000 measurement system.
- Integrate ISO 9000 measurement into other existing corporate systems (such as strategic planning, business planning, quality, etc.) and ensure that this is done in a simplified manner.
- Work with staff and management to assign accountability and ownership for results at all levels.
- Oversee the design of support systems and controls, including screen format and system prototypes, and the selection of application software, where required.
- Validate the integrity of measures and indices and ensure that measurements are working properly and accurately.

## Summary

The pursuit of ISO 9000 without an accompanying measurement system can resemble the proverbial shot in the dark: everyone knows where they want to go, but no one is sure of the miles traveled so far or the distance yet to go. Focused measurement can act not only as the integrator but also as the monitor of progress. We would never think of driving a car for long distances without checking the gas gauge. All too often, however, ISO 9000 can run out of gas because the gauges were not put in place at the beginning to track progress along the way.

# 12

# ASSESSMENT

## ELEMENTS OF A SUCCESSFUL ASSESSMENT

The culmination of an ISO 9000 project is successful assessment. The choice of an assessor and what the assessment process involves are discussed in this chapter.

### Choice of an Assessor

To become registered to ISO 9000, a company must have its quality system successfully assessed by an independent certification body. These bodies fall into two groups: those that are accredited by the Registrar Accreditation Board (RAB) and those that are not. The number of RAB-registered bodies is growing at a tremendous rate (see the profile at the end of Chapter 13 for the list of registered bodies); because the list continues to grow, it is worth contacting the RAB for an up-to-date version). In principle, anyone can set themselves up as an assessment body and hand out ISO 9000 certificates. However, accredited assessors are rigorously checked and regularly monitored by the RAB. Furthermore, accreditation is only for specific industry sectors where experience and competence can be demonstrated (known as the scope of accreditation).

Unfortunately, it may possible that no certification bodies are accredited for a particular activity. This will be the case if a company is an ISO 9000 pioneer. If no other company in a particular business has sought ISO 9000, it is unlikely that any of the assessors will have gone through the process to be accredited. However, as the coverage of ISO 9000 extends, this situation will change; the major assessment bodies are constantly extending their accreditation scope into new areas.

RAB-registered bodies are of two broad types: those offering assessment across a wide range of business activities and the specialists. Clearly, if there is a specialist body for a particular activity, it should be considered by companies involved in that same business, but otherwise it can be ruled out. In practice, therefore, the choice of assessor is from among any of those bodies who are willing to carry out an assessment in a certain area of activity (at least three of them will cover all fields). One or more of these assessors may be accredited for the activity in question.

Regardless of their specialization, or whether or not they are accredited in the activity, all assessors work in generally the same way. The assessment itself falls into two stages: an evaluation of the documented quality system to establish whether or not it meets the requirements of the standard and an on-site assessment to establish that the system is being followed. However, that is not the end of the matter. Achieving ISO 9000 is not like passing a driving test; a company is not licensed forever without retesting. After successful assessment, a company is, of course, expected to continue to keep its quality system working effectively, and the selected assessors check that this is done by regular surveillance visits. Some go further and work in a two- to three-year cycle of assessment, surveillance, and re-assessment, whereas others continue with surveillance visits. Either way, the relationship with the assessment body is continuous and long term, and this needs to be kept in mind when making the initial selection.

The assessors will provide a service; assessment and the process of selecting them should be basically no different from choosing any other service supplier with whom a company enters into a long-term contract. It should be established that the service offered, in all aspects, will meet the particular requirements and that the costs represent value for the money. As in any purchasing situation, this does not mean that the least expensive option is the best (as will be shown later, the charges vary widely); however, if a more expensive quote is accepted, it should be considered to offer, in some way, additional value. As a first step in making a selection, a written inquiry can be sent to a number of the NACCB-registered certification bodies, perhaps to all those that appear to be at all likely to cover a particular field. The inquiry can be a letter covering:

- What a company wants to be assessed for, i.e., ISO 9001, 9002, 9003, or 9004.
- An indication of the desired schedule, e.g., "We intend to implement our quality system on January 1st and would hope to be assessed by late April or early May."
- A very brief outline of the company and its field of activity, e.g., "We are

a specialist provider of market research services and have a staff of around 50 working from one office."

- A request for information on the assessor's experience in the field and whether or not the assessing organization has accreditation for this activity.

The timing of making this initial contact may be critical. Most assessors have a booked-up schedule of assessments and may be unable to start one for a new client within three or more months. Therefore, the assessor needs to be selected well before the planned assessment date. However, gestation or a "bedding-in" period is certainly needed between the date of implementing the quality system and assessment, and in practice many companies will find that the desirable bedding-in period is longer than the time scale the assessors offer. Around the time of implementation is usually early enough to make the initial inquiries, although there is no harm in doing so earlier—even right at the start of the project.

Once the inquiries have been sent out, the initiative moves to the assessors, and the speed and efficiency with which they respond could be a factor influencing the final choice (why deal with an organization that appears inefficient or lacking in quality in this respect?). Some of those contacted may respond negatively and state that they do not wish to carry out an assessment of a company in that business, but otherwise the response is likely to include brochures on the services offered and an application questionnaire to be completed on the company (to provide the assessor with relevant information in preparing a quote). There may also be a personalized reply, perhaps addressing the inquiry about accreditation.

After receipt of a completed application questionnaire, the assessor may suggest a preliminary visit before preparing a quotation. Obviously this allows the firm concerned to obtain a clearer understanding of what the assessment work will involve, but equally it gives the company to be assessed the opportunity to find out about the assessors, including in how much detail they carry out assessment work and their experience in the particular field. However, as a matter of policy, at least some of the general scope assessors do not make such preliminary visits to smaller companies (they may claim that the resulting savings in their own marketing costs are passed on to clients in lower assessment fees). Whether or not such a trade-off of lower costs against the more limited opportunity to make a judgment on the likely service to be provided is acceptable is entirely a matter for the potential client.

The next step in the process will be receipt of formal price quotes from the potential assessors. These will set out all the details of the service (e.g., number of visits for assessment, frequency of surveillance visits, policy on reassessment), the timing, the earliest date for assessment (there is usually no problem in putting it back) and the charges and payment terms.

A typical daily rate is between $1500 and $2000 per assessor day. Thus, a project involving ten assessor days in the first year, seven in the second year, and five in the third year would result in a consulting fee of $38,500 (on the average) over three years for a single-location assessment at a small to mid-size company. One final, and very important, point to bear in mind is that a review of many case studies on ISO 9000 certification rates the selection of an assessor as the most critical success factor. See the case study in Chapter 14 for additional details.

## The Gestation Period of "Breaking-In" the System

It is unrealistic to expect the quality system to work perfectly or even satisfactorily from the first day. There will certainly be defects in the design of the system: parts that either do not work well or do not work at all. Equally important, despite all the training, workers will find initial difficulties in following the system. Some will take time to come to terms with a formal quality system, including the important principle that even a bad procedure has to be followed until it has been changed. Bearing everything in mind, very few companies are likely to feel confident enough in their system to seek an immediate assessment.

There is also another consideration. The assessment will be mainly based on objective evidence of compliance with the quality system—the quality records that, at the point of startup, are nonexistent. Only as the processes of the company are carried out and the procedures followed are the quality records built up. A period needs to elapse, therefore, before the assessors can feel confident that compliance with the quality system can be demonstrated. The length of time needed to build up adequate records will depend on the nature of the business. A repetitive manufacturing process turning out hundreds of a standard product each week is clearly, in this respect, very different from a project-based business with job time scales of two or three months.

Taking into account both the need to fine-tune the system and its implementation and the need to build up sufficient records, probably very few companies are likely to seek an assessment in less than three months from startup, and many will want a breaking-in period of six to nine months. Generally, such time scales fit in well with the availability of assessors' staff for the work. Furthermore, breaking-in periods of three months or more are thought appropriate by most assessment bodies, and some will not consider an assessment in any shorter period.

The breaking-in period is certainly not just a waiting period. It is the time during which the system is really made to work and starts to produce some internal benefits. The key tool to achieve this is the quality triad: auditing to monitor compliance, corrective action to investigate problems and recommend solutions, and management review to decide on and implement change. The start of this cycle is the internal audit process described in Chapter 11. Auditing, therefore, must be carried out throughout the breaking-in period to identify problems and find solutions. The sooner this process starts the better, and the frequency of audit at this time should be higher than planned at other times. If possible, the entire system and its implementation should have been audited at least once before assessment.

There is also another advantage to auditing during the breaking-in period. Because the assessors are in effect external auditors, internal auditing helps prepare the company and its staff. If the auditors are doing their work well, their activities will be similar to those of the external assessors, who will examine quality records, observe staff at work, and ask questions.

The main evidence sought by either internal auditors or assessors comes from quality records. Attention should, therefore, be focused during the breaking-in period (and afterwards) both on keeping correct records and on their filing and safe-keeping. As described in Chapter 10, there should be a specific procedure for controlling quality records, and internal auditing should cover this part of the system, along with all other system control procedures (including the auditing of the audit procedure itself).

In addition to auditing, the other system control procedures should be followed throughout the breaking-in period; they should not be delayed. Obviously, the audit procedure will generate corrective actions, and, apart from the matters dealt with by the management representative alone, this will lead to the need for management reviews. However, irrespective of the need to discuss corrective actions, management reviews need to be held regularly to discuss the workings of the quality system during (and after) the bedding-in period.

As part of reviews during breaking in, controlled changes will almost certainly be needed to the quality system. Faulty procedures will need to be redrafted, and new procedures may need to be added. The formal approach to system control and change was discussed in Chapter 10. An additional point, however, is that staff training must cover changes to the system; it must be ongoing. It is pointless to make a necessary change to the system if staff are not informed of it. They cannot do what they do not know. Often this may, in practice, amount to no more than telling relevant staff that a change has been made and where in the procedures to find it. It is not a good idea to verbally paraphrase the modified procedure; staff should *read* it in full in a controlled copy of the procedure manual (which, when the change has been made, will contain the new version of the procedure, preferably with the revision highlighted in some way).

Ideally, the breaking-in period should last until the company is confident that the quality system is working well and is being followed in all but the most exceptional and occasional circumstances. Then, and only then, should assessment be sought. However, in practice, because most companies will want to achieve ISO 9000 sooner rather than later, and because the assessment has to be booked well in advance, a judgment will have to be made in advance that the company will be ready for assessment by a certain date. It is much easier to determine this date after at least some of the breaking-in period has elapsed and some experience with the operation of the system has been built up.

## Using the Dry Run

Before final assessment, some companies consider it worthwhile to have a dry run pre-audit assessment carried out. Some of the assessment bodies offer this as an additional service; other consultancies are also available for the work. If a consultant was used in developing the system, some form of this work may be offered as part of the overall package. Such pre-assessment audits are, in effect, dress rehearsals for the real thing. They help to correct problems rather than allowing them to be identified as nonconformities at assessment, which could lead to an initial failure to achieve ISO 9000. Apart from possible delays in the whole process and the additional costs entailed, it is difficult to argue a case against pre-audit assessment. However, the cost of this service may be quite substantial in relation to the total cost of assessment; if the assessors themselves are carrying out the work, they are likely to charge much the same rate as for carrying out a full-fledged assessment. Additionally, most problems likely to be identified during a pre-assessment audit should be spotted as part of normal internal auditing. With these considerations, the money spent on pre-assessment auditing might be better allocated to internal auditor training, where the benefits are longer term.

However, it is more than likely that any company designing and implementing a quality system on an entirely do-it-yourself basis will feel very vulnerable going into assessment if no outsider has critically reviewed the system. Also, because consultancy can be purchased in small blocks of time, there is a strong argument for using an outside consultant to test the system and its operation prior to assessment. This might best be done in two steps: a review of the documented system upon or just before implementation, followed by the consultant carrying out an in-house audit some time after implementation. This mirrors the methods of external assessors.

## The Desk Investigation at the Assessor's Office

As mentioned previously, the assessment takes place in two stages. The first is concerned with establishing whether or not the documented quality system meets the requirements of the standard, leaving to the second stage the question of whether or not the system is actually being followed. This first stage, commonly referred to as the *desk investigation,* usually takes place well before the on-site assessment (if the assessment is booked for three months later, the desk investigation may take place six weeks before the on-site assessment).

The practices of different assessment firms vary, but desk investigation is usually carried out off-site at the assessor's office. Soon after a formal application, the company seeking assessment will be asked to provide copies of all the quality documentation—the quality and procedure manuals—and it is on this evidence alone that conformity of the system with the standard is judged. In requesting copies of the documents, the assessors may make clear whether they require these to be controlled copies or up-to-date, but uncontrolled, copies. If they do not make this clear, the point should be clarified.

In a desk investigation, the assessors need to establish if the requirements of the standard are being addressed and, if so, whether or not the procedures in place provide a practical means of achieving this. These are two separate questions. If a company is seeking registration to ISO 9001, its quality system must include reference to design control. If this requirement has not been addressed, then clearly there is no possibility that ISO 9001 can be awarded. However, in addition, the system must include practical methods of ensuring that design control is exercised in day-to-day activities. In the approach to the documented system presented in Chapter 10, a clear separation was recommended, consisting of a quality manual made up of policy statements on how each requirement of the standard would be addressed, with cross-references to a separate procedure manual. The latter provides the practical means of carrying out the policy. This structure enables the assessor to carry out the desk investigation efficiently. The manual provides the bridge between the standard and the company's quality policies and leads easily into the procedure manual. As a result, without any familiarity with the particular business, the assessor can understand the particular quality system and evaluate its coverage against what is required.

There are really only two outcomes of the desk investigation: either the documented quality system is judged to meet the requirements of the standard or it is not. True, in the former case there might be some points of detail that the assessor questions or is unclear about, and these will be raised prior to site assessment. However, it can be assumed in this case that the assessor expects that any such problems can be resolved either before the site visit or soon afterward and that the problems in themselves are not so serious as to make it impossible to award ISO 9000 certification. On the other hand, when the assessor believes that one or more requirements of the standard are not met or adequately addressed by the quality system, there will be failure on these grounds alone. In such circumstances a site assessment would serve no purpose until a major revision of the quality system has been completed. How this situation is handled, and the implications in terms of additional charges, varies between assessors. However, the procedure that is followed should be known in advance of the assessment. In fact, it is an aspect of the service provided that should be clarified before the assessor is chosen and the contract signed. Whatever the practice, if this situation occurs it should, at worse, be only a setback to the schedule for gaining ISO 9000. The identified problem can be dealt with through a change in the system, the desk investigation then completed satisfactorily, and the postponed on-site assessment arranged.

When the outcome of the desk investigation is unfavorable, most companies will not feel in a position to disagree. However, in some circumstances, especially when the assessor is unfamiliar with a particular business, there can be legitimate doubts about how the standard should be applied. An example could be meeting requirement *4.11 Inspection, Measuring and Test Equipment* of ISO 9001 in a professional service company. The application of this requirement will be very different from the common practice in manufacturing. It may be felt that the need to apply this requirement simply does not arise, given the nature of the business. In cases such as this, it may be difficult to arrive at a clear-cut evaluation, and both assessor and company should expect to discuss and debate the matter before a final, and possibly adverse, decision is made on the basis of the desk investigation. The contract with the assessor will often include some type of appeals procedure, which can be followed as a last resort if the company strongly believes in its own interpretation of the standard. However, most will probably accept the assessor's recommendation and make such changes to the quality system as the assessor believes appropriate.

Where minor questions are raised as a result of the desk investigation, these should be carefully considered and changes instigated before the on-site assessment. In making any such changes, the formal change procedure must be followed. This involves initiating corrective actions leading, if appropriate, through management review to a controlled change of the system.

## On-Site Assessment

For a smaller company, the on-site assessment typically involves one or two of the assessor staff and takes about two days. Obviously, this will vary according to both the overall size and the number of operating sites of the company being assessed. The purpose of this part of the assessment is to establish whether or not the company is following its own quality system; the desk investigation will have determined whether or not the system itself meets the standard. The assessment work is, in principle, exactly the same as an internal audit. The assessor uses the documented system—especially the procedure manual—to establish what *should* happen at a specific point in a process and seeks evidence that this is what does happen in practice. There should rarely be any gray areas; either a particular requirement is being followed or it is not. Also, as in an internal audit, the primary evidence sought is from objective quality records, and much of the assessor's time will be spent in examining these. However, the assessor can also observe whether or not staff activities are in conformity with the procedures. If, for example, the procedures require an entry to be made on a job ticket as the batch leaves a department, observation may show whether this is being done or the records are incorrectly being created after the event. The assessor may also ask staff to describe how a certain process is carried out, with the purpose of establishing familiarity with relevant procedures. If the staff do not know what the quality system requires of them, how can the company be regarded as following its own system? This, however, does not mean that staff are expected to be able to recite procedures verbatim.

An important issue is what special preparation should be made immediately before the assessor's visit. The correct answer is not much. The staff should be fully trained in the operation of the quality system; no more can really be done. However, in practice, most companies will make an extra effort in the lead-up to the big day, paying particular attention to meticulous and retrievable records. The staff are also likely to receive coaching in how to handle auditors. One practical tip: if, during an assessment, an employee is are asked a question about a particular activity, the answer the assessor is looking for is in terms of procedures rather than the fundamental principles of wire bending or whatever. If the employee is unsure of the correct procedural answer to the question, the best response might be:

> I am not quite sure what we do in these circumstances, so I would look up the relevant procedure in the manual or consult my manager.

Another tip is to discourage staff from giving a long, involved answer that can result in self-incrimination, e.g.,

> How do we set the machine? Oh well, the procedure is…(etc.). At least, that is what we are supposed to do, but of course what we really do is take out this old notebook of mine I've had for years, and this tells me how to do it. To make things right, we enter up the setting records on the proper form when the machine is running. Another thing is….

Employees at all levels should be told to answer the assessor's questions as best they can, succinctly, and then say no more until another question is asked.

Most companies will undertake some such last-minute coaching, but realistically its effects will be, at most, marginal. If only lip service has been paid to the quality system up to this point, things will not be fixed in a few days. There is also the danger of making staff over-anxious. With a good quality system in place, no one should be made to feel that the future of the company hangs on his or her responses to an assessor.

Before arriving, the assessors will probably indicate their proposed schedule and timetable. Relevant staff will have to be available when each department is visited, because an assessment of the marketing department obviously cannot be carried out if the staff are all out seeing customers. Some disruption to routine business may have to be accepted. Normally, the key contact between the company and the assessors is the management representative. Indeed, this member of staff should expect to give all of his or her time to the assessment visit. Apart from direct discussions about the system in general and the aspects with which he or she is directly concerned (e.g., the system control procedures, such as auditing and corrective action), the management representative normally accompanies the assessors throughout their visit, takes them to each department, and introduces them. Also, very few management representatives would not want to be present at all times during the assessment. Because the management representative most likely has the best knowledge of the quality system in the company, he or she should be able to help the assessor interpret evidence in the best possible light.

Normally, the assessors will cover the whole company and the operation of the entire quality system. It is very unlikely that no problem whatsoever will be found, but a single deficiency, or even quite a few, does not have to result in failing to be certified. A basic distinction is made between major and minor deficiencies (or nonconformities). A major deficiency would be that a significant part of a quality system or a set of procedures is not being followed at all; for example, no quality records are kept for the cutting and bending department of the coat hanger factory, or there is no effective control over system documents with different versions of manuals in use. If such situations are found by the assessor, the company will fail ISO 9000 certification. Failure of this type, however, should hardly be a surprise. Auditing and management review should have identified these problems before assessment, and the date of the assessment should have been postponed until the problem was corrected. This would have been far better than failure.

Examples of minor nonconformities include entries missing from some job tickets, the failure to label some design plans, or the occasional oversight of a checking procedure. When problems such as these are found, the assessor logs penalty points against the company. If the total of such minor nonconformities is above a certain level, ISO 9000 will not be awarded, but if it is under this level, the company should still pass. Unfortunately, it is not possible to state precisely how many minor nonconformities are acceptable; if there are more than ten, the situation may start to become doubtful.

The precise procedure followed in cases where ISO 9000 is not awarded at the first attempt varies among assessment bodies and should be understood before a commitment is made (i.e., at any initial preproposal meetings, the company should ask for an explanation). Obviously, a further assessment visit will be required (at significant extra cost), but, depending on the situation found on the first visit and the policy of the assessors, the scope of this may be restricted to only those areas where the major problems were found. If the system was thought to be working well everywhere except in the cutting and bending department, for example, reassessment may be restricted to this one problem department.

Whether there are only a few minor nonconformities (rarely are there none) and ISO 9000 is awarded or there is a major deficiency requiring reassessment, the problems will, of course, be made clear. Not only will they be discussed with the management representative as they are identified, but a written statement will be prepared on what is effectively a corrective action form. These will be formally passed to the company and should then be dealt with in exactly the same way as internal corrective actions: an investigation is carried out, leading to a recommendation, followed by a management decision and, if appropriate, a change in the system. However, just as all internal corrective actions do not require a change in the system, the problems identified at the assessment might be a matter of better applying the existing procedures. Whatever the appropriate solution, the company will be expected to have taken effective steps to put matters right before the next visit by the assessors, whether this is a surveillance (following a successful first assessment) or a reassessment.

## AFTER PASSING ISO 9000: KEEPING THE MOMENTUM GOING

While some of the above may sound discouraging, the large majority of companies seeking ISO 9000 pass at their first assessment. One reason for this is that if the internal quality system is followed, it should be apparent to management when the company is ready for assessment. If the quality system has not matured sufficiently, there is little point going into an assessment in the hope that problems will disappear overnight or not be found on that day. A further point is that assessment firms would rather pass than fail a client. Of course, they have to follow their own strict procedures and maintain the standards set by the RAB, but every assessment body seeks to increase the list of firms they have successfully registered for ISO 9000.

Whether or not a company has passed ISO 9000 will be clear by the end of the assessment; the assessor should comment one way or the other. However, there will be some delay until, with the assessor's own paperwork complete, it is official and the certificate is on the wall. The intervening period can be frustrating because, strictly speaking, the company cannot yet claim to be ISO 9000 certified. It certainly cannot be claimed in press releases or other publicity, nor can the ISO 9000 certification mark be used. What can be done once it is official is discussed in the next chapter.

If all goes well, it's time for the champagne. The employees will more than deserve it. However, ISO 9000 is by no means over and done with. The quality system is ongoing, and so is assessment. Some six to twelve months after the initial assessment, the first regular surveillance visit will be made. The focus then will almost entirely be on whether or not the quality system is still being followed (the initial assessment will have established that the system meets the requirements of the standard). Normally, surveillance visits last a shorter time than the initial assessment visit and are narrower in scope. Any corrective actions raised as a result of the initial assessment may well be followed up, but in a shorter visit the operation of the system throughout the entire company cannot be covered; only certain parts will be selected. In other respects, the surveillance visit will be carried out in exactly the same way as the initial assessment.

Surveillance visits will then be repeated at the intervals specified in the agreement with the assessors. After three years it is the policy of some assessors to repeat the complete cycle, starting with a full reassessment. Other assessment firms continue surveillance indefinitely. Whatever the practice, neglect in adherence to the quality system can result in ISO 9000 registration being withdrawn. The negative impact of this could well exceed any initial benefits. The quality system *must* be kept in good working order.

## REWARDS AND CELEBRATION

Most companies that are awarded ISO 9000 certification find it important to celebrate the achievement in some visible way. In some cases, T-shirts, mugs, key chains, or the like are given to all employees. There almost always is a formal press release announcing the accomplishment.

# CHECKLIST OF BUILDING BLOCKS TO CONSIDER WHEN APPROACHING ISO 9000 CERTIFICATION AND ASSESSMENT

1. Obtain management commitment, including the Board of Directors as appropriate.
2. Appoint the Management Representative and obtain all ISO 9000 standards and guidelines.
3. Set up an ISO 9000 project implementation team; study the ISO 9000 framework and identify the major factors affecting your decision to proceed toward third-party assessment and registration.
4. Review your existing procedures against the appropriate requirements of ISO 9001 to 9004 and the ISO general guidelines.
5. Identify what needs to be done and build the ISO 9000 rollout plan.
6. Seek out industry experts, pioneers, implementers, etc. and exchange experiences with other companies.
7. Establish a formal project with appropriate authority and resources, including a project implementation budget.
8. Enroll the Management Representative in one of the lead assessor training programs, preferably one offered by an organization with experience in your industry.
9. Be sure that your calibration system conforms to ISO 10012 and other metric standards as appropriate.
10. Complete or upgrade your quality assurance manual and associated support documentation. Pay particular attention to your document control procedures, as procedure creation and document control problems constitute a significant portion of the barriers to registration.

---

*Source:* Loosely adapted from material by Michael J. Timbers (*The Journal of European Business*) as well as the ISO 9000 Forum's suggested items to consider for registration.

11. Define and implement any new procedures that may be required after an internal audit by your lead assessor.
12. Let the newly installed quality system operate for a period of time before considering assessment. This will highlight system weaknesses and shortcomings as well as generate the necessary records to demonstrate that the system does work.
13. Engage a consultant or assessor to perform a pre-registration audit to identify potential system weaknesses and provide authoritative interpretation of the relevant standard.
14. Initiate discussions with independent third-party registrars. Determine experience, fees, extent to which their registration is recognized, and the national registers in which your company would be listed. If your goal is recognition in the EC, be sure the registrar meets the requirements of EN 45012 (EC criteria for certification bodies operating quality system certifications). Surveys indicate that reputation, accreditation, and industry expertise are the most important factors when choosing a registrar.
15. After negotiating an agreement, meet with the registrar and lay out a schedule. Plan on having a "mock" audit using your quality assurance manual and associated documentation for review.
16. Modify your quality assurance manual and procedures based on the mock audit feedback and critique.
17. Prepare for the registrar's desk check and audit. The registrar's assessment team audits actual activities against ISO 9000 criteria and your quality assurance manual. Be sure the auditors meet the qualification criteria for auditors in ISO 10011-2.
18. Carefully review the assessment report; amend the system as required and undertake corrective actions in areas of noncompliance as quickly as possible; follow-up with the appropriate parties involved.
19. Review action on noncompliance with registrar.
20. Obtain Certificate of Registration on the first try, if possible, and within as short a time frame as possible.
21. Maintain your quality assurance system to the assessed standard; document through periodic internal audits; publicize as appropriate; obtain recertification within the appropriate time frames.
22. Seek creative ways to respond to ongoing quality system requirements and enhancements.

13

# MARKETING AND PUBLIC RELATIONS

## INTRODUCTION

The final chapter is about getting the best return from the investment of time and money spent on ISO 9000. However, a marketing department or regular advisers will undoubtedly be able to give better advice than can be covered in the few pages that follow.

It is assumed that the scope of registration for ISO 9000 is the entire company. If, as is possible, only a part of the business has been covered, any marketing connected with ISO 9000 must clearly refer only to the part of the business registered to ISO 9000. The ISO 9000 mark, for example, cannot be included on the company's letterhead if only one department has been assessed, although it may be possible to use it on a brochure that only relates to that department. The practical marketing problems raised by partial company registration, therefore, can be considerable and may be a good reason not to follow this route.

A marketing strategy for ISO 9000 is considered in the following pages, and some of the tools that can be used to meet the strategic objectives are described.

## DEVELOPING A MARKETING STRATEGY

A suggested strategy is summarized in Figure 13.1. Marketing activity can take place at various levels, each with a particular audience and appropriate tools. At all levels there should be a common message to communicate about the benefits conferred by ISO 9000. This message can be stated in different ways, but should include the following elements (although every communication does not have to cover the whole message):

- The company is committed to quality.
- The quality system in place both demonstrates that commitment and serves to enhance the quality of service offered.
- The quality system has been assessed to meet the stringent requirements of ISO 9000.
- Quality is no empty promise—the company's observance of its own system is proven through the assessment.

| Level | Objective | Audience | Tools |
|---|---|---|---|
| 1 | Awareness and image building | Customers<br>Potential Customers<br>Financial Supporters<br>Suppliers<br>The "Trade" | PR, Advertising<br>Routine communication |
| 2 | Stimulation of inquiries | Customers<br>Potential Customers | As 1 plus:<br>Direct mailing |
| 3 | Conversion of inquiries | Customers<br>Potential Customers | As 1 and 2 plus:<br>Quotation documents<br>Brochures, etc.<br>Face-to-face selling |
| 4 | Enhancement of customer satisfaction | Customers | Passing on internal benefits<br>Customer satisfaction monitoring and complaint handling<br>Customer mailing |

**Figure 13.1** Marketing ISO 9000.

At the first level, the objective is to create awareness and build the image of the company as a quality organization. The primary audience is customers and potential customers; in the longer run, through changing their perceptions, additional and perhaps more profitable business can be generated. However, there are others to influence as well, including organizations that support the company financially, such as banks, suppliers (possibly to stimulate their quality of service), and the trade. The latter includes competitors (for various reasons, most companies want competitors to be impressed) and possibly even potential buyers of the company; ISO 9000 certification may increase the value of the business when the time comes to sell.

The tools available at the first level include public relations (PR), advertising in its various forms, mailings, and routine communication (e.g., inclusion of the ISO 9000 certification body's mark on the letterhead). The objective at the second level is more focused: to stimulate inquiries. The audience in this case is potential customers and existing customers who may not currently provide all the business they could. The tools are much the same as for the first level, but with more emphasis on focused methods such as direct marketing.

Improving the conversion of inquiries into orders is the objective at the third level. It is not just a matter of the ratio; what also matters is obtaining more profitable orders. ISO 9000 may enable a firm to win orders from customers who, because of concerns about quality, might previously have placed only small, if any, orders. A projection of the quality of the service offered may also allow opportunities to charge more; customers are often willing to pay more for what they perceive to be better. The tools used in pursuit of the first- and second-level objectives will all have a trickle-down effect on inquiry conversion (the potential customer stimulated to make an inquiry through a mailing already has a positive expectation of the service offered). More specific tools here include the quote, which sets out the offer of a quality service, as well as other company literature that may be used in support. Finally, the quality message must be reinforced in any face-to-face selling activity. The salesforce should be well briefed and know how to use ISO 9000 in winning business. This has been one of the major shortcomings of the effect of total quality management to date—lack of knowledge of how best to capitalize on the marketing benefits it provides—and unless steps are taken to remedy it, ISO 9000 will fall victim to the same problem.

The final level is the enhancement of customer satisfaction, which in turn leads back to inquiries and orders. The most effective leverage available is that a quality system implemented to meet ISO 9000 requirements will produce a higher quality of service to customers. It is performance, rather than promises, that convinces. However, supplementary marketing tools also include customer satisfaction monitoring (which should be built into the system) and, should things go wrong, complaint handling. Finally, customers should be contacted routinely through such means as newsletters and mailings to tell the ISO 9000 quality story.

## USE OF THE ISO 9000 MARK

The right to use the ISO 9000 mark of an accredited assessor is a very valuable asset. It has not been mentioned up to this point simply because virtually all ISO 9000-related literature will feature it.

The value of the mark might seem a small thing. It is not. Unfortunately, as ISO 9000 has increased in prominence and become a criterion for supplier selection, some companies have made doubtful, if not misleading, statements. Examples include:

> "We're working towards ISO 9000." (You can work toward something forever without either real effort or commitment.)
>
> "We provide quality to ISO 9000 standards." (Then why not get ISO 9000?)
>
> "We recognize ISO 9000 as an appropriate quality standard." (Okay, but have you achieved it?)

The effect can be made even more impressive by prominently displaying a statement in large type:

*Working toward*
*ISO 9000 certification*

Legitimately or not, such claims are made. However, unless its quality system has been successfully assessed by an accredited certification body, a company cannot use that assessor's ISO 9000 mark. Because this is their mark, the assessors will vigorously pursue any who use it wrongfully. It should be noted that it is the assessor's mark that is used, and not ISO itself. ISO as an organization does not offer certification of any kind at the present time.

Each assessor body has detailed rules governing the use of its own mark. These rules should be read and clarification requested where there is any doubt; on surveillance visits, the assessors check to make sure that the mark is not being misused. However, assessment for ISO 9000 also gives rights to use the equivalent British and European standards marks, and these may be used by certificate holders in addition to, or even instead of, the ISO 9000 mark. This right may be particularly important for an exporting company.

Whatever the detailed rules, the ISO 9000 mark (or the British or EN equivalents) can be used by registered companies in a wide variety of ways, including:

- **Letterhead:** The mark can be included on company stationery.
- **Company literature:** As long as it is not implied that any specific product is covered by ISO 9000, the mark can be used in most literature and brochures.
- **Media advertising:** Media advertisers can also carry the mark, subject to the restriction on product links.
- **Vehicles:** ISO 9000 registration can be shown on the delivery fleet or other vehicles.
- **Buildings:** Flags and other methods can be used to display the accrediting body's mark on or near the company's premises.

Although the mark can be used in any of these ways, it might be wise to be selective. For various reasons, it may be thought inappropriate to include it on the letterhead, for example.

The one place the ISO 9000 mark cannot be used is on products or their packaging; by extension, it must not be suggested in other ways that a product meets ISO 9000. ISO 9000 is a standard for quality management; it is *not* a product standard. An ISO 9000 company is clearly committed to quality, but as such, registration to the standard implies nothing about the product specification or method of manufacture. When a physical product is produced, there should be no ambiguity about the prohibition on relating ISO 9000 to the product. In some service companies, however, the matter may be less than clear-cut. If there is any doubt, the matter should be discussed with the assessors.

A final comment on the use of the ISO 9000 mark: if the quality system is not maintained and eventually registration is lost, the mark can no longer be used. Removal of the mark from literature, vehicles, and the building could be very expensive—another reason it is important to keep the registration intact.

## PUBLIC RELATIONS

The ISO 9000 certificate can, of course, be mailed to a company. A more formal presentation, however, might involve a press release. The person making the presentation can be almost anyone, but the better known the presenter, the greater the impact of the story. Some presenters to consider include:

- A representative of the assessor firm
- A high-profile person in the industry (the chairman of the trade association, for example)
- A senior representative from a major customer or a large company in the market that the company supplies
- A local politician, such as the mayor or a city councilman (this type of presentation is most appropriate if the market is mainly local)
- Someone nationally known, e.g., a major politician (this is not out of the question if the individual can be persuaded that the story will benefit him or her as well)

The actual presentation does not have to be a formal affair; just a photo session will do, unless it is to be an event for the employees as well. By all means, a professional photographer should be hired.

A story should be written up for the press release. This should not be overdone; a page or two at most is enough, possibly with different versions tailored to fit the interests of different publications. The content of the story depends on the company and its business, but themes could include:

- The company's business and a brief history
- Why ISO 9000 was sought
- How it was obtained (The hard work and commitment should be mentioned, but it is perhaps better to suggest that many of the quality procedures were already in place in some form.)
- What ISO 9000 means for customers—the most important angle of all

If the company is an ISO 9000 first in its industry, this also should be featured and may encourage especially good coverage.

Target media for the press releases include the trade press of the business, the trade press of the major markets supplied, and the local press. Each should receive a copy of the story, preferably tailored to their specific interests, together with a labeled, high-quality photograph. The national press is always a possibility, but unless there is a really special story and professional PR help is available, the chances are very slim.

In addition to the presentation, other PR opportunities are available. One is to follow up in the trade press by offering articles on the benefits of ISO 9000 to the industry or on how the company obtained the registration. If sufficient writing talent does not exist in house, a ghost writer can be hired inexpensively. Writing a letters to the editor in the trade publication is another possibility.

If the company regularly issues press releases, it should consider including an ISO 9000 angle in other stories. In a press release about winning a major order, for example, the company can mention ISO 9000 registration and perhaps imply a connection with the new business.

PR activity can be wider in scope than press releases. Almost anything that gets the company name into circulation can be considered. Articles on ISO 9000 can be followed up with participation in seminars and conferences. Events such as customer days can also be considered.

## Using Publicity Material

Virtually all firms have some existing publicity material, and this should be changed to feature ISO 9000. Just to include the ISO 9000 mark is not really enough in many cases—not all recipients of the material will fully understand what it means. At least a paragraph on the quality policy and what this offers customers should be included. The expense of the design work and reprinting, however, may be considerable; therefore, it might be more economical to phase in the new edition as the old stocks run out. Alternatively, including an ISO 9000 reference might be seen as a good opportunity to replace existing, outdated material.

If the company regularly advertises in the trade or other press, the ad copy should be changed to include the ISO 9000 mark. Special advertisements might also be considered at the time the standard is gained or the long-term focus of the advertising is shifted to feature quality of service. If the original advertising copy was professionally designed, the ISO 9000 mark should not merely be inserted in the only blank space available; the ad should be redesigned properly. If it was not designed professionally in the first place, now is a good opportunity to upgrade.

In addition to adapting existing literature, a company could consider having some material specific to ISO 9000. This might be used for a special launch mail-out to existing and potential customers. One suggestion is to use the quality policy. This can be printed attractively and can include the ISO 9000 mark. Either a special edition of the company newsletter or a one-time edition can be considered. This can cover how and why the company sought ISO 9000 and can give an outline of the quality system and what it offers customers. Even a simple letter to customers is better than nothing; ISO 9000 will not generate additional business if no one knows about it.

As mentioned earlier, the quality manual (not the procedure manual) can also be regarded as promotional material, although it is better used selectively to meet a specific request or perhaps sent to a few major customers. This is not just a matter of the expense of reproducing it. Frankly, recipients will find the average manual a little on the dull side. Of course, it should be designed and produced to appear as professional as possible.

One other important document to consider is the proposal or price quote. This can take various forms, depending on the nature of the business, from a one-page letter up to a lengthy proposal document. It should, in all cases, be seen as a selling document, rather than just as a contract offer. Customers should be given reasons to buy from the firm. ISO 9000 should, therefore, be mentioned in the quotation. Certainly the mark should be included, but something should be said about the quality system as well, what ISO 9000 registration means, and what benefits are offered to customers.

### Monitoring Customer Satisfaction

Monitoring customer monitoring and complaint handing will be built into the quality system to provide an external measure of whether or not requirements are being met. However, the contact with customers entailed should also be seen as a marketing opportunity. Mailing a short satisfaction questionnaire is another opportunity to keep in touch with customers, perhaps with a follow-up letter to address any comments made. This demonstrates that the company values customer care and interaction. However, monitoring does not have to be only by mail. Key customers, at least, can be followed up personally by a senior manager, who can use the need to monitor the quality system as a reason for making contact.

Even with an effective quality system in place, some customers will complain. This will of course trigger some quality system procedures, including an investigation into a long-term solution to the problem. However, the fact that such a complaint is taken so seriously should be turned to a marketing advantage, with the particular customer left believing that, although an error occurred, everything possible was done to put the matter right and prevent a recurrence.

### Educating the Salesforce in ISO 9000

In many businesses the salesforce is the major source of both inquiry generation and order conversion, with business dependent on their face-to-face selling skills. It is important, therefore, that they be trained to tell customers the ISO 9000 story. How this is done needs careful thought, with time set aside to make sure they are adequately briefed. This should cover the use of publicity material to reinforce the quality message.

## A FINAL WORD

An organization should not pursue an ISO 9000 quality system for the anticipated marketing edge. Rather, it should adopt a quality system to attain and maintain a competitive advantage through improved customer satisfaction. On the other hand, ISO 9000 can offer enormous marketing opportunities. It can also be a burden: the company must live up to the commitment to quality. Promises are a start in any business dealing, but they soon become empty if performance does not measure up. It is not enough, therefore, to tell customers that the ISO 9000 registration offers an enhanced quality of service; they must experience it as well. In the long term, the quality system must be used to produce continual quality improvement. Marketing activity can then communicate what has actually been achieved. Only in the very short term can marketing be an alternative to real service. Despite what they are told, customers will soon realize that the claims are false.

Quality also must extend to the marketing activity itself. It is, for example, false economy to mail out the quality policy in the form of an unprofessional-looking photocopy. In addition, the marketing should reflect that attention to detail has been built into a quality system. In one case, as soon as the particular company was certified, a mailing was organized, with a copy of the quality policy to be included with a letter. One recipient took delight in pointing out that his envelope contained the letter, but not the quality policy. Perhaps a review of the mailing procedure would have been wise.

## ISO REGISTRATION FIRMS

As explained in Chapter 12, the number of firms performing ISO 9000 registration audits is growing at a tremendous rate. Unfortunately for companies seeking registration, not all auditing firms are certified by the national registration bodies. In selecting an auditor, a company must be careful to ensure that the auditor has been approved by the national registration body, so that the registrar's stamp will be approved by the company's suppliers.

This profile contains a list of registrars that had been certified by the U.S. registration governing body, the Registrar Accreditation Board (RAB), as of early 1994. An up-to-date list may be obtained by calling the RAB at (800)-248-1946. Ask for Julie Michalsky at extension 7426.

## Quality System Registrars

This is an "unofficial" listing of registrars based in the United States and Canada. Note the following designations:

♦ Registrars accredited by the Registrar Accreditation Board (RAB) prior to the implementation of the American National Accreditation Program for Registrars of Quality Systems (a joint ANSI-RAB program). These accreditations are being processed for reissuance under the ANSI-RAB program.

◊ Registrars that have applied for accreditation under the ANSI-RAB program.

♦ **ABS Quality Evaluations, Inc.**
James O. Ricks
16855 Northchase Drive
Houston, TX 77060-6008
Phone: 713-873-9400
Fax: 713-874-9564

♦ **American Society of Mechanical Engineers**
David A. Wizda
345 East 47th Street – 39W
New York, NY 10017
Phone: 212-605-4796
Fax: 212-605-8713

♦ **A.G.A. Quality, A Division of A.G.A. Laboratories**
Stephen Gazy
8501 E. Pleasant Valley Rd.
Cleveland, OH 44131
Phone: 216-524-4990 ext. 8349
Fax: 216-642-3463

American Association for Laboratory Accreditation (A2LA)
John W. Locke
656 Quince Orchard Road #704
Gaithersburg, MD 20878
Phone: 301-670-1377
Fax: 301-869-1495

American European Services, Inc. (AES)
Eric Thibau
1054 31st Street NW, Suite 120
Washington, DC 20007
Phone: 202-337-3214
Fax: 202-337-3709

◊ American Quality Assessors
Frank Degar
1201 Main Street, Suite 2010
P.O. Box 1149
Columbia, SC 29201
Phone: 803-254-1164
Fax: 803-252-0056

♦ **AT&T Quality Registrar**
John Malinauskas
650 Liberty Ave.
Union, NJ 07083
Phone: 908-851-3058
Phone: 800-521-3399
Fax: 908-851-3360

♦ **Bellcore Quality Registration**
Edward M. Barabas
6 Corporate Place
Piscataway, NJ 08854
Phone: 908-699-3739
Fax: 908-336-2244

♦ **Bureau Vertias Quality International (NA) Inc.**
Greg Swan
509 North Main Street
Jamestown, NY 14701
Phone: 716-484-9002
Fax: 716-484-9003

Canadian General Standards Board
Quality Certification Branch
Berne Geiger
222 Queen Street
Suite 1402
Ottawa, Ontario, Canada
K1A 1G6
Phone: 613-941-8669
Phone: 613-941-8657
Fax: 613-941-8706

◊ Davy Registrar Services (DRS)
Leroy W. Pfennigwerth
One Oliver Plaza
Pittsburgh, PA 15222-2604
Phone: 412-566-3402
Fax: 412-566-3407

Det norska Veritas (DnV) Industry, Inc.
Steve Cummings
16340 Park Ten Place
Suite 100
Houston, TX 77084
Phone: 713-579-9003
Fax: 713-579-1360

♦ **DLS Quality Technology Associates, Inc.**
James A. Kalitta
Rocco Lupo (315-655-8710 ext. 336)
108 Hallmore Drive
Camillus, NY 13031
Phone: 315-468-5811
Fax: 315-637-2707

GBJD Registrars Limited
(SIRA Certification Services)
Raymond F. Grayston
32 Clarissa Drive, Suite 822
Richmond Hill, Ontario, Canada L4C 9R6
Phone: 905-508-9417
Fax: 905-471-0822

♦ **Intertek Services Corporation**
William E. Airey
9900 Main Street, Suite 500
Fairfax, VA 22031-3969
Phone: 703-476-9000
Fax: 703-273-4124

◊ KEMA Registered Quality Inc.
Theo Stoop
4379 County Line Road
Chalfont, PA 18914
Phone: 215-822-4283
Fax: 215-822-4285

♦ **KPMG Quality Registrar**
Daniel L. Brennan
Three Chestnut Ridge Road
Montvale, NJ 07645-0435
Phone: 201-307-7991
Fax: 201-307-7443

◊ Litton Systems Canada Limited
Quality System Registrars
John Womack
25 City View Drive
Etobicke, Ontario, Canada M9W 5A7
Phone: 416-249-1231 ext. 2406
Fax: 416-246-2049

♦ **Lloyd's Register Quality Assurance Ltd.**
c/o Lloyd's Register Shipping
Joseph Marchese
33-41 Newark Street
Hoboken, NJ 07030
Phone: 201-963-1111
Fax: 201-963-3299

MET Electrical Testing Company
Robert Ryan
916 W. Patapsco Avenue
Baltimore, MD 21230
Phone: 410-354-2200
Fax: 410-354-1624

◊ NSF International
Garry Puglio
P.O. Box 130140
Ann Arbor, MI 48113-0140
Phone: 313-769-8010
Fax: 313-769-0109

♦ **National Quality Assurance, U.S.A.**
James P. O'Neil
1146 Massachusetts Avenue
Boxborough, MA 01719
Phone: 508-635-9256
Fax: 508-266-1073

National Standards Authority of Ireland (NSAI)
Richard Bernier
5 Medallion Centre
Greenley Street
Merrimack, NH 03054
Phone: 603-424-7070
Fax: 603-429-1427

OTS Quality Registrars, Inc.
Andrew J. Bergman
10700 Northwest Freeway, Suite 455
Houston, TX 77092
Phone: 713-688-9494
Fax: 713-688-9590

◊ Performance Review Institute Registrar
Glenn L. Anderson
402 Commonwealth Drive
Warrendale, PA 15096-7511
Phone: 412-772-7170
Fax: 412-776-0002

Quality Certification Bureau Inc.
Julie Press
Suite 208, Advanced Technology Centre
9650 – 20 Avenue
Edmonton, AB, Canada T6N 1G1
Phone: 403-496-2463
Fax: 403-496-2464

Quality Management Institute
Malcolm J. Phipps
Suite 800 Mississauga Executive Centre
Two Robert Speck Parkway
Mississauga, Ontario, Canada L4Z 1H8
Phone: 416-272-3920
Fax: 416-272-3942

♦ **Quality Systems Registrars, Inc.**
Marshall L. Courtois
13873 Park Center Road, Suite 217
Herndon, VA 22071-3279
Phone: 703-478-0241
Fax: 703-478-0645

QUASAR
Quality Systems Assessment Registrar
A Division of the Canadian Welding Bureau
Richard B. Kitney
7250 West Credit Avenue
Mississauga, Ontario, Canada L5N 5N1
Phone: 905-542-1312
Fax: 905-542-1318

SGS International Certification Services, Canada Inc.
Diane Pryde
9 Gough Road
Markham, Ontario, Canada L3R 5V5
Phone: 905-479-1160
Fax: 905-479-9452

◊ SGS International Certification Services, Inc.
John Brookes
1415 Park Ave.
Hoboken, NJ 07030
Phone: 201-792-2400
Fax: 201-792-2558

♦ **Steel Related Industries**
Quality Systems Registrar
Peter B. Lake
2000 Corporate Drive, Suite 450
Wexford, PA 15090
Phone: 412-935-2844
Fax: 412-935-6825

♦ **TRA Certification**
Thomas R. Arnold
700 E. Beardsley Avenue
P.O. Box 1081
Elkhart, IN 46515
Phone: 219-264-0745
Fax: 219-264-0740

♦ **Tri-Tech Services, Inc.**
Auditors/Registrar Division
Joseph A. Fabian
4700 Clairton Boulevard
Pittsburgh, PA 15236
Phone: 412-884-2290
Fax: 412-884-2268

TUV America, Inc.
Manfred A. Popp
5 Cherry Hill Drive
Danvers, MA 01923
Phone: 508-777-7999
Fax: 508-777-8441

RTI/TUV Essen
Robert Sechrist
1032 Elwell Court
Suite 222
Palo Alto, CA 94303
Phone: 415-961-0521
Fax: 415-961-9119

TUV Rheinland of North America, Inc.
Martin Langer
12 Commerce Road
Newtown, CT 06470
Phone: 203-426-0888
Fax: 203-426-3156

◊ Underwriters Laboratories, Inc.
Harvey Berman
1285 Walt Whitman Rd.
Melville, NY 11747
Phone: 516-271-6200
Fax: 516-423-5657

Underwriters Laboratories of Canada
Quality Registry Division
Howard J. Spice
7 Crouse Road
Scarborough, Ontario, Canada
M1R 3A9
Phone: 416-757-3611
Fax: 416-757-1781

AV Qualite
Terry Heaps
2900 Wilcrest
Suite 300
Houston, TX 77024
Phone: 713-465-2850
Fax: 713-465-1182

14

# THE BAILEY CONTROLS CORPORATION: A CASE STUDY IN CREATIVITY AND SHORTENING THE REGISTRATION LIFE CYCLE

## INTRODUCTION

In 1991, the Bailey Controls Corporation successfully achieved ISO 9000 registration in a nine-month period from start to finish, which is about half as long as it takes most organizations to accomplish the same task. This fast-track registration was a major accomplishment for the 78-year-old company, and their story was first documented in a *Quality Digest* article by Ted Kinni in October 1993. Since then, the company has continued to move ahead in their ISO 9000 journey, as described in the following case study. The material for this profile is based on information provided to Frank Voehl by their Quality Assurance Director, Ed

Mahoney. Special thanks also goes to Sandy Edwards, quality assurance staff specialist at Bailey Controls, who helped coordinate and provide materials for this case study.

## OVERVIEW

Bailey Controls Corporation is located in Wickliffe, Ohio and has a manufacturing facility in Williamsport, Pennsylvania. The three primary industries they serve are electric utilities and oil and steel production. They are suppliers of controls, instrumentation, computer systems, and software for process applications and have earned an international reputation for their creative and innovative solutions to highly complex, high-tech control problems.

## BUILDING BLOCKS FOR SUCCESSFUL ISO 9000 REGISTRATION

The Bailey Controls ISO 9000 story is presented in the framework of the registration checklist introduced in the profile at the end of Chapter 12, which provides a useful framework for any organization seeking ISO registration in a speedy time frame. The following is a summary of their success story.

1. **Obtain management commitment, including the Board of Directors as appropriate.**
   Bailey's decision to implement ISO 9000 was simple. Having been purchased in 1988 by Finmeccania (an Italian high-tech conglomerate), ISO 9000 registration was viewed by management as a necessary process to improve business operations as well as to achieve competitive advantage through continuous improvement and superior customer satisfaction.
2. **Appoint the Management Representative and obtain all ISO 9000 standards and guidelines.**
   The Bailey management representative was the Director of Quality Assurance. Bailey chose not to name an ISO program coordinator. This decision was made to ensure that ISO became more than a program. Bailey chose to train in the ISO standard an individual with broad corporate knowledge and a solid QA and TQM background. This individual became the ISO "guru" (or in-house ISO expert) and served as the one-point contact for each department as well as its department quality coordinator (DQC). One caution here is to make every effort to select the best person for the job, rather than the most available. ISO 9000 standards and guidelines were obtained from Canada's Quality Management Institute (QMI).

3. **Set up an ISO 9000 project implementation team; study the ISO 9000 framework and identify the major factors affecting your decision to proceed toward third-party assessment and registration.**

   A project team was not used until much later in the process, as the approach was more top-down management driven. As mentioned earlier, the new owners issued a broad challenge to develop a quality strategy capable of moving the company into the 21st century; part of that strategy was the implementation of an ISO 9000 quality system.

4. **Review your existing procedures against the appropriate requirements of ISO 9001 to 9004 and the ISO general guidelines.**

   In 1990, a broad review of the ISO 9000 standards, coupled with the results of previous customer satisfaction surveys, resulted in choosing ISO 9001 to cover the company's Wickliffe, Ohio headquarters and ISO 9003 for the Williamsport, Pennsylvania manufacturing facility. Since that time, the decision was made to upgrade the Williamsport facility to ISO 9002.

5. **Identify what needs to be done and build the ISO 9000 rollout plan.**

   The rollout plan was developed by the Quality Assurance Department and submitted to management for approval. In addition to ISO 9000 and ISO 9003, it contained a requirement of incorporating Canada's CAN 3 Z299.1 and Z299.2 standards, which feature heavy emphasis on operator readiness and in-depth analysis of root causes of problems. As part of management requirements, the team was told to implement in ten months or less at no additional cost to production.

6. **Seek out industry experts, pioneers, implementers, etc. and exchange experiences with other companies.**

   The Bailey Controls total quality journey was influenced in the early stages during the late 1980s by the Florida Power & Light Vendor Quality Improvement (VQIP) effort, which was a pioneer in the supplier quality management aspects of the quality movement. At the time Bailey began the ISO 9000 journey, most of the industry was below average in delighting customers and was having a rough time surviving the recession. Very few were pursuing ISO 9000. In fact, of the companies that had achieved certification, none qualified on their first audit. The rollout plan timeline included a milestone that allowed for a minor failure.

7. **Establish a formal project with appropriate authority and resources, including a project implementation budget.**

   As previously mentioned, Bailey initially used a top-down stance and delegated a lot of authority to the ISO guru, who in turn leveraged his time and energies through the DQCs, who did most of the work. A project tracking mechanism was used to track milestones and cost. Bailey's DQCs were middle and upper managers with authority for business operations. Through this activity, these managers were able to clearly define and improve some processes while taking on program enforcement responsibilities. By tracking cost and improvement using a measurement system approach, Bailey was able to show that the activity was self-supporting and actually recovered its cost prior to completion of the project. (See the profile at the end of Chapter 11 for general information on ISO measurement systems.)

8. **Enroll the Management Representative in one of the lead assessor training programs, preferably one offered by an organization with experience in your industry.**

   The ISO guru was enrolled in a full battery of lead auditor assessor training courses offered by QMI (which eventually served as the company's registrar). This individual then showed the DQCs how to document their processes in an acceptable format. The guru became the final authority on compliance with the ISO 9000 standards.

9. **Be sure that your metrology and calibration system conforms to ISO 10012 and other standards as appropriate.**

   The Bailey quality system contains over 25 different types of standards or specifications, including 10CFR50 Appendix B, CAN 3 Z299.1, FDA GMPs, and other less known standards. Due to the very precise and exacting nature of control system products and services provided to industries such as nuclear power, many of Bailey's policies exceeded the minimum requirements for ISO. Because of the concerns for continual compliance, Bailey's single manual needed to satisfy all requirements. Some documentation on non-nuclear activities was eliminated, but the process was essentially identical.

10. **Complete or upgrade your quality assurance manual and associated support documentation. Pay particular attention to your document control procedures, as procedure creation and document control problems constitute a significant portion of the barriers to registration.**

    The key to Bailey's success was to spread the responsibility for document preparation and control throughout the organization from virtually day one. In many U.S. companies, the road to ISO means sequestering the QA Department with the standards for two weeks or more and telling them to start writing the manual. The Bailey approach was just the opposite. Each manager was responsible for writing his or her own manual with help from the ISO guru. Buy-in was high, resulting in an empowered workforce using real documents that addressed real departmental needs. The manuals contained fewer errors and were connected in a corporate-like daisy chain, which resulted in very powerful synergy and empowerment.

A restriction to the procedure development process was that departments could not tell each other what to do. This forced the DQCs to approach the process as they would a customer, inquiring as to needs, wants, and desires. This activity also resulted in the elimination of nearly $10,000 worth of unnecessary documentation and process steps.

11. **Define and implement any new procedures that may be required after an internal audit by your lead assessor.**

    Most of the improvements and enhancements to procedures were performed from within by the people involved with the documentation. This resulted not only in high buy-in, but also in substantial cost savings as hand-offs from department to department were documented, reviewed, and streamlined. Much of this occurred during the "getting ready" stage leading up to the mock audit and then the actual audit.

12. **Let the newly installed quality system operate for a period of time before considering assessment. This will highlight system weaknesses and shortcomings as well as generate the necessary records to demonstrate that the system does work.**

    As previously mentioned, a short time frame was built into the process to allow for minor failure. Bailey had a quality system based on inspection that covered its complete product line. They had no quality assurance systems for 75 percent of their activities.

    Each process was documented, employees were trained, and the process was implemented. Some procedures were modified before the complete manual was released.

13. **Engage a consultant or assessor to perform a preregistration audit to identify potential system weaknesses and provide authoritative interpretation of the relevant standard.**

    Choosing the right registrar—the one who is right for your organization and its direction, vision, and values—is the most important management decision you will make. Bailey Controls used a five-criteria matrix to rank the following:

    - Credibility
    - Familiarity with industry
    - Ability to work together
    - Proximity
    - Cost

    See item 14 and *Quality Digest,* October 1993, page 28 for additional details.

14. **Initiate discussions with independent third-party registrars. Determine experience, fees, extent to which their registration is recognized,**

**and the national registers in which your company would be listed. If your goal is recognition in the EC, be sure the registrar meets the requirements of EN 45012 (EC criteria for certification bodies operating quality system certifications). Surveys indicate that reputation, accreditation, and industry expertise are the most important factors when choosing a registrar.**

The following five factors were key to the Bailey Controls choice of a registrar:

- *Marketplace credibility:* Is the registrar recognized by our customers and the certification bodies of the countries where we conduct business? "When you buy these guys, you are buying credibility. They better be able to deliver," emphasizes Mahoney.
- *Familiarity with the industry:* Is the registrar knowledgeable about our business processes and products? Familiarity confers a cost savings because you do not need to spend extra time educating the registrar about the business. It also helps to ensure a rigorous, relevant audit.
- *Ability to work together:* Can we develop a good working relationship with the registrar? Is the registrar responsive to our needs? The business relationship with the registrar will continue long after the initial registration. Be sure that you can establish a long-term cooperative partnership.
- *Proximity:* Is the registrar located near our company? Bailey Controls interviewed five registrars. QMI was the only one that met the other criteria and had a focus in North America. The company realized substantial savings in travel expenses and also maximized face-to-face contact.
- *Cost:* Finally, are the registrar's fees reasonable? Registration fees are fairly standard, and the registrars' quotes should not vary by more than 5 to 10 percent.

15. **After negotiating an agreement, meet with the registrar and lay out a schedule. Plan on having a "mock" audit using your quality assurance manual and associated documentation for review.**

The Bailey Controls DQCs participated in a half-day pre-assessment visit by the lead auditor during which they familiarized themselves with QMI's approach to audits. A secondary benefit was the learning transfer to the in-house staff on how to conduct audits (compliance reviews). It is critical to allow time in the schedule for troubleshooting and corrective action prior to the actual audit.

16. **Modify your quality assurance manual and procedures based on the mock audit feedback and critique.**

The internal pre-assessment mock audits were conducted over a long enough time period to allow for feedback and corrections. (Approximately two to three months was allowed for this activity.)

17. **Prepare for the registrar's desk check and audit. The registrar's assessment team audits actual activities against ISO 9000 criteria and your quality assurance manual. Be sure the auditors meet the qualification criteria for auditors in ISO 10011-2.**

    Because of the timeline, Bailey chose to have the manual reviewed in stages as it was being completed. This increased the desk check cost by about 20 percent, but provided invaluable experience as the manual development process continued.

18. **Carefully review the assessment report; amend the system as required and undertake corrective actions in areas of noncompliance.**

    A total of nine areas of noncompliance were detailed in the assessment report, most of which were of a minor nature. It took about thirty days to correct these areas.

19. **Review action on noncompliance with registrar.**

    All nonconformance items were corrected within a short time frame, and the results of each were discussed with the registrar.

20. **Obtain Certificate of Registration on the first try, if possible, and within as short a time frame as possible.**

    Bailey Controls obtained its certificate on the first try, within a nine-month time frame. This was accomplished by compressing the development cycle, taking a top-down approach, and using mock audits to uncover disconnects early in the cycle. A total of 7 man-years of internal time was needed, as well as $20,000 in registration and consulting fees.

21. **Maintain your quality assurance system to the assessed standard; document through periodic internal audits; publicize as appropriate; obtain recertification within the appropriate time frames.**

    Maintaining the quality system is the responsibility of local area management, who have the ownership and the commitment to move forward with recertification activities that are in the process of being finalized.

22. **Seek creative ways to respond to ongoing quality system requirements and enhancements and to deal with technical problem areas.**

    Management buy-in and accountability for compliance are two of the keys to success. Buy-in is essential so that the process becomes the managers. Avoid the tendency to delegate this authority to a consultant.

    The quality manual must support your business first and then the quality system audit and not the reverse. Because the nuclear market is extremely rigid, the Bailey Quality Assurance Manual contains 18 sections that mirror the requirements of 10CFR50 Appendix B.

Another example of a creative response was to include a listing of all relevant test fixtures, documents, and drawings required at each operation in the MRP system. Thus, the manufacturing router became a quickly changed process control document and was properly controlled. Bailey could also quickly implement required changes because the MRP and financial system already knew the product status.

At the start of this process, the Bailey Quality Assurance Manual contained over 7 inches of paper and was a stagnant document. Since registration, it has been revised more than 30 times and is currently less than 2 inches thick

Finally, the Bailey challenge for 1994 is to eliminate all references to ISO in the manual other than on page one. The manual has been rewritten as the Bailey Quality Management System and is commonly used as a training document.

# INDEX

## A

## J



## K



## L



## M



## N

## Q



## R

## S



## T

## U



## W